A More Perfect Union

A Novel by Fred McKibben

Copyright – Fred McKibben, 2020

This book is a work of fiction. Except as described in the Author´s Note at the end of this book, the names, characters, places, and events depicted in this book are a product of the author's imagination or are used fictitiously. Any resemblance to actual events, locations, or persons, living or dead, is entirely coincidental.

Chapter 1

May 22, 1787
Philadelphia, Pennsylvania

Sara Sullivan threw the covers off the bed and swung her feet to the floor. A drop of sweat trickled its way between her breasts beneath the thin cotton shift she had slept in. Gradually, she gained control of her breathing, reminding herself that the nightmare was only a dream now. Still, the image of the monster looming over her and her own father's withered hands holding her down haunted her. Her heart thundered inside her chest as she remembered the brutal rape by the man she'd been forced to marry.

Eight years, a new name, and a large ocean separated her from that horrible night. The monster was dead. Her father was probably dead too, but still, the images followed her.

With her hand, she brushed a red curl away from her eyes and took two steps to the window. A faint glow washed across the eastern horizon, but daylight was at least a half-hour away. She looked at the porcelain clock on the table beside her bed but couldn't make out the time in the dim light. She could go back to bed and wait for the morning sun to flow through the window, but the dream might come back. Bile rose in her gut at the memory of that night, but a glance around the semi-dark room reassured her. She had escaped that evil.

Sara peered out the window again. Only the earliest risers were on the streets, those who prepared the homes and businesses of the city for the fortunate ones who would rise with the sun, or later. The ones who would expect tea and toast on a tray; a copy of the Pennsylvania Chronicle folded next to the teapot. The darkened city with its few scattered lights reminded Sara of her last view of Dublin from aboard a Dutch freighter sailing out of the harbor well before daylight.

Her hands swirled around the little table until she found the tinderbox. She removed the cover and took the flint and steel from its little chamber on one side. Henrietta would have made sure there was a low fire burning in the kitchen downstairs, but Sara hated trying to tread the narrow staircase in the dark. She tapped the steel on the flint rock several times before a decent spark appeared in the tinder.

She returned the flint and steel to their compartment and took one of the sulfur-tipped sticks from its slot. The sulfur ignited when she touched it to the spark. Sara knew how fast the sulfur would burn away so she deftly lifted the globe and lit a whale-oil lamp on the table.

She took her robe from the bedpost and slipped it on over her shift. The light from the lamp cast a yellowish glow as she descended the staircase and proceeded along a short hallway toward the kitchen. She stopped and tapped on the last door before the kitchen.

"Yes'om," came a groggy reply from the room.

Sara pushed the door open and leaned inside, "You sleep in a while this morning, Hennie," she said. "I'll take care of breakfast for Mr. Martin."

"Yes'om," the black woman acknowledged.

Sara closed the door and went into the kitchen where she stoked the embers in the iron stove and added kindling, then two chunks of coal from a box by the stove. Like many colonial homes, the "kitchen" at Sullivan House was the place where they stored foodstuff and where they made meals ready for serving. The small stove in the room was for heat and to warm kettles of water for tea or wash basins. Roasting, baking, and frying took place in a small "cookhouse" separated from the main house by several yards.

Despite her entreaties, Sara knew Henrietta would be up and ready to work before daylight. The aging black woman came with the house when Sara purchased it four years earlier. She had not realized that a slave would come with the house until her agent announced the completion of the transaction.

Sara understood something of slavery, having lived some months in Martinique before she arrived in the colonies. The notion of it repelled her. On the occasion of their first meeting, she informed Henrietta that she was free to leave. Henrietta had other ideas, though. While she liked the idea of freedom, she also knew that the handful of freedmen in Philadelphia endured difficult lives. They lived in camps or hovels and begged for the most menial work. So, Sara and Henrietta agreed that, while the black woman was free, she would continue to live and work at the boarding house, which Sara intended to call Sullivan House. They agreed upon a small salary and the agent prepared a simple document declaring Henrietta's freedom. Like most slaves, Henrietta had no last name, but as the agent prepared the document, she announced that her name would be Henrietta Washington, taking the name of the most famous American.

Looking back now, Sara realized Hennie was a godsend. She'd made it possible for a twenty-three-year-old Irish girl from the slums of Dublin to make Sullivan House a success. While Sara knew something of cooking and cleaning, she knew nothing about hosting boarders, or cooking to please the strange American taste.

Sullivan House was just one of over a hundred

boarding houses in Philadelphia. Older ladies, many widowed during the recent war of independence, ran almost all the other establishments. In the beginning, rumors and innuendo flew around the town. Why would a beautiful, young, unmarried woman want to run a boarding house? For the widow-ladies the answer seemed obvious; the world's oldest profession was expanding from the waterfront to the heart of the city.

The widow-ladies watched the comings and goings at Sullivan House, and they prodded the mayor and various constables to do so, as well. But, after four years, everyone realized Sullivan House was just what it presented itself to be.

If anything, though, the fact that Sullivan House was not a house of prostitution only deepened the mystery of Sara Sullivan herself. In the beginning, the widow-ladies reaction to her mystified and hurt Sara, but over time, her bewilderment turned into amusement. So much so she sometimes started rumors herself just to see how far they spread and how they came back to her.

Sara understood that her appearance gave her an advantage against the widow-ladies when men came to the city on business and sought accommodations. Her hair was the first thing people noticed. It was red, but with enough blond to soften the color and catch the sunlight. She was fair skinned, as were most with such hair, but unlike most, she picked up color from the sun without showing freckles. When she chose the right clothing, she could show off a fine figure, but she rarely chose such clothing, preferring to dampen the effect instead. It wasn't that Sara didn't enjoy being pretty. She did, but she had learned from experience being pretty could be dangerous.

Guests at Sullivan House usually stayed for a few days, or a few weeks at most, before concluding their business and leaving the city. While many of the houses in the city took on permanent renters, Sara was never inclined to do so and priced her accommodations to discourage men seeking permanent quarters. As a result, Sullivan House often had vacant rooms. It was less profitable than most other establishments and that was fine with Sara. She'd come to Philadelphia with some money — something else for the widow-ladies to speculate about — but she doubted it was enough to live on indefinitely. Anyway, she'd rather have something to do besides wait for a husband or become a seamstress. The income the house produced, along with her savings, was enough to assure her independence.

Sara touched the stove top with a fingertip and judged it warm enough for the teapot which she filled from a water bucket hanging from a peg on the wall. While she waited for the water to steam, she retrieved butter and jam from the larder and sliced the remains of yesterday's bread. In the dining room next to the kitchen, she spread the curtains open and noted daylight had begun to erase the darkness. She hoped it would also erase the dream.

A low hum from the teapot drew her back to the kitchen where she prepared herself a cup of strong tea. She added a pinch of sugar and sat down at a small table near the stove. As she tasted the first sip of the dark liquid, Henrietta's petticoats rustled in the hallway. A second later, the slender black woman was in the kitchen rearranging the food Sara had just set out.

"Sit down, Hennie," Sara suggested. "Have a cup of tea."

"I got to poot some ham out, Miss Sara. You know Mr. Martin love dot ham." Sara loved the rhythm of the woman's speech. Despite nearly twenty years in Philadelphia, she still spoke with the melodic accent of her Caribbean upbringing.

"Yes," Sara conceded.

"Cheese too," Henrietta added.

"You're right," Sara agreed. In four years, she couldn't remember a single time she'd laid out a meal that exactly met Henrietta's standards.

Henrietta cocked her head, "I think I hear the man stirrin' about now."

"He's leaving today," Sara said. "I expect he'll want to get started early."

"So he will," Henrietta said, "and I won't be so sad to see his backside goin' down the road."

"Nor will I," Sara agreed. In fact, during the two weeks Henry Martin had been a guest at Sullivan House, he'd resurrected all the fears and resentments Sara sometimes felt in the company of men. Most of the time, she had no trouble assuming the posture of a businesswoman and keeping the men at arms-length, and she had done so with Henry Martin. It was a necessary skill since almost all her guests were men.

Martin had finally received the shipment of British goods he had come to retrieve and had hired wagons to haul them to Western towns where he expected to sell them at an enormous profit. British goods were difficult to come by in the colonies so soon after the war, but Martin had arranged the shipments through a cousin in Trinidad.

"When dot fancy lady come visit?" Henrietta asked.

"Ten o'clock this morning," Sara answered. She almost giggled at the notion of Sarah Bache referred to as a "fancy lady". As the daughter of the famous Benjamin Franklin, she was the most distinguished woman in Philadelphia. But by the standards of the English ladies Sara had seen in her youth, Mrs. Bache was rough around the edges. Still, it was an important event for Sullivan House and Sara had been nervous and excited since the messenger had come yesterday.

"Make sure Mr. Martin is out before ten," Sara instructed Henrietta, whom she knew would be far more effective at dislodging the boarder than she would be herself.

*****

She needn't have worried about Mr. Martin. He was down from his room almost as soon as the daylight was full, his bags packed and ready to leave. He gulped down his tea with a bit of the bread and ham, paid for his last week of lodging, then headed out to find his wagons loaded with goods, presumably thinking of the small fortune he was about to reap.

Sara examined herself in the mirror atop the dresser in her bedroom. She judged the plain blue skirt with a single petticoat and white blouse — buttoned all the way to her neck — to be just the right attire to greet the distinguished lady. She smiled at her own image. The blue was particularly pleasing since her father never allowed her to wear it in her youth. Even though the English repealed their sumptuary laws nearly two centuries earlier, her father feared alienating the powerful British nobility in Dublin.

Henrietta agreed that the look was just right while she pinned a mass of red curls behind her head before running downstairs to escort Mrs. Bache into the parlor and offering tea. Sara peeked out the window to verify that the lady's carriage was parked in front of Sullivan House. She took two deep breaths to calm her nerves, then started down the stairs.

She shouldn't be nervous, she told herself. When the British abandoned the city in 1778, they took anyone still loyal to the crown with them. And she doubted the daughter of one of the most famous

American rebels would give her secrets away even if she learned them.

"I'm honored by your visit, Mrs. Bache," Sara said as she entered the parlor.

"The honor is mine," Sarah Bache said. "Folks speak highly of your establishment."

Henrietta had placed cups of tea on the small table between them and Sarah Bache took a sip from one, her eyes wandering around the neatly furnished parlor.

"You're very kind."

"Please call me Sarah, Mrs. Sullivan," Mrs. Bache insisted.

"Then you should call me Sara, as well," Sara responded.

"It seems there's a bit of Irish in your accent."

"Yes," Sara acknowledged. "I grew up in Dublin." Since leaving Ireland, she'd managed to hide the Irish brogue from her new neighbors, except for the occasional I or R. The less they knew about her past, the better.

"What you have accomplished here is impressive," the older woman observed. "Especially after being widowed at such a young age."

"Business could be better, I suppose." Somehow the story had developed over her four years in Philadelphia that Sara was the widow of a Caribbean sugar planter, and being Irish, detested the English. Parts of the story were Sara's own creation and other parts the creation of rumor mongers. Some variations of the story even had Mr. Sullivan alive in an English prison. She made no effort to dissuade either version of the story, especially since the latter provided a reason for not remarrying.

"Perhaps business will be better," Sarah Bache said. "I've come on behalf of my father and the Congress," she added.

"Oh?"

"Yes. You may have heard there is to be a gathering of delegates from all the states to discuss revisions to our Articles of Confederation."

"I did hear that Mr. Madison is in town and that some meetings are planned."

"Very important meetings," Sarah Bache said. "The future of the United States lies in the balance. The Articles simply are not sufficient to make a nation."

"How can I be of assistance?"

"We still lack suitable lodgings for some delegates," Sarah Bache explained. "If you could take in at least two delegates — and their servants — it would be enormously helpful. The Congress has agreed to pay a fair board for the duration of the convention."

Sara suppressed a groan. Not paying its bills was about the only thing the Congress of the United States was famous for; not too surprising since the Congress of the United States of America had no source of income other than begging the individual states for funds. She suspected that many of the boarding establishments in the city had already declined to provide boarding for that very reason.

"I'd be delighted," Sara said. If nothing else came of it, she expected Sullivan House would gain a measure of prestige.

"Thank you, Mrs. Sullivan," Sarah Bache said, reverting to the more formal address. "I expect Mr. Oliver of Connecticut and his servant to arrive tomorrow or the next day. Will you be ready to accommodate them on such short notice?"

"It isn't a problem," Sara said. "Who else should I expect?"

"That we shall see as the delegates arrive."

Chapter 2

May 22, 1787
Trenton, New Jersey

John Oliver examined the horizon. The sun was low in the sky; an hour to sunset, he judged. Despite the remaining daylight, his aching backside assured him it was time to get out of the saddle for this day.

"We'll stop here for the night," he said to Ned Foster.

"That sure sounds like a good idea to me, Mr. Oliver," the slender black man said. Like Oliver, the valet hadn't spent so many hours in the saddle in years. Now, they'd ridden for nearly a solid week, sleeping on the ground for nights of fitful rest.

The road widened as they entered Trenton and

before they'd gone far into the town, John Oliver saw a stable advertising livery for hire. His legs ached as he dismounted his horse and led it to the open barn door, Ned Foster following close behind, tugging along his mount and the pack mule tethered to it.

A large man emerged from the barn to greet them, a leather blacksmith's apron tight against his bulging chest. Underneath the apron, a plain white shirt had turned a dingy gray from the soot of the bellows. Sweat glistened on his powerful forearms and dripped from his dark hair and mustache.

"You fellas looking for a place to rest those animals?" the smith asked.

"That we are," Oliver replied. "We're looking for a place to rest our own bones for the night, too."

The smith looked from Oliver to Ned Foster, then said, "Tenth house straight ahead on the left. Mrs. Alston's got a nice place, and she's got slave quarters for your boy."

Oliver stared at the smith for several seconds before replying. "Mr. Foster is not a slave, sir. He will need quarters the same as mine."

"Well, that's going to be up to Mrs. Alston, I guess," the smith said, "but, she's particular 'bout her reputation."

"In case we don't meet Mrs. Alston's particular requirements, can we bed down in your hay loft?" He really wanted to sleep in a nice, soft bed, but the hay loft was certainly better than sleeping on the ground as they had for several nights in a row.

"Yep," the blacksmith said. "Be a dollar for each of you fellas. Spanish dollar, none of that Continental junk," he added.

"Don't worry about me, Mr. Oliver," Ned Foster said in his deep, smooth voice. "You get a good night of sleep."

John Oliver knew his valet would say something along those lines and he knew the man meant it sincerely. But Oliver had no intention of taking quarters in a house that would deny a decent room to his servant, a free man by the laws of the state of Connecticut.

"We'll see what the lady says," Oliver said to the smith, "but I expect you'll have two guests in your hayloft for the night."

"Yep," the smith agreed. "There's an oil lamp hanging on the post up there. Be sure you don't catch the loft afire."

*****

Mrs. Alston's warm smile faded the moment she realized Oliver intended for the black man to sleep in one of her rooms. She told them that the slave quarters behind the house were clean and warm. Again, Ned Foster assured Oliver he was fine with sleeping in the quarters for one night. Still, Oliver declined the offer, and the two sauntered back to the livery barn with two pails containing roasted chicken, biscuits, and turnip greens provided by

Mrs. Alston's kitchen for a small price.

Dim light from the lantern gave the strewn hay of the loft a golden glow as the two men sat on their bedrolls finishing the meal. Despite her frostiness toward Ned, Oliver had to admit that Mrs. Alston's kitchen put out a first-class meal, which he hoped would erase the memory of dried meat and molded bread from the night before. John Oliver wasn't a stranger to rough living. He'd spent five years as a captain in the Continental Army, sleeping when and where he could, and sometimes going days without a meal of any kind, much less Mrs. Alston's roast chicken.

For Oliver, the war ended on September 5, 1781, at the Battle of Chesapeake, when a dying British officer put a pistol ball into his backside. During his recuperation in Baltimore, the French and American armies forced the British to surrender at Yorktown on October 19, effectively ending the war. A month later, John Oliver hired a small carriage and driver to take him back to his farm northwest of Hartford. The bumping, jostling ride had convinced him that there should be very few reasons ever to leave the farm again.

"You got something on your mind," Ned Foster said. "That I can tell." By now, Oliver was accustomed to Ned's odd accent and sometimes unusual way of speaking. He was born in the islands but had spent most of his thirty-five years as a household servant for a quarrelsome British nobleman who was bitter at being marooned in the new world. The resulting speech pattern could sound melodic at times, but more often it was stiffly English.

"I was thinking about the war," Oliver said.

"You got better things to think about, now," Ned Foster said.

"I suppose I do," Oliver agreed.

In fact, thinking about anything was better than thinking about the war and everything that happened. Victory was sweet, but the price had been high for John Oliver. The wound to his buttocks was the least of it.

"That business is finished," Foster said. "Now, you and those other gentlemen are going to make a new nation."

"You're right about the nation, Ned," Oliver said, "but that business won't be finished until I have my son back."

"Sir William got scared when the fires started. He was sure those rebels would come running through New York looking for him. He panicked and he convinced Mrs. Becky and the boy to escape to Staten Island with him. She sent me to find you and tell you she'd be back as soon as she could, but what with the fire and the riots, I didn't find you for four days."

"She never came back," Oliver lamented. "I went to the house and one of the maids told me they went back to England. She was crying because they didn't take her with them."

"The British held the city after all, so Sir William and Mrs. Becky could've stayed until the war was over," Foster said.

"Sir William didn't want to stay," Oliver said. "He never wanted to be here. He didn't trust his brother, always worried he would somehow cheat him out of inheriting the title. Now, I'm not sure Becky wanted to stay either."

"She wanted to stay," Foster tried to reassure him.

"Two days after that, the British hung Wilton Rogers. He wasn't even a rebel."

"They were looking for someone to blame and Wilton Rogers was handy," Foster reminded Oliver.

"In two days time, I'd lost my wife, my son, and my best friend to the English. I hadn't cared much for the revolt before that time, but it became my passion."

"Tomorrow we will be in Philadelphia, and you can start working on a new passion, building a great nation."

"Sometimes you're a dreamer, Ned," Oliver said. "Making a nation from these states will be no easy task. The states won't be amenable to surrendering their sovereignty."

"If they don't unite, the British will come back one day," Foster said. It wasn't the first time Ned had expressed such a sentiment and John Oliver respected the valet's understanding of politics and international affairs. Sir William and his household staff in England and New York educated Ned, and he read every book, pamphlet or newspaper he found.

"That is truth without doubt," Oliver agreed. "If we continue this useless confederation, the British, or the French, or the Spaniards will splinter the states into their own dominions."

"Yes."

"We must hope that good men of strong purpose will hold forth at this convention and unite us in spite of our differences."

"There are many things they will agree on," Ned Foster said, "and one they will not."

"Slavery, of course," John Oliver acknowledged.

"Yes."

"It must be reckoned with somehow, Ned. If we should form a nation without resolving the issue of slavery, the abscess will continue to fester."

"The Southern states will not join a union that deprives them of their wealth," Ned Foster said.

"And an honorable nation cannot countenance the notion of human property."

"Who are these honorable nations, I wonder?" Ned Foster questioned. "It seems to me that just about every nation is happy to profit from slavery, whether by practicing the trade or by trading with those who do."

John Oliver lowered his head and let out a long

sigh. The wiry black man knew far more about slavery than he ever would. For most of his life, Ned Foster had been a slave, including twenty years in the household of John Oliver's father-in-law, Sir William Black.

"You have seen that with your own eyes," Oliver conceded. He'd only learned of Sir William's interest in slaving ships after his father-in-law had escaped New York with Becky and Caleb, not even two-years-old at the time.

"I never understood how a man could be so kind on the one hand, and so evil on the other," Foster said.

"He thought nothing of taking my wife and child with him."

"Mrs. Becky thought they would be back in a few days," Foster observed. "The fire was a scare, but the British held the city."

"She didn't come back," Oliver said again. "I got a letter from her some weeks later. She was in England and her father had convinced her she and Caleb could never be safe in America again."

Ned Foster stared toward their shadows thrown on the hayloft wall by the light from the lantern. In the years since those days in New York, John Oliver had learned that Ned Foster always weighed his words before speaking. He waited. Finally, Ned turned back to him. "That letter made you a slave owner," Foster said.

"I was a slave owner for a single day," Oliver

said. That was true because Becky's letter had gifted ownership of Ned Foster to John Oliver. The next day, he found a magistrate who signed a document declaring Ned Foster a free man. "You're free now," Oliver added.

"You're a good man, John Oliver," Ned Foster said, "but you don't understand what makes a man free. Folks like Mrs. Alston don't care about that document we made. They just look at the color of my skin and think I'm a slave, or something that amounts to the same thing."

Oliver opened his mouth to speak, but nothing came out. He knew Ned was right. If, against all odds, the convention decided to free all the slaves, it would only be the start of a new kind of problem. "We have to find a way, Ned," he finally said.

"It won't be easy to undo the evil that's been done."

"We must undo it, though," Oliver observed. "Repatriation to their native countries, perhaps?" It was an idea he'd heard many politicians expound in recent months.

"Repatriation won't work," Ned Foster explained. "Most of the slaves don't even know what place they came from. They don't have any family there and they don't speak the language. Besides, the plantation owners won't give them up. The white men will say they're free, but they'll have no place to go, no job to feed themselves, except to stay and work the land for pennies."

Oliver shrugged and reached for the lantern. "Let's get some sleep," he said.

*****

The hayloft had indeed proved to be superior to those nights of sleeping on the ground. John Oliver awakened before sunrise and nudged Ned Foster awake soon after, and by the time faint red sunlight illuminated the eastern sky, the pair rode out of Trenton. With fair weather and good riding conditions, they reached Philadelphia by mid-afternoon.

He had given little thought to what sort of reception he would get upon arrival at the Pennsylvania Statehouse, but he supposed he had expected someone to be there to greet arriving delegates. Instead, he'd awakened a sleeping bailiff who'd gone off to find Mr. Madison's aide at a nearby tavern. A short time later, the aide, smelling of rum, had recorded the particulars about John Oliver in a brown ledger book, and given him a letter he was to present to his hostess, Mrs. Sullivan.

Sullivan House was one street north and two streets west of the Statehouse, also known as Independence Hall. Oliver and Ned Foster walked the short distance with their horses and pack mule in tow. When they reached the house, Ned unloaded the luggage onto the walkway by the street before leading the three animals to a nearby livery barn

Mr. Madison's aide had suggested. Oliver watched as Ned led the animals away, then lifted the heavy door knocker.

Chapter 3

The acrid scent of strong ale and halitosis assaulted her nostrils such that she turned her head away from the old priest, hoping the smell would pass her by, and maybe his words as well. But it didn't work. The odor remained strong and Father O'Malley's words swirled around in her head.

"Ye must marry him," the old priest said.

"I won't," Sara Byrne insisted.

"Aye, ye must, and ye will."

"Why must I?" Sara asked. "Am I not a free woman?"

"Is any Irishman free, I wonder?" the priest mused. "And, if a man be not free, then certainly a woman be not."

"I despise him," Sara spit out.

"Aye, maybe ye do," Father O'Malley said. "But a marriage to a high-born Englishman is a very rare thing for a young woman of your station, and ye willn't be the first woman to despise a husband."

May 23, 1787
Philadelphia, Pennsylvania

The sound of the metal knocker against the heavy oak door aroused Sara. She wasn't sure if she'd been asleep or merely daydreaming, but the image of Father O'Malley, and the smell of him, had been as distinct as her memory could produce. She thought of the despair she felt that day as she walked back to the tiny house her father rented for the family. Before that day, she considered Father O'Malley a decent man who drank more than he should. But now she understood the priest had taken Alfred Carlisle's money to bless the marriage, just as her father had done. She didn't know how much money, but assumed it was impressive. The amount didn't matter though, her father and two worthless brothers would soon waste it on drink. Father O'Malley would probably do the same.

The sound of the front door swinging open and Henrietta's voice offering a greeting to someone prompted Sara to get up from the comfortable settee where she'd been napping. She hurried to the entrance hall where she found Hennie closing the door behind a tall man in need of a bath and a shave.

"Mrs. Sullivan, I presume," the man said, as he removed his rumpled broad-brimmed hat and bowed a dirty mop of brown hair in her direction. As he straightened, he extended a folded paper toward her.

She perused the short letter quickly. "I was expecting you, Mr. Oliver," Sara said. She hadn't thought much about what a delegate to the great meeting would look like but had supposed they would be distinguished gentlemen of their state. She knew little of Connecticut, but it was hard to believe the man she saw before her now was one of their most prominent. His breeches must have been white once, but were now a dusty brown, almost matching the color of his knee-high leather riding boots. Though fashionable, his black coat and brown waistcoat were as dirty as the breeches. It was a warm day, and beneath the unbuttoned waistcoat, a once white shirt clung to his chest, yet the cravat around his neck was still tied perfectly. He was tall and shaped well enough, slender at the hips and wider at the shoulders. His square jaw was covered with a scruffy beard in need of attention.

"That is correct madam," Oliver said.

"Welcome to Sullivan House, Mr. Oliver," Sara said. "I trust you will be comfortable here."

"Thank you, Mrs. Sullivan," he said. As usual, Sara felt his eyes linger on her cleavage a bit too long.

"I was told you have a servant, as well," Sara said.

"Yes, he's gone to take the horses to the livery."

"We have excellent quarters in the attic for our guest's slaves."

"I'm sure those quarters are quite nice, but Mr. Foster is not a slave. He is my valet and if possible, he should have a room near my own."

Sara did a quick mental calculation. There were two bedrooms on the first floor, one of which was Hennie's room, and four on the second, one being her own room. The attic had four beds in two rooms.

"I am expecting another delegate in the next few days," Sara said. "Mrs. Bache said the Congress would pay, but I don't know if they will pay for an extra room."

"Mrs. Sullivan," Oliver said. "The Congress may have difficulty paying for one room, let alone two. But don't concern yourself of that. I shall pay in Spanish gold for both rooms while we are here."

"Very well then," Sara said. He might look like a simple wayfarer, but Spanish gold meant she wouldn't have to worry about the nearly worthless currency the congress would try to pay with. Then to Hennie, she said, "Show Mr. Oliver to his room, Hennie, and set up the room next to it for his valet."

"Most grateful, madam," Oliver said.

"I'm sure you'll be wanting a bath," Sara said. "Henrietta will bring a wash basin and warm water up to your room."

Oliver bent at the waist and examined his lower half. "I suppose I could use a wash," he grinned, his smile showing two rows of perfectly even, white teeth.

Ten minutes after Hennie had led John Oliver to the largest bedroom on the second floor, she opened the door for an equally dusty black man. Sara watched from the hall as he easily hauled two large packets into the anteroom. About the same height as Mr. Oliver — six feet almost — but leaner, he introduced himself to Hennie, while also eying Sara in the hallway behind her. He was younger than Oliver, but his curly black hair showed a sharply receding hairline above the temples. As he lowered the packets to the floor, she noticed a wide round bald area on the crown of his head.

"We're expecting you, Mr. Foster," Sara said before Hennie could answer. "Henrietta will show you to your room, it's next door to Mr. Oliver."

"Thank you, ma'am," he answered. His accent surprised her. There was enough Englishness to put her off, but something else that was pleasant. Then, she realized what charmed her, the island dialect. The way he said "ma'am" was just the way Hennie said the word.

"I jus' taken a wash basin to Mr. Oliver. Ye'll be needin' a bath ye'self, man," Hennie said to him. "I bring a basin to ye."

"Thank you, ma'am," Foster nodded to Hennie.

While Henrietta led Ned Foster upstairs, Sara returned to the comfortable settee in the parlor. Two days with no boarders in the house had been restful. She understood she needed boarders to make a living, but an empty Sullivan House was the most peaceful place she'd ever lived. Sometimes she sat in the parlor and read from the books that were on the bookshelves when she purchased the house. Other times, she helped Henrietta with the housework or the laundry. On warm sunny days, she and Hennie would walk around the town, usually with no particular destination in mind, but often stopping to admire the goods in various shop windows.

Sara walked to the parlor window and looked out on Third Street. A rustic wagon pulled by an ancient ox clacked its way slowly toward Market Street with a load of hay probably bound for the livery barn on Dock Street. She heard footsteps on the wooden floor above her head, then she listened as the same footsteps came down the stairs. She turned around as Hennie entered the parlor.

"What do you make of our guests, Hennie?" Sara asked.

"I'll hold onto my judgemen' bout Mista Oliver till I see 'em cleaned up a bit," the older woman answered. "That Ned Foster, though. He make an old girl want to be young again."

"I thought I saw those eyes of yours lingering on that man," Sara laughed.

"Linger they did, Miss Sara," Hennie said. Henrietta had always referred to Sara as "Miss Sara" even though she was supposedly the widow of Mr. Sullivan, and Sara had never corrected her. They had never discussed the matter, but Sara suspected Henrietta knew that Mr. Sullivan was simply a ruse.

*****

With Henrietta's help, Sara had learned to keep meals simple at Sullivan House. At home in Dublin, her father and brothers drank away what little money came in, leaving almost nothing for the pantry. Besides, her mother had died without ever teaching the girl the skills needed to cook over the small open fireplace in their little house. Sara was more adept at stealing apples, potatoes, and other tidbits from the market than she was at cooking them. While hiding out in the French countryside, the cook at the chateau where she worked taught her the essentials of French cooking, but her American customers had more basic tastes.

The sun was low in the sky when Sara and Henrietta carried warm trays of fried chicken, roasted potatoes and bread from the cookhouse to the kitchen where they separated the portions onto plates for themselves and their guests. Most of the time, her guests ate a large meal at midday, usually at one of the many public houses in the city. In the evening, the fare was usually something simple and light such as salted meats, cheeses and bread. But

Mr. Oliver and his valet hadn't had time for a large meal earlier in the day and they would be hungry now. Besides the main course, a freshly baked shoofly pie was cooling on a shelf by the stove, next to a pitcher of fresh ale.

When she was satisfied with the presentation, they transferred the meal to the dining room and Hennie went to fetch their guest from the downstairs parlor. Since only the four of them would be dining, Sara decided to seat everyone at the big table in the dining room instead of having the servants eat in the kitchen as they normally would.

As Henrietta led the two men into the spacious dining room, Sara noted that the clean and well-dressed version of John Oliver was a decided improvement over the version she had greeted in the hallway two hours earlier. His thick brown hair was clean now and brushed back behind his ears from a part in the middle of his crown. He had tied it into a neat ponytail at the top of his neck. The scruffy beard was gone, and his strong square jaw glowed in the light from the candles. He wore a clean white shirt beneath a buttoned tan waistcoat, with clean white breeches and no topcoat. The heavy riding boots from earlier had been replaced by black shoes with large gold buckles and white stockings. She had noticed the bright hazel eyes earlier when they lingered on her chest.

"I hope you don't mind, Mr. Oliver," Sara said. "I've set the table for the servants to join us for supper rather than eat in the kitchen."

"Certainly not," Oliver said. "I have shared many a meal with Ned, and Miss Washington is a delight."

They arranged themselves at one end of the large table, John Oliver and Ned Foster on one side, and Sara and Hennie on the other. Henrietta poured four mugs of the ale and passed them around. Then Sara said, "We don't usually do any blessing of the food, Mr. Oliver, but if you wish to, please go ahead."

"To be honest, I'm not a churchman," Oliver said.

"Well, that's fine by me," Sara assured him. In fact, the last religious man she had known was Father O'Malley, and he had helped her father sell her to the English pig, Alfred Carlisle. "You must be starved so enjoy your supper, it's Hennie's famous island fried chicken."

Chapter 4

John Oliver was certainly hungry when he and Ned Foster followed the tiny black woman from the salon to the dining room. They'd had a cup of campfire coffee and a piece of stale bread courtesy of the blacksmith before they'd ridden out of Trenton a short time after dawn. Along the road, a farmer had offered bread and cheese, along with cups of bitter tea. In the war, he'd sometimes gone days without a real meal, but that was years ago and now a good meal was the cornerstone of a good day.

Seeing the food on the table and smelling the fresh bread and seasoned chicken almost made Oliver dizzy as he pulled a chair back from the table. Mrs. Sullivan said something about the servants joining them at the table and Oliver was fine with that. In fact, he would have sat down with

George III himself, and laughed at his bad jokes, if it meant he could start eating.

Then she had mentioned skipping any before meal praying, and that was fine, too. Before Sir William took Becky and young Caleb away to England, they had often attended the Methodist Church in Hartford, or the Anglican Church when they were in New York. But since then, his interest in organized religion had waned, and he hadn't attended a service in years.

Oliver took his eyes off the victuals and realized Mrs. Sullivan was staring at him. She looked away quickly when she realized he'd noticed her gaze. Since Becky left, he'd mostly avoided romantic situations with women. At first, he'd believed his wife would return once the war was over. He sent her letters through diplomats but got no replies. Then, he received a letter from a solicitor telling him his marriage had ended.

Over three years had passed since the colonies and Britain signed the formal treaty in Paris ending hostilities and now he knew Becky would never return. Perhaps, some day, he would trust a woman again, but he wasn't ready for that yet. But the look Sara Sullivan gave him raised his curiosity to a level he hadn't felt in some time. Now, as he looked at her, he wanted to know more. Her red hair caught the light from the candles at each end of the table and reflected it back brighter than the original source. It framed her flawless face with bright ringlets that were cinched together below her cheekbones and rested beautifully on her chest, accentuating the play of light and shadow between the curved tops of her breast and the cleavage between them.

Now, it was her turn to catch him staring. He felt his face flush as he spun his head back to the plate in front of him and stabbed at a potato with his fork, a utensil he was not particularly accustomed to, but found quite useful.

"It's all delicious," Oliver said, between bites. "I must have the recipe for the chicken."

"Do you cook, Mr. Oliver?" Mrs. Sullivan asked.

"On occasion," Oliver said. "I enjoy it."

"In France, a lot of men cook."

John Oliver noted that the pile of fried chicken on the platter in the center of the table was disappearing fast. As far as he could tell, Mrs. Sullivan had eaten a single piece, and her cook, Henrietta, was still picking at her first one. He had finished two and begun a third himself, which meant Ned Foster had devoured at least four pieces.

"I think Ned really likes the chicken," he said to Henrietta.

"Is good to see a mon eat like dat," the old woman said in her island style.

Oliver turned to Sara Sullivan and said, "When were you in France, Mrs. Sullivan?"

"A few years ago," she answered. "It was during

the war."

"You must have been quite young," Oliver observed.

"I was eighteen when I arrived in France."

"You were lucky to be away from the war," Oliver said.

"I grew up in Ireland, Mr. Oliver. The war meant little to me then, although I hated the English as much as you did."

"When did you arrive in Philadelphia?" John Oliver asked.

"September 1783."

Oliver glanced around the spacious dining room, "It appears you have done quite well in our new nation," he observed. "It couldn't have been easy for a young *widow* to make her way." As soon as the words were out of his mouth, he feared he had overstepped. He'd emphasized the word "widow", hoping she would elaborate as to what had become of Mr. Sullivan.

"I was fortunate to find an honest and reliable agent to help me along," she said. Apparently, there would be no enlightenment on the fate of Mr. Sullivan. *It's none of my business, anyway,* Oliver thought, yet his curiosity only increased.

"You were lucky," Oliver agreed. "The country was in disarray then, no real currency or court system. I suppose it isn't much better now, and that's why we are here to make some changes."

"I wish you great success in your efforts, Mr. Oliver," Mrs. Sullivan said.

"I wish I could be more optimistic, but I am afraid the slavery issue will be a very difficult one to get passed."

"Surely everyone understands the practice of slavery is contemptuous," Mrs. Sullivan observed.

"They may understand that it's contemptuous, Mrs. Sullivan," Oliver offered, "but that doesn't mean they will give it up. They've invested their fortunes in human beings, and their leaders, both political and religious, tell them there is nothing wrong with the practice."

"I understand your meaning, Mr. Oliver," Mrs. Sullivan said. "I came here from Martinique where slaves die in the cane fields every day."

"Perhaps it's a less brutal proposition in our nation," Oliver said. "Perhaps not."

"I have seen very few slaves in Philadelphia."

"There is little profit to owning slaves in a city such as Philadelphia," Oliver observed. "It is in the Southern states where the practice is so rewarding to its proponents."

"Does everyone in the South own slaves?" Mrs. Sullivan asked.

"No, but the powerful landowners do, and they control the territory like feudal lords might have done in old England."

"I have some experience with the English and

their manor of owning things," Mrs. Sullivan said. "In my home country, ordinary people are not much more fortunate than slaves."

"I have heard stories of English brutality in Ireland and in Scotland," Oliver acknowledged. "Maybe one day, the Irish will throw them off, as we have."

"You speak as if you have done great things, Mr. Oliver," Sara Sullivan said, "but is anyone better off for what you've done. Slaves are still slaves. Farmers must still hope for rain. Merchants still need customers. Was anything accomplished?"

"Yes," Oliver said. "Whether brilliant, or whether fools, at least we draw our own path forward." Oliver leaned back and smiled at the young lady across the table from him. She had drawn him into a much more complex conversation than he had expected, and he found it exhilarating.

Chapter 5

May 23, 1787
Off the Coast of Maryland

Susannah watched quietly as Hugh Marlow's breathing changed from rapid and uneven to smooth and soft. Then, it changed again as a muffled snore sounded at the end of each exhalation. She knew the snores would get louder soon, then Marlow would sleep hard for three or four hours.

She looked around the small cabin and took a mental inventory of the things she could have used to kill Hugh Marlow if Simon wasn't watching from a chair leaned against the port side hull of the small coastal schooner. Simon would kill her the instant she reached for the meat knife that had come on the tray with Marlow's supper, or the heavy candlestick beside it.

She didn't know who she hated more, Simon or Marlow. Simon was a slave, too, but for reasons she now understood, he was fiercely loyal to Marlow, and Marlow was just as loyal to Simon, who had become his de facto slave master. The one hundred or so other slaves on Marlow's indigo and rice plantation feared Simon as much as they feared any of their white bosses.

Susannah had lived all her twenty-two years at Hallow Hill. At least, she believed she was twenty-two. Her mother told her she was fifteen the year her father died from wasting sickness. The next summer, Hugh Marlow traded her mother and sister to a neighboring plantation owner in exchange for Simon. Six summers had passed since then and Susannah never saw her mother or sister again.

In those six years, Susannah grew to be a beautiful young woman. She was petite and slim, but strong, like her father had been. But she had her mother's lighter skin, green eyes, and deep brown hair. By the time she was seventeen, her body had taken a shape that drew the eyes of men in such a way that made her self-conscience. The white men on the plantation took notice of her, as well. Hugh Marlow had taken notice, too, and brought her into the manor house to live and work.

She grimaced at the thought of Hallow Hill. Why had Marlow named the place that anyway? There were no hills anywhere on the place, or anyplace else in the low country as far as she knew. Much of the land was wet for a good portion of the year, making it an inviting home for alligators, snakes, and dangerous wild hogs.

Until three days before, Susannah had never been further from Hallow Hill than Charleston, about fifteen miles from the plantation. She'd heard of Philadelphia but didn't know where it was. Since they were traveling by boat, she assumed it must be an island. In any event, it wasn't part of South Carolina.

She was sick the entire first day after they left Charleston harbor, but Marlow didn't care. He still expected to have his legs and feet massaged with warm oils. That was the reason he insisted Susannah come along. She was still young and pretty, but Marlow didn't care about that anymore. Not very often anyway. Now, he just wanted relief for his arthritis and gout.

She shuddered thinking about the times Marlow had raped her. The law wouldn't call it rape because Susannah was Marlow's property. He could do what he wanted with her. But Susannah knew she was violated. Being owned, knowing she couldn't resist didn't matter. It was rape.

Maybe those days are over for good, she thought. The last time was more than four months past now. He'd called her to him a couple of times, but nothing happened when his flaccid tool wouldn't respond. But even then, she felt violated. In her mind, she would never be this man's property.

She felt Simon's hand squeeze her bicep and

brought her mind back to the present situation. "Time to go, girl," Simon said. He squeezed her arm again and directed her toward the door to the small cabin connected to Marlow's. Susannah said nothing as he guided her through the door and locked it behind them.

The tiny compartment barely afforded room for two narrow cots and a privy bucket the both of them used. Susannah was accustomed to having little privacy, but Simon's close proximity made her uncomfortable. He was an imposing man. The top of her head was just even with his shoulders, which were broader than any man she'd ever seen. She didn't know his age, but assumed he was a few years older than herself.

Simon slipped the key into the pocket of his dirty white shirt, which was open to the waist where he'd tucked it into equally dirty brown breeches cinched at the waistband with a thin rope. He wasn't skinny like most other slaves but was well-fed and fit. His skin was lighter, too, not having to spend day-after-day in the broiling heat of the fields.

"You best sleep now, girl," Simon said to her. "We gon' get to that Philadelphia place tomorrow mornin'." He smiled at her, showing two rows of even, white teeth.

She'd seen the smile many times before. She knew it wasn't meant in friendship or kindness, but still the smile could be disarming. When Simon had first arrived at Hallow Hill, most of the young girls on the plantation had advertised their interest in him, but he'd shown no interest in return. Then, a couple of weeks later, an injured young boy had crawled home to his cabin. The boy wouldn't say what happened to him, but others had seen him with Simon earlier. Now, everybody knew Marlow kept one or two young boys at the main house to entertain Simon in exchange for his insuring that the other slaves weren't planning a revolt.

"You know anythin' 'bout Phil'delphia, Simon?" Susannah asked. She hated Simon and usually avoided conversation.

"Nope," he responded.

"Why we goin' dar?"

"Mr. Marlow say it's a big important meetin'. Theys men coming from all over goin' to make some new laws."

"Them laws ain't gon' mean nothin' to us," Susannah commented. "So, whys I goin' to Phil'delphia?"

"You gon' rub Mr. Marlow's feet when he want you to," Simon said. "You gon' do whatever else he want, too."

"And you goin' along to make sure I do what he want?"

"Mr. Marlow, he like you, girl, but he don't trust you none," Simon said. "I don't trust you none, either, so I be keepin' close watch on you."

Susannah lowered her eyes and sighed, then glanced toward the privy pot. "You mind not watchin' whilst I use the pot?" she asked.

"I don't care nothin' 'bout watchin' a girl pee," Simon said, "but like I says, I don't trust you none."

She lifted the well-worn dress Marlow had given her before they left Hallow Hill and squatted over the pot. She stared at Simon, who never looked away while she relieved herself.

*****

May 24, 1787
Philadelphia, Pennsylvania

Susannah shielded her eyes from the early afternoon sun with her right hand and watched as the schooner's crew lashed the vessel to a sturdy wooden pier. Beyond the pier, laborers pushed heavily loaded carts between the long row of ships tied up to the quay and the long, narrow buildings that fronted the piers. Other men loaded cargo onto mule-drawn wagons waiting to haul it into the city beyond the yard.

"Theys all white men workin' here," she said to Simon. She hadn't meant to say it aloud, but her astonishment overwhelmed her caution. She'd seen white men doing hard labor before, but it was damned uncommon in the low country.

"Mr. Marlow say they ain't got many slaves in these parts. White folks got to do the work."

"Them white folks must be mad about that. I bet they want some slaves to do that work for 'em."

"No," Simon said. "I been talkin' to Mr. Marlow this mornin'. He say they don't want nobody to have slaves."

"Well, I think I like Phil'delphia," Susannah said, peering beyond the dockyard. From what she could see so far, Philadelphia was very different from South Carolina.

"Don't get no ideas 'bout runnin' off," Simon warned. "I got my eyes on you." Simon was again the loathsome creature she knew him to be.

Beyond the row of warehouses, she could see a busy cobblestone avenue lined with two-story wooden buildings. Most of the structures looked as if they needed a fresh coat of paint, or at least a bucket of water and some soap. The only other large city Susannah had seen was Charleston, where majestic brick and stone mansions overlooked the harbor.

Closer to the schooner, she saw Marlow on the wide wooden pier. He was speaking to a young man in a stylish waistcoat with matching breeches, clearly not one of the dockworkers she'd been observing. The man pointed toward a carriage and Marlow nodded in agreement. A few seconds later, she saw two of the dockworkers loading Marlow's heavy trunks into the back of the carriage.

*****

The carriage was a simple wagon with one wooden bench near the front and an open deck behind it where the luggage was loaded. Marlow sat on the bench beside the young man who had met them on the dock and Susannah and Simon sat on the trunks in the back. The cobblestones beneath the wheels caused the solid wooden axles to bounce continually up and down.

A short distance from the dock, Susannah saw an encampment of makeshift tents and huts set up on the opposite bank of a small creek. Three black men and a woman milled about outside the tents. Marlow and Simon also saw them.

"Those are freedmen," Marlow turned around and said to Susannah. "In case you get ideas, take a good look at 'em. They ain't no better off than slaves."

Susannah said nothing but looked at the freedmen again. Marlow couldn't know if they were better off or not. He wouldn't understand the difference between being owned and being free.

As the wagon traveled further from the dock, the homes and buildings got statelier and more impressive. Gardens were better maintained, recent paint on buildings, finely dressed ladies walking beside the street. Even the roadway was smoother, sand having been spread to even out the rough cobblestones.

Finally, the carriage made a turn to the right and proceeded along a broad avenue lined by Oak and Elm trees. In some places, the residential look of the buildings gave way to large red brick structures that reminded Susannah of the banks and society halls she'd seen in Charleston.

After two more turns, the little wagon stopped in front of a large, three story wooden house. It was well-maintained with a front garden bursting with spring flowers. A broad front porch shaded the white exterior of the first level. Two large rocking chairs hinted at the comfort to be found within the house. A wooden sign stood beside the street. Susannah tried to remember the letters her mother had taught her years before. S… U… L. She recognized an N, an H and another U.

Chapter 6

Sara's heart thumped faster as she watched her husband's eyes staring at her cleavage from across the dining table. She'd chosen the blue dress because she knew the effect it would have on Alfred Carlisle. She understood how to control him now, and though she hated Carlisle as much as ever, she must control him.

May 24, 1787
Philadelphia, Pennsylvania

Sara wondered if the memories would ever stop. The simple task of slicing bread for the mid-day meal had brought on the image of Carlisle's hungry stare. It wasn't regret. Carlisle got what was coming to him. But her own efforts to start a new life were always muddled with her past life.

Once again, the heavy door knocker interrupted her thoughts. Hennie was away looking for fresh vegetables and meat, so Sara hurried to open the door for her new guests. Just an hour earlier, a messenger had come from Mrs. Bache to alert that a new guest would arrive soon.

As she swung the door open, she saw a dour, puffy-faced man whom she guessed to be in his late forties or early fifties. He was only slightly taller than herself and carried an obvious excess of girth. He was pale and the tip of his nose and the ridge of his cheeks were tinged red and showed tiny blood vessels coursing through them.

She'd expected her new guest to arrive road weary and filthy, as had Mr. Oliver, but the man before her now wore clean gold breeches and an immaculate blue waistcoat over a spotless white ruffled shirt. Polished black shoes, each with a sparkling gold buckle in the center, and white silk stockings completed his outfit. She noted the familiar scent of a freshly powdered wig as the man extended a folded parchment toward her.

"Hugh Marlow of South Carolina, Madam," the man said as she took the parchment from him. "You must be Mrs. Sullivan."

"Yes."

"According to this letter of introduction, you are to provide accommodations for myself and my two attendants for the duration of this meeting," Marlow said.

"That is correct Mr. Marlow," Sara said. She glanced over his shoulder and saw a well-dressed young white man and a tall, powerfully built black man unloading two large trunks from the carriage that had delivered Hugh Marlow. A slender young black woman stood beside the carriage. "Won't you come in Mr. Marlow," she added. "You must be exhausted from your travels."

"I'm well-rested Mrs. Sullivan," Marlow assured her. "I came by coastal schooner from Charleston. It was quite comfortable."

"Good then, I'll show you to your room and send your man up with the trunks."

"Thank you," Marlow said. "And when my girl, her name is Susannah, comes inside, send her up with a fresh cup of tea."

"By the way, I hadn't realized you would bring a female servant, so I had planned to put both in the same attic room," Sara told him. "It isn't a problem, though, I have another attic room she can use."

"It isn't necessary, Mrs. Sullivan," Marlow said. "They are slaves. They sleep where and when I tell them."

"But surely the girl needs some privacy?" Sara questioned.

"Too much privacy is not a good thing for slaves, Mrs. Sullivan," Marlow said.

"Are you afraid they'll run away, Mr. Marlow?" Sara asked. She remembered it had been a constant concern of slave owners in Martinique.

"Simon would not run," Marlow said, "but the girl might. Simon will keep an eye on her."

Sara looked at the girl again. She was pretty in the way many of the creole girls of Martinique had been, with lighter skin and brown hair rather than black. To Sara, she looked delicate and vulnerable, but if Marlow feared she would run, there must be plenty of inner strength in the girl.

She wondered why Marlow had brought the girl to Pennsylvania if he feared she might run away. It was well known the state had been the first to enact an abolition law, declaring that children of slaves born after 1880 would become indentured servants until age 28, after which they would be free. Also, many Pennsylvanians, particularly the large German and Quaker populations, vehemently opposed slavery and had pressured slave owners to free many not covered by the new law. But even such a progressive law had its limitations. Slavery could still exist, and the state was party to a confederation that required it to assist in capturing runaways.

The girl turned a little to gaze down Market Street. Her dress wasn't fashionable by any means, but it was a pretty shade of gray and showed off a very fine shape. She couldn't help but think of her own young shape that had infatuated an older man. At least she hadn't been a slave, although Alfred Carlisle had thought of her as his property.

"Very well," she said to Marlow. She would tell Hennie the situation as soon as the older woman returned to Sullivan House. Together, they would try to protect Susannah as much as possible.

She led Marlow to his room on the second floor opposite John Oliver's, then back downstairs to tell Simon where to take Marlow's trunks. She watched as the big man directed Susannah to go up the stairs ahead of him, then easily lifted one of the trunks and followed after her. A few seconds later, he came down the stairs alone and retrieved the second trunk.

The sound of the kitchen door opening and closing told Sara that Henrietta must have returned from her shopping. "Is it you, Hennie?" she called out and walked toward the kitchen.

"Yes'om," came the reply.

"Our new guests arrived while you were out," Sara said upon entering the kitchen where she found Hennie stowing away the carrots and onions she'd purchased.

"Woot they be like?" Hennie asked.

"I shouldn't make assumptions before we get to know them better, but I don't think we will like Mr. Marlow," Sara said. Then she relayed her initial impressions of Hugh Marlow, Simon and Susannah.

"No Miss Sara," Hennie agreed.

*****

John Oliver returned to Sullivan House midafternoon. He dispatched Ned Foster, who had spent the day reading in his room, to a laundress recommended by Mrs. Bache with a large basket of the dirty clothing the two had used in their travels from Hartford to Philadelphia. Upon returning to the boarding house, he had accepted Mrs. Sullivan's invitation to early tea. A new guest had arrived, another of the meeting delegates, and their host would facilitate their introduction.

He considered wearing the waistcoat he had worn to the state house that morning but rejected the idea. The convention could last as long as three weeks and he would likely spend a lot of time with the other delegate at Sullivan House. No, it was better to start their relationship in a more relaxed manner. He glanced at his image in the mirror. The plain white shirt he'd worn since morning still looked clean and starched. He decided on comfortable boots rather than shoes and stockings.

In the hallway, his eyes settled momentarily on the doorway across from his own. He heard muffled voices through the heavy door but couldn't make out what was being said. In any event, the man in that room was not traveling alone.

In the parlor he found Mrs. Sullivan standing next to a round table with a teapot, sweet biscuits, and fruit. Late afternoon sunshine streamed though large windows, illuminating the red curls above her shoulder. She wore a simple green dress buttoned all the way to her neck.

"Good afternoon, Mrs. Sullivan," Oliver said.

"Good afternoon, Mr. Oliver," she responded. She smiled now, replacing the pensive stare he had noticed upon entering the parlor.

"I understand that another delegate to our convention has arrived," Oliver observed.

"Yes," Mrs. Sullivan confirmed. "Mr. Marlow will be down in a few minutes."

"Marlow?" Oliver mused. "I don't recall ever meeting anyone of the name."

"He is from Charleston, which is in South Carolina I believe."

"Indeed, it is in South Carolina," Oliver noted. "What was your impression of Mr. Marlow?"

Before she could formulate an answer, Hugh Marlow strode into the parlor still dressed in the fancy attire from his arrival.

"Good afternoon, Mr. Marlow," Mrs. Sullivan said. She offered a formal introduction of the two men as she poured tea and handed a cup to each, along with a small plate for the biscuits.

"Connecticut, you say," Marlow observed, not to Mrs. Sullivan, but to John Oliver. "I believe Mr. Shays' rebellion in your neck of the woods is the reason we are attending this matter."

"Excuse me, gentlemen," Sara Sullivan said. "I must attend to other matters in the house." She slipped quietly out of the room.

"The rebellion occurred in Massachusetts, but I understand your meaning Mr. Marlow," Oliver said. "The rebellion shed light on the fact that the Articles of Confederation, as they now exist, are inadequate to protect the nation against such uprisings."

"Why should South Carolina send its men and riches to save Massachusetts from its rabble?"

"Because the discontent of the rabble, as you refer to the poor farmers of Massachusetts, would soon spread to the poor farmers of other states, including South Carolina," Oliver countered.

"The people of South Carolina understand their place, Mr. Oliver," Hugh Marlow said. "The lowborn are satisfied with their lot and will protect the property of others with their lives if necessary."

"Are the slaves satisfied?"

"Yes, they are," Marlow stressed.

John Oliver stared at Marlow but said nothing. Then, Marlow spoke again.

"The paramount reason Governor Pinckney asked me to attend this assembly was to see that South Carolina's sovereignty is protected," Marlow said.

"Then you wish to perpetuate the Articles of Confederation in their current state?"

"Some minor corrections may be in order," Marlow offered.

"What corrections do you have in mind?" Oliver asked.

"We must protect property rights with more vigor," Marlow said. "Under the present regime, a man may lose his property all together if it should turn up in another state."

"You are referring to runaway slaves, I suppose," Oliver said.

"Yes."

"All the states in the Confederation recognize the rights of other states to regulate the practice of slavery," Oliver pointed out. "Even Pennsylvania acknowledges South Carolina's right."

"Acknowledgement and action are different things. Many of the states north of Maryland have been lax in their efforts to recover the property of slave owners from the Southern states."

"The officers of those states have a full agenda, Mr. Marlow," Oliver said. "They don't have the time or manpower to chase and capture men who should be free anyway."

"Would you abolish the practice of slavery completely?" Marlow asked.

"If it were in my power to abolish slavery in the Confederation's entirety, I would certainly do it," Oliver acknowledged.

"And how would you compensate men like me for the loss of our property?" Marlow asked.

"I don't know the answer to that yet," Oliver said. "But I hope it will be a question that we must resolve as a nation one day."

Before Marlow could respond to Oliver's last statement, the pounding of the heavy door knocker sounded, and Henrietta Washington hurried to open the door for Ned Foster. She stepped back to make room for the valet to enter carrying a large bunch of freshly cut flowers.

"I bought these from a flower seller," Foster said to Henrietta. "Perhaps they will cover the aroma of too many men in the house."

"I likes the smell of men in dis house," Hennie giggled to Ned. "I get these in some wota' and put 'em in the dinin' room." She took the flowers from him and walked toward the back of the house.

When Hennie had disappeared into the back of the house, Oliver called to Ned. "Come and meet our new housemate, Ned."

As the black man walked toward them, Oliver turned to Hugh Marlow. "Mr. Marlow, I'd like to introduce my valet and companion, Mr. Ned Foster." Then to Ned, "Mr. Foster, please welcome Mr. Hugh Marlow of South Carolina to our company." He hoped that by introducing both men as "mister" he was sending the message he considered them equals.

"Welcome, Mr. Marlow," Ned Foster said in his most refined voice and offered his hand to shake.

Marlow sneered at the black man for several seconds. Finally, his glare softened, "Very well," he said, but didn't take the offered hand.

Foster turned to Oliver, "Unless you need me, I'll go up to my room and take a nap for a while before dinner," he said.

"Enjoy your nap, Ned," Oliver said.

Just as Ned Foster reached the hallway to the staircase, he turned to the two men still in the parlor, "I'll see you this evening, Hugh," he said to Marlow. John Oliver smiled to himself. He knew Ned's familiarity would infuriate Marlow.

"Since you oppose slavery, I should assume that your man is a freedman," Marlow said once Ned Foster had disappeared into the hallway.

"Yes, he is," Oliver acknowledged.

"Free man or not, he should learn proper respect for his superiors," Marlow scowled.

"I've known Ned for many years," Oliver said. "I'm sure he afforded the respect *he* thought proper."

"I see that sharing this accommodation may be difficult for us both, Mr. Oliver," Marlow said.

"Yet, we shall soldier on," Oliver said. He placed his cup on the table and started for the hallway.

"Just a moment, Mr. Oliver," Marlow called out to him.

Oliver stopped and turned to meet Marlow's gaze. "Yes?"

"Your man may be free, but I am accompanied by two negroes who are not free. I want your assurance that your man will not try to influence the behavior of my slaves."

"I'll relay your concerns to Mr. Foster," Oliver said. He whirled and left the room.

Chapter 7

Sara's heart raced as Paul leaned toward her and kissed her on the lips, gently at first, then harder. As his hand slid slowly up her inner thigh, one small part of her mind wanted to scream "Stop", but the larger part, the part that wanted to love, told her to relax, enjoy.

Her nipples swelled against his bare chest as Paul gently eased her down onto the cot and lay beside her. He rolled her onto her back and kissed each nipple and the space between them. His curly blond hair smelled like the fresh bread baking in the kitchen a few steps away.

She felt his lips on her abdomen and giggled a little when the tip of his tongue made little circles around her navel. He moved further down her torso and now his breath caused the hairs around her womanhood to vibrate. One second, two seconds, three seconds, more. Her hips moved upward with anticipation.

May 25, 1787
Philadelphia, Pennsylvania

Sara's body shuddered from the orgasm. She threw the covers aside and sat on the side of the bed, her nightgown bunched around her waist. As she stood and walked to the washbasin, the gown fell into place.

She looked out the window onto a bright Philadelphia morning. She'd slept later than normal, but then she'd lingered in bed a while longer, her mind flooded with memories of Paul Barré, as it often did.

Memories were so much better than dreams. She could control memories, select the good ones and delete the bad ones. Memories of Paul were plentiful, both good and bad. She used the good memories for pleasure and the bad ones to remind herself that men, even the ones she loved, were not to be trusted.

The porcelain clock on the bedside table told her it was almost nine o'clock. She should go downstairs and at least make an appearance as host before her guests went about their business for the day. But thoughts of Paul Barré had turned her mood inward, and, as she often did, Sara reflected on her journey from a Dublin slum to a fine house in Philadelphia.

In a way, the man she'd hated more than anything in the world made her transition possible. Alfred Carlisle had stolen thousands of pounds from his family's enterprises in Ireland and hidden the money in a secret compartment in his study. But her husband never realized Sara was watching every move he made.

After months of planning, the time was finally right. She stuffed over ten-thousand pounds of Bank of England notes into the false bottom of a travel case and made her way in the early morning hours to a Dutch trading ship that would take her to France. In addition to the money, she carried three dresses, assorted undergarments, and the hope of a new life.

What she did not carry with her that night was guilt. Alfred Carlisle got what he deserved, and Sara had no regrets about serving it to him. But there would be repercussions and the sooner she was away from Ireland the better. It wouldn't be long before Alfred's father, Lord Carlisle, grasped the events of that evening and exercised his enormous power within the kingdom to bring her to justice.

Sara stayed in her cabin for the entire voyage. The man who arranged her voyage had paid a sizable bribe to the captain to ensure her safe passage, but there was no reason to take chances. Late in the afternoon of the fifth day at sea, the little freighter tied up to a pier at the port of Brest in France.

Once the vessel was secure, the captain sent his

crew ashore to enjoy a pint of ale before the work of unloading began. As soon as they were out of sight, he escorted Sara down the gangplank and gave her directions to a tavern run by a Scotsman. She would find lodging and people to help her there.

Two days later, a young Scottish girl told her that Robert Murray, a wealthy Scottish expatriate was looking for an English-speaking maid to work in his chateau outside the city. She convinced the tavern owner to arrange a meeting with Murray for her and a few days after that, Sara was employed in Robert Murray's household.

Remembering Murray always brought a smile to her face. At first, she'd worried the man, who was forty-five and single, would be like Alfred Carlisle. But she soon realized that Murray was more attracted to men than to women and over the next three years, she came to love him as the father image she never saw in her own father.

From the beginning, Murray sensed there was more to Sara's story than she had told, and when he learned from an English captain that Lord Carlisle was offering a large reward for a young Irish girl, he confronted her. She decided to trust Murray and told him the whole story of her marriage and escape. Murray vowed to protect her secret.

Sara proved adept at mastering the language and was able to move about the town as any young French woman would. Murray himself had lived in France since the age of ten when the family fled to France after the last Jacobite uprising. But he was never able to shake the strong Scottish brogue he'd learned from his father. He had no trouble understanding the French, but they could never understand his strange pronunciation.

After almost two years in Robert Murray's service, he asked her to work in the kitchen as an assistant to a new chef. Paul Barré was well-known for his work in Paris and his presence on Murray's estate would enhance business opportunities for Murray's trading and shipping businesses. But Barré didn't speak any English.

Sara agreed enthusiastically. Soon, she was learning to bake bread, create flavorful sauces, and plate a dish properly. At the same time, she was teaching Barré to speak English and falling in love. Two years had passed since the nightmare of Alfred Carlisle ended. Maybe all men were not evil. Certainly, Robert Murray wasn't evil. He wasn't a romantic possibility either, though. Paul Barré was.

Paul was handsome in ways she'd never thought of. He was graceful, with never a wasted step as he moved between stove, oven, and prep table. He was always clean, and his curly blond hair smelled of fresh bread rather than the perfumes and powders men often wore. At thirty-seven, he had avoided the most obvious hazard of his profession, the potbelly. Instead, his width was in good proportion with his height, which was just a few inches taller than Sara. The smoothness of his cheeks and forehead belied his age, as did a nearly hairless chest.

The attraction was mutual, too, and it was only a

matter of weeks before they shared the small cot in Paul's room. That was the first of the erotic memories that often aroused her, as it just had. At those times, it was easy to push away the bad memories. She had imagined a life with Paul Barré, but it wasn't to be. Still, Sara realized love was possible for her.

She sat on the edge of the bed as those memories raced through her brain. But the sound of the door closing downstairs brought her back to the present. She stood and looked out the window onto Third Street, where she saw John Oliver and Hugh Marlow walking side by side in the direction of the Pennsylvania Statehouse.

Sara slipped out of her nightgown and into the dress she had worn the evening before, but without the undergarments and the three petticoats that made it so stifling. She would have to climb into that rig again soon enough, but for now, she opted for comfort. When she reached the kitchen, she found Hennie at the kitchen table with Ned Foster and the two slaves who had accompanied Hugh Marlow.

"Good morning, Mrs. Sullivan," Ned Foster was the first to speak.

"Good morning, Mr. Foster," Sara said. "Good morning, Hennie," she added.

"Mornin' ma'am," Hennie responded.

Sara turned to the two newcomers on the other side of the table, "Mr. Marlow neglected to make introductions yesterday," she said. "I am your host, Mrs. Sullivan."

The girl didn't speak but looked to the large black man beside her. "I am Simon and dis girl be called Susannah," he said.

"Welcome to Sullivan House Simon and Susannah," Sara said. "I hope you have found the accommodations comfortable."

"It's fine, ma'am," Simon said.

Sara looked at the girl, but again, she didn't speak. "I could arrange a separate room if you need more privacy," she told the girl.

"The 'commodations is fine, ma'am," Simon said before Susannah had a chance to respond.

Sara ignored Simon's answer and continued to look at Susannah. Finally, the girl said, "It's fine, ma'am."

Simon smiled and Sara felt her face flush with anger. She glanced to Ned Foster, who shook his head slowly.

Chapter 8

May 29, 1787
Sullivan House

"South Carolina will never accept the Virginia Plan," Hugh Marlow insisted.

"What is your concern with Governor Randolph's plan?" John Oliver asked. He poured himself another cup of tea and took one of the maple cookies Mrs. Sullivan had placed on the table.

"It isn't Randolph's plan; it's Madison's plan," Marlow said. "And the reason I object is that South Carolina cannot allow the federal legislature to veto laws put in place by the state."

"You are referring to slavery?"

"Yes."

"Randolph and Madison are Virginians and slaveowners themselves," Oliver objected. "Surely they would protect the institution which is so important to South Carolina."

"They put too much faith in the goodwill of others," Marlow said, "people such as yourself, Mr. Oliver. You would deprive us of our property and offer nothing in return. No, South Carolina is better served if we simply make a few needed changes to the Articles of Confederation. That was, after all, the pretext for this gathering."

"I am sure your objections will be well aired in the coming days," Oliver offered. Marlow was right about one thing. The pretext of the meeting had been to amend and repair the Articles in order to make the existing confederation more stable. The Congress of the Confederation authorized the gathering in February for that purpose. Four days earlier, on May 25th, representatives from seven states had reported to the assembly and they declared it in session. The proceedings began with the unanimous election of General Washington as presiding officer and the election of a secretary, messenger, and doorkeeper.

The delegates present soon realized the project they were to embark on would be much more important and more difficult than they imagined. On the previous day, May 28th, a committee proposed rules that required absolute secrecy during the course of the meeting, and, in spite of the coming summer heat, Washington had the windows nailed shut to prevent eavesdropping. Additionally, they decided that they would release no official record of the proceedings to the public in any form.

On Tuesday, May 29th, the official business of the convention commenced when Edmund Randolph, the young governor of Virginia, presented the Virginia Plan, which envisioned repudiation of the Articles of Confederation and replacing them with a new constitution. The weaknesses of the confederation had become obvious to many. The central government was little more than a symbolic institution with no power to collect taxes, regulate commerce, conduct foreign affairs, or defend the nation from its adversaries. Still, a large contingent of delegates favored limited revisions to the articles to protect the sovereignty then enjoyed by the states.

As Randolph outlined the plan, the new federal government would be comprised of three branches: an executive, two legislative bodies, and a judicial branch. The plan envisioned that each branch would act as a check on the power of the other branches. The source of authority would be derived from the people through public election of the larger house of the legislature, who would then select the members of the smaller house. The combined legislature would then select the executive. Also, the legislature would have veto power over state laws that it considered unconstitutional, which appeared to be the root of Hugh Marlow's objections.

"The sovereignty of the states is not my only

objection, Mr. Oliver," Marlow said. "I do not care for the notion of general elections of the primary legislative body."

"The people will not stand for anything less," Oliver argued. "They have made great sacrifice to throw off the ruling aristocrats of England. They will not accept establishment of a new ruling class."

"I believe the people select their state representatives in every state. To me, that seems to be quite enough democracy."

"How then do you suggest we select the members of the federal legislature?" Oliver asked.

"If such a federal system is to be established," Marlow offered, "the representation of the states should be selected by the duly authorized officers of the states."

"Such a plan might be viable if all of the states provided their citizens with the same rights," Oliver argued. "But many states have severe restrictions on voting."

"Sensible restrictions," Marlow countered.

"That is a matter of perspective. In many states, only those fortunate enough to own property may vote. Is that fair to those who have been less fortunate? Your own state of South Carolina requires confirmation of religious beliefs. Is that fair to those of different beliefs?"

"It isn't intended to be fair, Mr. Oliver," Marlow answered. "South Carolina wishes to preserve a certain way of life."

"No matter the cost to anyone else?"

"That is correct. Randolph himself said the chief danger to our nation arises from the failure to put a proper check on democracy."

John Oliver shook his head and placed his teacup on the table. There was nothing left to say. At least, not in this conversation. There would be others, but he'd had enough for this night. As he climbed the stairs to his room, the task before the convention struck him as a nearly impossible one.

He pushed open the door to his room and saw that Ned had lit an oil lamp on the table next to the window. He sat in a chair next to the table, pulled boots off his tired feet, leaned back and closed his eyes. In the days and weeks ahead, there would be many conversations like the one he'd just had with Hugh Marlow.

Oliver opened his eyes at the sound of a tap on his door. "Yes," he said.

"I'd like a few words with you," Ned Foster said as he closed the door behind himself.

"What is it, Ned?"

"That girl, Susannah, Mr. Marlow's slave," Ned began. "She's in a bad situation."

"All slaves are in a bad situation, Ned," Oliver said.

"Some situations are a lot worse than others."

"Tell me what you think," Oliver said.

"I was sitting in my room and I could hear

Simon and Susannah talking up in the attic," Ned Foster started. "I couldn't make it all out, but the gist of it was that Susannah is here to perform personal services for Marlow."

"Sex?"

"Probably," Ned said.

"Mrs. Sullivan expressed a similar concern," Oliver said. "She also said she thought Simon was here to keep Susannah from running away."

"That may be," Ned agreed. "Simon kept saying he was watching her."

"I don't like it Ned," Oliver said, "but what can we do."

"I want to talk to the girl," Ned said, "find out what's going on."

"That reminds me, Marlow asked me to keep you away from his slaves. He's afraid a freedman will give them ideas."

"Well, you've asked me," Ned said. "Now, I'm going to do it anyway."

"I assumed you would," John Oliver said. "Just be careful. Simon can't be trusted and he's probably dangerous."

*****

The tinkling of a little gold bell roused Susannah from a light sleep. The bell was attached to a wire connected to a metal ring in Hugh

Marlow's room on the second floor. The purpose of the bell was to alert servants or slaves in the attic rooms that their masters required their presence below. Other bells were connected to metal rings in the other guest rooms, but since she and Simon were the only servants in the attic, those other bells wouldn't be ringing.

The bell woke Simon as well. On the voyage from Charleston, she had not seen him sleep even once, but since they arrived at Sullivan House, he nodded off often, but never for more than an hour or so.

Once, he'd awakened and found her staring at him. *"If you gonna kill me girl, you better be quick about it, 'cause if I wakes up, you gonna be dead,"* he had said. There was no fear in his voice, but he had taken precautions, having removed any item she could have used as a weapon, and he'd locked the door and put the key inside the crotch of his pants. She had no intention of trying to fish the key out of there.

"Come on, girl," Simon said. "Mr. Marlow wants you."

"Might be he just wan' you," Susannah suggested.

"Ain't nothin' he want from me this time o' e'nen."

She knew Simon was right when they entered the second-floor room. Marlow sat on the edge of the bed in his nightshirt. "Take that chair and wait outside, Simon," Marlow said.

"Yes sir, Mr. Marlow," Simon said.

Once Simon had clattered into the hallway with the chair and closed the door, Marlow patted the bed beside where he sat. "Sit here, Susannah," he instructed.

She hesitated for a few seconds and then sat down next to Marlow. She cringed as he cupped her left breast with his right hand through the thin dress she wore. "Did you wash today?" Marlow asked.

"No," she lied.

"Hmmm, I'll ask Simon about that. I instructed him to be sure you washed today."

Marlow moved his hand from her breast and began to slide it slowly up her thigh beneath the dress, "You feel clean enough to me," he said. "Take the dress off."

She glanced at a half empty whiskey bottle on a chest-of-drawers near the bed and knew Marlow was in a low mood. She knew she couldn't hesitate long, or his somberness would turn to anger. She stood and pulled the dress off over her head. She was naked underneath since underwear was a luxury of the rich.

She turned to face him and stood completely still as his eyes drifted up and down her body. Marlow stood and pulled his own nightshirt off before crawling onto the bed and lying face down. "It's not as bad as you think," he said to her. "I just need my backside massaged."

In her mind, Susannah debated the relative disgust she should feel. On the one hand, intercourse — if he were able to achieve an erection — would take less than five minutes, but the massage could take an hour or more, depending on his mood. And she hated it even more when he required her to be naked throughout the work. She straddled herself across his bare thighs and began to knead his buttocks and hamstrings with her hands.

When he first summoned her to work in the house, Marlow had treated her in much the same way he treated the other house slaves, courteous most of the time, but with occasional fits of anger. But, after six or seven months in the house, she noticed him watching her more often, sometimes making her uncomfortable with long stares. A short time after that, Simon came to her tiny room in the attic to fetch her to Marlow's bedroom.

More than four years had passed since that night and Marlow had sent for her many times, sometimes for intercourse and other times for personal services such as the massages or keeping his bath water hot.

Once, she'd tried to refuse him and gotten a powerful backhand across the cheek and he'd threatened to turn her out into the fields to harvest rice among the cottonmouths and copperheads. That's when she decided to talk to Winnie, the cook and de facto head of the household slaves.

"Everybody on the plantation know what been

hap'nin to you, chile," Winnie had said.

"Do they hate me?" Susannah asked.

"No chile, they don' hate you," Winnie assured her. "You a slave, girl. You ain' got no say in what happen to you. Er'body on dis farm know dat."

"I don' wanna get with chile from that man, Winnie."

Winnie smiled, "Now, dat somethin' I can help you with."

Winnie gave her a small bag of pumpkin seeds and instructed her to place one seed in a second bag each day after her menstrual period began until the beginning of the next period. When her next period began, she would know the length of her menstrual cycle. Now, she could move one seed a day from one bag to another during each cycle. She was to try to avoid intercourse during the middle third of the cycle. But they both knew that Susannah would have little control over Marlow's urges, so Winnie had concocted a disgusting mash that Susannah was to drink as soon as possible after intercourse during the danger period.

Whether due to her own calendar or Winnie's potion, Susannah avoided pregnancy. Then, during her third year in the house, Marlow began experiencing impotency. At first, Susannah feared that he would express his anger toward her, but instead, he sought comfort in rum and brandy. Soon, she learned that the massages soothed his darkest moods.

She slowed her manipulations of Marlow's buttocks and leaned forward enough to hear a soft snore coming from his nose. She sat still for several seconds and listened again. The same soft snore. She gently lifted her leg over him and slid off the side of the bed. She found the edge of a blanket and pulled it over Marlow, then slipped her dress on over her head. She opened the door quietly and exited into the hall where Simon waited.

Chapter 9

June 4, 1787
Pennsylvania Statehouse

As the second week of the gathering began, John Oliver reflected on the discussions of the first few days. Many ideas had been presented and discussed, but almost nothing decided.

Finally, the convention made a significant advancement a few minutes earlier with a decision that the "executive" would be a single individual, as opposed to a committee or commission. The idea of an executive was a big change from the Articles of Confederation, which had no such position. It required considerable discussion to get the delegates comfortable with the notion that enough checks would be in place to prevent the executive from gaining too much power.

Except for their brief experiment with the Confederation, monarchy was the only form of government most had known, and many of the delegates assumed that America would one day be a monarchy as well. Yet, most were firmly committed to establishing a republic, albeit one that gave substantial preference to wealth and property.

George Washington was the most famous and beloved American of that time, and if anyone could assume the role of king, it would be the general who had willed his rag-tag armies through a war against a much stronger foe. But Washington had no desire to be king and had only reluctantly agreed to take part in the meeting in Philadelphia. On the first day, the delegates selected Washington to preside over the proceedings. He accepted the task, but participated very little in the debates, preferring to appear non-partisan.

Most of the delegates, however, engaged in the debates with vigor. Thus far, the conference had not been "in session" for most of the many hours spent in the chamber. Instead, Madison suggested an approach he referred to as a "committee-of-the-whole", which fostered a more open discussion of ideas. Washington would gavel them into session for votes and other formal matters.

After determining that the executive would be a single individual, the committee-of-the-whole took up the matter of how the executive would interact with the legislative branch. The Virginia Plan called for a limited "negative", or veto of legislation, to be exercised by a Council of Revision made up of the executive and members of the judiciary.

The first to speak on the issue was Elbridge Gerry of Massachusetts. "I think the judiciary ought not take a part in the making of law," he said, "as they will surely be called upon to make judgements about its appropriateness in later proceedings."

"What do you propose in place of such a council?" Madison asked.

"I have given that a measure of thought sense first reading these proposals," Gerry said. "I move that the executive shall have a right to negative any legislative act which is not subsequently passed by a substantial part — a number we must ultimately determine — of each branch of the national legislature."

Rufus King, also of Massachusetts, stood to comment, "I concur that judges ought to be able to expound the law as it comes before them without the bias of having been a part of its creation. Therefore, I second Mr. Gerry's proposal."

"If the branches are to be equal," James Wilson of Pennsylvania observed, "then the executive should have an absolute negative."

"Mr. Gerry's motion has been seconded," George Washington interjected. "We must consider the proposal in good order."

"Very well," Wilson said. "I move that the last clause of Mr. Gerry's proposal — the legislative override — be struck."

"I second Mr. Wilson," Alexander Hamilton stated. "There is no danger of such power being too much exercised. The king of England has such a veto and has never used it against Parliament."

"I see no necessity for so great a control over the legislature," Gerry countered. "The two branches will be comprised of the best men in the community."

Roger Sherman of Connecticut offered his thoughts. "No one man should have so much power as to stop the will of the whole," he stated. "We should avail ourselves of his wisdom in revising the laws, but we should not permit him to overrule the cool and thoughtful deliberations of the legislature."

Madison agreed with Sherman, but further added that he thought the executive would never feel so empowered as to try using his negative when so large a portion of the legislature supported the law.

Pierce Butler of South Carolina took the floor. "As you have witnessed today, I cast my vote in favor of a single executive. But, had the idea of a complete negative of legislative endeavors been presented beforehand, I would have viewed it differently."

"Hear, hear," Oliver heard an unidentified voice shout.

Pierce continued his speech, "Some gentlemen seem to think we have nothing to fear from abuses of the executive power, but why might not a

Cataline or a Cromwell arise in this country as in others."

Gunning Bedford opposed any veto power at all, and George Mason worried that an executive might abuse the power to coerce the legislature. "We are not constituting a British government, but a more dangerous monarchy, an elective one," he said. Mason added that he could see the value of a negative, but such power in the hands of one man would be dangerous.

"The first man put at the helm will be a good one," Dr. Franklin said from his position near the dais. "Nobody knows what sort may come afterwards. If he would possess an absolute negative, the executive will always be increasing power here, as elsewhere, until it ends in monarchy."

John Oliver looked toward Wilson and Hamilton, the two men who had proposed the absolute negative. Hamilton looked as if he intended to rise and speak, but out of respect for the elder Franklin, remained silent. After several seconds of silence in the room, the chair brought Wilson's motion to give the executive an absolute negative to a vote where it was unanimously defeated.

Next, Washington proposed a vote on Gerry's original motion, and after some discussion, they passed it with language inserted to set the legislative override at two-thirds in each house. Madison still was not satisfied and again proposed that the judiciary be part of the process. Mr. Gerry and Mr. King reiterated their objections to this, and the matter was not brought to a vote.

*****

"I prefer something stronger, Mrs. Sullivan," Hugh Marlow rejected her offer of tea.

"I have a little rum and some peach wine," Sara Sullivan offered.

"While peach wine sounds delightful," Marlow replied, "My girl is bringing down a bottle of excellent Kentucky whiskey."

"I'll get a glass for you," Mrs. Sullivan said to him. Then, turning to John Oliver, "Will you need a glass as well, Mr. Oliver."

"Tea will be fine for me," Oliver replied.

"Nonsense," Marlow said. "Bring a glass for Mr. Oliver, too." He turned to Oliver, "Have you drunk Kentucky whiskey, Mr. Oliver?"

"I've had whiskey from Pennsylvania and the western area of Massachusetts, but not Kentucky."

"Well, you shall see that it is remarkable whiskey, particularly given that the area has only been settled for a few years."

By the time Mrs. Sullivan returned with two glasses and a pitcher of water, the girl, Susannah, had delivered the liquor. The first thing John Oliver noticed about it was its dark brown tint, the color of French cognac. It looked nothing like the clear

Pennsylvania "moonshine" he had occasionally drank with his friends in Connecticut.

Marlow thanked Mrs. Sullivan for the glasses but offered no similar appreciation to the slave girl. "Go back to your room now," was all he said.

Oliver watched her leave the room. They had lived under the same roof for ten days and nights, yet he'd only seen the girl one other time and that a fleeting glance. But Ned Foster's description of her was correct. She was pretty in a clean printed dress without petticoats to hide her shape. The girl said nothing when she handed the bottle to Marlow, but her stare toward the man said plenty. She hated Hugh Marlow.

Marlow extended a glass of the brown liquid in Oliver's direction. "We should drink to a day of accomplishment I suppose," he said.

"I suppose we accomplished something," Oliver conceded.

"If we continue at this pace, we shall be in Philadelphia for Christmas celebrations." Marlow raised the glass to his mouth and took a long draw on the dark liquid, then held the glass away and admired it. "This is quite good, isn't it?"

"Yes," Oliver agreed after taking a small sip of the whiskey. "The question of how the executive will be a check on the power of the legislative, and visa-versa is critical," Oliver suggested.

"As long as men of property control both, then they should have no need of checks and balances.

They will act to protect the property of all."

"We must strike a balance between the rights of property and the rights of those without property."

"Why should those without property have rights?" Marlow asked.

"Because we have said 'all men are created equal' in our Declaration of Independence from the King of England," Oliver stated.

"Perhaps all men are created equal," Marlow retorted, "but that doesn't mean they have accumulated wealth equally."

"There are many thousands of men and women who never had the opportunity to accumulate wealth."

"Are you referring to slaves, Mr. Oliver?"

"Yes."

"Slaves are property," Marlow said.

"Slaves are humans," Oliver retorted.

"I think I will agree with you on that score," Marlow said. He took another long sip of the whiskey and placed the glass back on the table.

"Then they should have rights," Oliver stressed.

"They will have rights, Mr. Oliver," Marlow offered. "They will have the right to be represented by elected legislators."

"Are you saying you will support giving slaves the right to vote?"

"No," Marlow answered. "But, if you have read

Mr. Madison's plan, you will know that he proposes to set the number of representatives to the larger house based on the population tallies of the various states. Thus, in order for the Southern states to achieve fair representation, the slaves must be counted in such tallies."

"So, your hope is that the slaves will count for purposes of determining how many representatives South Carolina may elect to the federal legislature, but those same slaves will have no voice in who is elected?"

"Exactly," Marlow confirmed.

"Connecticut will never agree to such a plan," Oliver said. "Nor will the other states in the Northern region."

"Then we shall have two nations instead of one," Marlow said as he rose from his chair. "I won't see you at supper tonight for I shall dine in my room. Good night, Mr. Oliver."

Chapter 10

June 11, 1787
Sullivan House

Sara Sullivan frowned as she examined herself in the mirror above the dresser in her bedroom. She slid her hands down her sides to her waist and then further down to her hips. She cupped her hands to the underside of each bare breast to see if they needed support for their weight. They didn't. She moved the hands slowly down her naked torso, stopping to squeeze the tips of her fingers into her flat abdomen.

She'd been told many times she was beautiful naked. First by her brother, then by Alfred Carlisle. But hearing it hadn't pleased her until Paul Barré said it. She smiled for a moment, then the frown returned. Men might find her beautiful, but they couldn't see the scars. Paul, wherever he was now, knew about the scars.

Again, she pressed her fingertips into her abdomen. Four years was time enough to erase some memories, but others haunt for a lifetime. She turned away from the mirror and threw herself facedown onto the bed. When she rolled onto her back, a tear trickled down her cheek. She laid a hand on her belly and remembered the tiny bump that had been there once.

She thought about the joy she had felt that day when she knew for sure she had Paul's child inside her. She had rushed to the kitchen, took Paul's arm and pulled him into a quiet corner where no one else could hear. She expected him to be as excited as she was. He wasn't.

Sara was certain that Paul loved her and would be happy about the baby. Instead, she watched as his head sank, and his normal smile faded to a look of frightened dejection.

"What's the matter, Paul," Sara had asked.

"This is so unexpected," Paul had told her.

"How can it be unexpected?" Sara asked. "We've had sex a lot of times."

"I know, but I didn't think I could," Paul explained.

"Why not?"

Paul looked away from her and didn't speak for several seconds. "Marie has not conceived in more than ten years," he finally said.

"Who is Marie?" Sara asked.

"My wife," Paul answered.

At that moment, the fantasy she had concocted shattered. Her lover of more than a year had kept from her the one thing that made their relationship impossible. She had never considered the possibility that Paul was married. But, looking back, maybe there were signs she had missed. He often went away for a week or two at a time, but never asked her to come along. When she'd asked him about it, he had said he went to visit relatives and that she wouldn't enjoy it.

There were things she hadn't told Paul, as well, but not things that would prevent them from being together. He knew her only as Sara Sullivan and she saw no need for him to know of her past marriage, or how that marriage ended. If they married in France, there was no chance at all the registrars would link Sara Sullivan to Sara Byrne or Sara Carlisle.

Both France and Ireland remained staunchly Catholic and forbade divorce except in the most compelling circumstances. Since Paul and Sara were both Catholic, any application for a divorce would invite the Vatican to investigate, and Sara knew the risks that would entail.

After she left the kitchen in tears, Robert Murray stopped her in the hallway to ask what the problem was. She sobbed harder and threw her arms around Murray, the one man she knew she could trust.

When the sobbing lessened enough, she told Murray the entire story. By the time she finished, her own tears had stopped, but Murray seemed on the verge of crying. Instead, he gripped her shoulders and held her at arm's length.

"We must decide what to do, Sara," Murray said.

"I have no place to go to have the baby," Sara said, "and I can't stay here with Paul. It wouldn't be fair to him and it would be too painful for me."

"I could send Paul away," Murray offered. He released her and put his hands on his hips.

"No, you can't. A great chef like Paul is good for business. You've said so many times."

"There are other chefs," Murray said.

"No," Sara was stern. "I must find a place to go to have this child."

"There are convents where girls can go," Murray said. "I can find one for you."

"I can't go to a convent," Sara said.

"Why not?"

"Lord Carlisle is one of the most important Catholics in England," Sara said. "I'm sure the entire Church is watching for me."

"That's true, I'm sure," Murray agreed. "That's why you never go to mass with the other staff."

"I have other reasons to avoid the church, too," Sara said. "I've seen how it really works."

Murray stroked his chin with the fingers of his left hand and thought for a moment. "There is another alternative," he finally said.

"What?"

"There is a man in Brest who has been known to provide abortion services to unwed girls," Murray said. "He did it for one of our maids a few years ago."

"Abortion isn't legal is it?"

"No," Murray agreed, "and it isn't safe either. The maid nearly died, and she can never have children again."

"If Lord Carlisle finds me, I won't have children anyway," Sara sighed.

She told Murray she would think about it and headed toward her room two floors above. Through her entire life, the Catholic Church had told her that abortion was a sin, but her own experience with the church had taught her their ethics were pliable. The church demanded that such children come into the world, but then offered no help for the difficult lives the poor and illegitimate faced. Besides, for as long as Lord Carlisle lived, her child could become an orphan at any moment.

Her mind was made up before she reached the top of the stairs. She turned around and went back in search of Robert Murray, who she found in his office near the library.

"If you're sure it's what you want, I'll arrange it," Murray said when she told him she wanted to end the pregnancy.

"Yes," Sara said, and went on to explain her reasoning.

"Very well," Murray said. "I'll arrange it. And, by the way, I have another idea for you as well."

"What?"

"A new life for you in the new world," Murray said.

It was something she had thought about when she first left Ireland, but the American colonies were at war with Great Britain, which meant she could still be within reach of Lord Carlisle. "Tell me," she said.

"One of my vessels leaves next week for Martinique in the West Indies. A business associate of mine has a large estate on the island. I'll give you a letter of introduction and I'm sure you can stay there as long as you need to."

"Martinique?"

"It's a small island," Murray informed her. "Hot as blazes in summertime, but they speak French and you would be safe there until you can go somewhere else."

"Paul said the American colonies are winning the war with England," Sara said.

"Thanks in no small part to Louis XVI," Murray said. "The French treasury is empty because of Louis's spending on the American war. Some say there could be a revolution."

"Perhaps I could make my way to the colonies from Martinique once the fighting has ended."

"My captain tells me the fighting is over as far as the armies are concerned," Murray said. "The British still control the seas around their ports, though."

She often thought of that day, and how the decision she made would affect the rest of her life. She had been lucky in the procedure, experiencing only strong cramps during the three days that followed. Within weeks, her menstrual cycle returned to normal, and although there was no way to be sure, she was confident she could conceive again.

It was mid-afternoon, and the house was quiet. Mr. Oliver and Mr. Marlow likely wouldn't return until near sunset. Sara rose from the bed and slipped a simple dress on without undergarments, a habit she had developed in France. She would dress more formally by evening, but for now, comfort was of the first order.

She picked up a brush from the dresser and began pulling it through her hair when a crashing sound from the main floor below caused her to stop mid-stroke. She stood still and listened to the sound of male voices, raised in anger. She dropped the brush onto the dresser and hurried to the stairs.

Sara followed the voices to the main parlor at the front of the house where she found Ned Foster and Simon glaring at each other near the center of the room. Near the window, a small round table had been moved and a vase lay on the floor near it. Henrietta Washington watched the two men from the other side of the room.

"What's going on here?" Sara demanded.

"We were just having a difference of opinion, Mrs. Sullivan," Ned Foster said without changing his glare toward the other man. The two were about the same height, but Simon's shoulders were wider, more powerful.

"If this difference of opinion will involve violence, you must go outside," Sara said to both men.

"Ain't got nothin' to do with no 'pinion ma'am," Simon said. "Mr. Marlow don't want dis nigga talkin' to Miss Susannah. I's jus' remindin' him o' dat." He gave Sara a slight nod of the head and left the room. The three who remained stood silently until they heard Simon's footfalls receding up the staircase.

"We need to talk," Sara said to the others. "Put the tea kettle on, Hennie."

A few minutes later, Hennie placed a tray with three cups, a teapot, and a jar of sugar on the small table in the kitchen. She poured a cup of the strong tea for each of them, then took one of the empty seats. When everyone had tasted their tea, Sara spoke. "What did Simon mean when he said you weren't to talk to Susannah?"

"Marlow is afraid I'll fill her head with ideas about freedom," Foster said.

"Have you talked to her?" Sara asked.

"I tried, but Simon woke up," Foster said. "Susannah pushed me away when she realized he was awake. I came downstairs, but he followed me."

"What were you going to say to her?"

"I just wanted to know what was going on in Marlow's room," Foster said. "I wanted to know if she was OK."

"In Marlow's room?" Sara wondered.

"Yeah. Three or four times since they got here, Simon takes her to Marlow's room at night. Simon waits outside."

"How long is she in Marlow's room?"

"About an hour I guess," Foster said.

"What do you think is happening in that room?" Sara asked.

"What men usually do with a pretty young woman in their room," Foster said.

"Does that sort of thing happen a lot with slaves?" Sara asked. She hadn't noticed it in Martinique.

"When it come to wat down dare, men gets cola' blind real quick, Miss Sara," Hennie offered.

"I don't like this happening to that girl in my house," Sara said.

"If you send Marlow somewhere else, it's not going to help the girl," Ned Foster said.

"Ned's right, Miss Sara," Hennie said.

"All right, what do we do to help the girl?" Sara asked.

"Dat Simon, he watch dat girl all the time," Hennie said.

"Simon falls asleep sometimes," Foster said. "That's about the only thing Susannah was able to tell me before he woke up."

"Everybody sleeps sometimes," Sara put in.

"Susannah thinks Simon has been drinking a bit of Mr. Marlow's whiskey," Ned said. "That's why he's falling asleep more than normal."

"You mean dat whiskey he got up in his room there?" Hennie asked.

"I guess," Ned said.

"Well, I got jus' da ting gonna make dat man sleep real good," Hennie said with a smile. "The island powder."

"If you put it in the whiskey, won't Mr. Marlow get a dose as well?" Sara asked.

"Yeah," Hennie conceded. "But, I thin' Mr. Marlow need a good night sleep, too."

Chapter 11

June 19, 1787
Sullivan House

Hugh Marlow took another sip from his whiskey glass and glared at John Oliver. "On the whole, I prefer the New Jersey Plan," Marlow said.

"Oh, I thought you might prefer Mr. Hamilton's plan, given your admiration of all things British," Oliver suggested.

The "plans" he referred to were put before the convention as alternatives to the Virginia Plan. The New Jersey Plan was essentially a modification of the Articles of Confederation. It put an executive — to be composed of more than one person — in place and gave the executive some powers to compel states to comply with federal legislation, but otherwise placed few limitations on the sovereignty of the states. Hamilton's proposal was a near replication of the British system, with an executive and legislators who would serve for life. Furthermore, the Hamilton Plan would eliminate the states altogether.

"I admire the British markets, Oliver," Marlow said. "Before the war, England bought all of my produce and paid a fair price for it. The French are more difficult to deal with."

"Our nation exists because the French gave us so much," Oliver said. "Without their money, ships, and soldiers, we would not have prevailed."

"King Louie was a fool," Marlow asserted. "He bankrupted the French treasury in the belief that the United States would become his great trading partner. But we are still Englishmen at heart and England will be our foremost trading partner again someday."

"Did you support the war?" Oliver asked. He doubted that South Carolina would send a loyalist to the meeting, but it had never occurred to him to inquire.

"I supported the notion of more independence from Britain," Marlow said. "I am a selfish man, Oliver, as you have no doubt realized by now. My primary aim was protecting my property. The slaves got it in their heads that George III would set them free."

"The enemy of my enemy is my friend," Oliver commented.

"Exactly," Marlow agreed. "And because of that, I needed to raise a squadron of men to guard the property."

"Did your men engage the British?"

"During the siege of Charleston, my men engaged the British a few times as they passed near Hallow Hill. I believe there was a skirmish with a troop of Hessians, as well."

"Charleston surrendered in May 1780, I believe," Oliver said. "A lot of slaves joined the British in exchange for their freedom, but you kept yours. How did you manage it?"

"General Clinton believed I would join his force of loyalist and bring my men with me," Marlow said. "I did nothing to discourage his belief, yet I never actually joined them. In any event, by the end of 1780, Clinton was bedeviled with problems in the upstate and they never bothered us again."

"If the Carolina loyalist had joined up with Clinton in the way he expected them to, his Southern strategy might have worked," Oliver observed.

"It likely would have worked," Marlow agreed. "But I will admit that my actions, and those of many others in similar situations, weren't exactly altruistic. We simply wanted to preserve our options."

"Whether England rules us or whether we rule ourselves, slavery will end one day," Oliver told him.

"Certainly, when the time is right," Marlow agreed. "Slavery will cease when there is no longer an economic benefit from it. The good people of Massachusetts and Europe clamor for abolition, but they also want cheap cotton and indigo."

"Some things are more important than economics," Oliver observed. "Perhaps it is government's job to make those decisions."

"Make no mistake," Marlow said as he leaned toward Oliver. "While I would value the security provided by national unity, I will do all in my power to prevent South Carolina from joining a government which would make such a decision."

"And I will oppose any plan that perpetuates the abominable practice of slavery," Oliver responded.

Marlow sat his empty glass on the table and stood. "On that matter, I think we shall never agree," he said. "Now, I must retire as sleep beckons."

"Good night," Oliver said as he watched the other man stumble slightly toward the stairway just outside the parlor.

He continued to sit alone on the settee, wondering if he should have partaken of the whiskey himself. The past two days were particularly disturbing. After almost a month of slow, frustrating work on the Virginia Plan, suddenly two new plans were thrust before the delegates and many seemed willing to throw the

Virginia Plan aside and start anew.

It was true that the reason put forward for convening this conference was to revise the Articles of Confederation, and that is what the New Jersey Plan did. But, in the opening session, Randolph and Madison had put forth a plan that was more appealing to Oliver. For one thing, it created a nation rather than a confederation. For another — although it may not have been Madison's intention — the debate over slavery was opened.

Hamilton's plan was of little concern. It would be short-lived. While many of the delegates might view themselves as aristocrats, they knew that the farmers, laborers and shopkeepers who had so recently freed the colonies from monarchs would be ill disposed to empower a new monarchy. Hamilton stressed that his plan was based on republican principles as the king would be elected but that would sooth few among the populace. Oliver knew that the first such king would likely be George Washington, but eventually, men of little character would gain power. Hamilton suggested that only a permanent body of power could check the impudence of democracy, but Oliver was just as sure that only the impudence of democracy would protect freedom.

*****

For almost four weeks, Sara had heard the footfalls on the stairs as the two men made their way to their rooms on the second floor. Usually, she attended to things in the kitchen, or read in the small parlor off the dining room, until her guests retired. Then she would go to her own bed.

She recognized the heavier step of Hugh Marlow as he made his way up the stairs and assumed she would hear John Oliver's softer step a few minutes after. But ten minutes passed and Oliver still hadn't gone up. Perhaps this was the right time to have a conversation with a man who had been a guest in her home for almost a month.

She tiptoed toward the parlor. She didn't want to startle him in case Oliver had fallen asleep. He wouldn't be the first guest to do so. But Oliver wasn't asleep. He sat quietly on one end of the settee; hands clasped behind his head.

"Is something wrong, Mr. Oliver?" Sara asked as she slipped into the chair Marlow had recently vacated.

"You should call me John, Mrs. Sullivan," Oliver said. "We have been acquainted for some weeks now."

"And you should call me Sara," she responded.

"Very well, Sara," Oliver said. "Something is indeed wrong, and I'm not sure any of us have the answers required to fix what is wrong."

"I've sensed the meeting isn't going well," Sara said.

"No, it isn't going well," Oliver lamented. "I am beginning to believe failure is inevitable, that we are destined to be a continent of separate nations."

"Is that so bad?" Sara asked. "There are dozens of nations in Europe."

"Yes, and the nations of Europe are constantly at war with one another."

"I suppose that's true," Sara conceded. Robert Murray had taught her much about the history of Europe and its wars, often fought over events that no one even remembered.

"If we are to form two nations out of these thirteen states, then war will be inevitable," Oliver mused. "It isn't only the abomination of human slavery that the North will detest, they will also detest the economic advantage given to the slave states."

"Then you must find a way to form a single nation," Sara said. She moved to the settee and clasp Oliver's hand. She sensed him flinch as she laid her hand over his, but then felt him relax.

"I am afraid any solution will require such a compromise that neither side will be satisfied. The same resentments will surface, and they will fester until the union splits apart and civil war destroys us."

He gazed directly toward Sara with a sad but steady expression, as if he accepted the bleak fate he had just outlined for his nation. It was Sara's nation too, and she supposed she should be sad, too, but that wasn't the emotion she felt at that moment. Instead, she wanted to lift John Oliver out of his moribund state.

"You should get away from it for a time," Sara suggested.

"There is so much to do, and we have accomplished so little up to now, I feel a duty to be present each day," Oliver said. "There are others who have spent time away, though, and I suppose I could do it."

"I haven't been out of the city in weeks, myself," Sara said. "Perhaps we might take a ride in the countryside. Just for a day."

She watched his reaction. She didn't intend to be forward, but maybe that wasn't a bad idea. When she first saw Oliver, filthy and covered with dirt from days in the saddle, he had not made a great impression on her. But, in the weeks since then, her initial impression had faded and now she regarded him as a smart, dedicated man of principle.

In the first few days of his stay, Oliver had smiled often — it was a nice smile — and laughed along with her when Hennie dished out one of her island sayings. But, as the convention ground on, his smiles and laughter had mostly disappeared.

Also, there was the matter of Hugh Marlow. The two men could not be more ill-suited as house mates. Still, she wondered how Oliver would react if he learned of the plot she, Hennie, and Ned Foster had formed to help Susannah escape her enslavement.

"That sounds nice," John Oliver said.

"Good," Sara said. "Day after tomorrow." She realized is sounded more like a command than a scheduling suggestion, but Oliver didn't seem taken aback. He nodded his assent.

Chapter 12

June 21, 1787
Philadelphia, Pennsylvania

Sara pulled the curtain back and saw a cloudless sky beginning to glow with the first light of morning. The air was cool for a midsummer morning, but she knew it would be sunny and warm before they reached the little grove of trees on a hillock south of Chestnut Hill. She hadn't ridden there since the previous summer, but she was sure it would be as pleasant as she remembered.

She had convinced John Oliver that a day away from the frustration of the convention would be good for him, but she thought it would be good for her, as well. A few hours on horseback in the rolling countryside around the city always cleared her mind of the cluttered thoughts that accumulated over time.

Usually, she was alone on her rides. In the beginning, Hennie tried to talk her out of riding alone, warning her of soldiers still finding their way home after the war. Such men could be dangerous, Hennie had said. But Sara wouldn't be deterred, and while she did occasionally see forlorn soldiers on the road, she never felt threatened by any.

As a poor girl growing up in Dublin, the only horses she saw were pulling carts through the muddy streets or carrying a stout — and often drunk — constable. It was Paul Barré who had shown her the joy of galloping across a field of fresh green grass, or ambling through a still forest, hearing only the chirping of birds and the rustle of leaves overhead.

She hadn't ridden with a man since those days with Paul. Solitude had been her choice as there had been many offers of companionship. Those men's intentions had been clear, and Sara was not ready for that, even with the ones she found attractive. Oliver was different though. Clearly, he found her attractive. The way his eyes lingered assured her of that, but he seemed as reluctant as her to move beyond lingering gazes and fleeting thoughts.

She had learned from Ned Foster that Oliver had been married before the war, but Ned had declined to provide any more information. "That's Mr. Oliver's story," Ned had said. "He should be the one to tell it."

She stripped off her nightshirt and examined

herself in the mirror over the dresser. She was pleased that nothing had disintegrated since the last time she had made such an examination. She was a sound sleeper and lately she'd noticed puffiness around her eyes in the mornings.

She took a cloth from beside the wash basin, dampened it, and rubbed her face with the cool water. *That's better*, she thought as she replaced the cloth on the washstand. Even though she was only twenty-seven, Sara had come to respect the passage of time. It seemed only weeks had passed, not five years, since she'd lain in bed with Paul Barré.

She pulled a white chemise over her head and sat down in front of the mirror. After applying a light dusting of rice powder to her cheeks and bosom, she appraised herself again. *Good enough*, she thought, glad that Americans had not adopted the French obsession with extreme white skin. Fortunately, Robert Murray had warned her against using the common powder derived from a mixture of lead and vinegar.

Next, she applied several brush strokes to her red hair. Thanks to a night scarf, the few tangles she encountered pulled out easily and the normal glow returned to her curls. But Sara had no plans to show off the curls today. Instead, she pulled the mass of hair behind her head and secured it with a broad silver clip, which might have been the only possession she still had from the home of Alfred Carlisle. Well, that and a few thousand British Pounds.

From the armoire, she extracted her riding clothes and began to pull them on, hoping the months since she had last gotten into them had been kind to her waistline. Once all was in place, she glanced again at the mirror and gave herself an approving smile. She would soon see just how liberal Mr. Oliver was.

*****

John Oliver watched through the parlor window as Ned Foster tied two horses to the fence in front of Sullivan House. He recognized his own gelded bay and realized the dapple-gray mare next to it must belong to Mrs. Sullivan. At first, he had assumed that Sara meant they would take a carriage ride for their foray into the countryside. Only when she asked Ned Foster to retrieve the horses did he realize she intended to ride. Also, he noted that both animals were tacked with standard saddles which meant she wouldn't be riding side-saddle.

The clop-clop of boots on the parlor's wooden floor caused him to turn around. Sara's amused laugh told him that his face must have displayed his shock.

"You look a little surprised, John," Sara said.

"I don't think I've ever seen a woman wearing trousers," Oliver said.

"Why should men be the only ones to enjoy comfort and practicality?" she asked.

"I shall propose we add exactly such language to our new constitution," he announced.

"Are you willing to be seen in the company of a woman in trousers?" she asked while turning to show him a profile.

"I'll be the talk of the town, I suppose," he responded. "But I believe I can handle that."

"Perhaps everyone will assume I'm a man," Sara offered, again turning to the side.

"No, I don't think they will," he assured her.

"Ain't no mon look like dat in a pair o' britches," Hennie said from behind Sara.

Sara turned to Hennie and took the two leather pouches being offered. "Thank you, Hennie," she said, then to John Oliver, "I know a wonderful place to stop and enjoy a midday repast."

*****

They had walked the horses slowly out of the town until they came to a narrow river where a well-traveled trail led away to the west. Sara turned her mount onto the trail and nudged it into a gentle trot.

Oliver took his cue and encouraged his own horse into a similar pace, following a few strides behind. From that position, he observed how easily she moved with the animal, almost as if they were one creature. Although he had ridden since childhood, he never attained that level of horsemanship. Instead, he bounced and wobbled as if the next moment might find him on the ground. Another thing apparent from his position behind her was that Henrietta Washington was absolutely correct: No one would mistake Sara Sullivan in trousers for a man.

After trotting for half a mile, Sara slowed her mount to a walk and turned to Oliver, who slowed and pulled alongside her. "That was refreshing," she said to him.

"My backside might have a different opinion," he joked.

"Ha," Sara laughed. "Well, we have a few more miles to go. My apologies to your backside," she added and then nudged her horse forward again.

A mile further along the river trail, they turned north on another trail next to a small creek that flowed into the river. A short time later, the creek and the trail turned west again and began a slow ascent from the Philadelphia basin. After an hour of alternating between slow trots and even slower walks, Sara turned her horse away from the trail and trotted up a small hill toward a grove of oak trees.

*****

They walked their horses to a halt and dismounted at the edge of the grove where Sara loosely tied one rein to a low tree branch. "There's plenty of grass for them here," she said. "Just make sure he can reach the ground."

Oliver dismounted and fastened his horse to the same tree. From behind her saddle, Sara took the two leather bags Hennie had given her along with a blanket they had lain across. "That looks like a nice spot," she said to Oliver, pointing to a well shaded area of the grove.

They spread the blanket in a small clearing under the oaks where only small patches of sunlight reached the ground, the rest filtered through the thick oak leaves overhead. Once she was satisfied with the position of the blanket, Sara unloaded the contents of the leather bags.

"We've got bread, cheese, cured ham, pickled onions, apples, and some wine to wash it all down," she said, as she laid out each cloth wrapped packet along with tin plates and cups.

"It looks very good," Oliver observed. "I am hungry after that ride."

"We can eat well, and have a nice rest before we ride back," Sara said.

Oliver lowered himself to the blanket and sat cross-legged on the opposite side of the feast, "Where did you learn to ride so well?" he asked.

"In France," she said. She could have told him that her husband had spent a considerable amount of money on riding lessons when she lived in Ireland, but she didn't. She'd had no interest in it then, maybe because she despised the husband.

"You said you spent three years in France," Oliver inquired. "Is that where you met Mr.

Sullivan?"

She knew the question would come. It always did. *What became of Mr. Sullivan?* Sometimes, she gave a simple answer: Mr. Sullivan had died in a flu epidemic, or, Mr. Sullivan had drowned on the voyage to Martinique. Most times, she avoided answering and let questioners draw their own conclusions. Today was different, though. She wanted to learn some of John Oliver's secrets, too, and she felt a strong urge to share her own secrets, at least some of them.

"No," Sara said. She wasn't quite ready for more disclosure. She turned her eyes away from him and selected a small piece of the ham, the cheese, and the bread.

"I have heard many speculations around the town as to the circumstances of Mr. Sullivan," Oliver said.

"The people of the town are bored and search for interesting topics," Sara said. In time she might want to disclose her secrets to John Oliver, but for now she enjoyed the banter of hide-and-seek. She had a few questions of her own.

"I've done a bit of speculation myself," Sara said after swallowing some bread. "Ned Foster mentioned there was a Mrs. Oliver, but she was in England."

"Yes, that's right," Oliver said. There may have been a note of irritation in his voice.

"When will she be returning?" Sara asked.

He looked at her for several seconds, lips pursed, a slight flush on his cheeks. Then, his face relaxed into a resigned smile. "She will not be returning," he explained.

"Oh?"

"That's right," Oliver said. "She took our son, too."

"I had no idea," Sara offered. "I'm so sorry."

"I haven't seen my son in nearly twelve years," Oliver said. "I wonder what he looks like now."

"I'm sure he is very handsome," Sara said.

"I'm sure he's a proper English nobleman," Oliver said, with a note of disgust. He went on to describe that day in 1776 when Lord Black had lost his nerve and fled New York for London, taking his daughter and grandson with him.

"Have you thought of going to England to find her?"

"Not long after the war ended, I got a letter from a judge in England to notify me he intended to grant Becky a divorce. I found out later that Lord Black had demanded it and that Becky was betrothed to marry again."

"Oh, I'm sorry," Sara said. "Ned didn't tell me that part."

"Ned doesn't know," Oliver said. "Now, I have told you my story. I want to hear yours."

Sara took one deep breath and closed her eyes. She had trusted Robert Murray, and he had been faithful to that trust. She was about to trust John Oliver and she hoped he would be equally faithful.

"There never was a Mr. Sullivan," she blurted out.

Oliver cocked his head, "You weren't married?"

"I was married," Sara answered, "but not to someone of my choosing. In fact, my father forced me to marry someone I loathed from the first day."

"So, you ran away," Oliver speculated.

"I went to France," Sara said. "I took some money from his safe and left."

"I assume you don't want this man to find you," Oliver stated the obvious.

"Alfred Carlisle is dead," Sara said. "But his father is Lord Carlisle of England and the family wants to find me." As she told this to Oliver, Sara wondered if she had said too much. As far as she knew, Lord Carlisle's reward offer was still out there and how did she know it wouldn't tempt this man.

"Lord Carlisle?"

"Yes."

"That's the man Becky married," Oliver said. "Not Lord Carlisle himself, but his son. I think his name is Dennison Carlisle."

"I met Dennison once," Sara told him. "He was Alfred's older brother and the heir to the title. He was an arrogant bastard." She relaxed now, realizing they had a mutual enemy in the Carlisle family.

"So," Oliver said after finishing a slice of the bread and a large chunk of cheese, "I still don't know who taught you to ride."

"I worked on the estate of a Scotsman while in France," Sara said. "He taught me to ride." Up to that point, everything she had told Oliver was true, with many omitted details. But she wasn't ready to tell him about Paul Barré.

"Why did you leave France?" Oliver asked.

"Mr. Murray, the Scotsman, knew that Carlisle wanted to find me. He had a business associate in Martinique, and he thought I would be safer there."

"But you decided to come to America instead," Oliver surmised.

"I stayed in Martinique for a few months," Sara said, "but I hated the place. Also, the French and the British had swapped control of the island several times. If the British took control of the island again, Lord Carlisle would have eyes and ears there."

"How did you get to Philadelphia?"

"A sympathetic acquaintance introduced me to the captain of a Portuguese ship that stopped in Martinique on its way back from Brazil," Sara explained. "The captain told me that the British fleet had abandoned the blockade of Philadelphia, and he wanted to secure a cargo of rum and other goods to deliver to the city."

"And the captain let you come along?"

"Better than that," Sara said. "I bought half the cargo and we split the profits."

By this time, they had finished the wine and most of the food. The conversation had been serious, but the mood warm and pleasant. Each time they shifted their positions on the blanket, it seemed they got closer to one another.

"I suppose we should start back to the city," Sara sighed.

"Yes, I suppose," Oliver agreed.

Chapter 13

John Oliver's backside hurt more in the mornings than later in the day. Once he moved around a bit, the pain diminished. But, on this occasion, there was no choice. He knew his effort was nothing more than symbolic, but he had to do it.

A thin strip of daylight spanned the Eastern sky as Oliver gazed across the flat surface of Baltimore Harbor. He didn't care much for boats and normally he would feel comforted by the calmness of the water, but the absence of wind meant the little sailing vessel would take hours to reach his goal.

Finally, he felt a light breeze glance off his cheek and heard the mainsail snap to attention. He looked over his shoulder at the Continental Navy sailor standing at the helm on the rear of the twenty-foot vessel. The sailor pulled from the water a long pole he'd been using to propel the vessel and pointed to the sail thankful for the newfound power source.

Oliver gave a "thumbs up" to the sailor and surveyed the city that was receding behind them. The rooftop of the Baltimore Convalescent Hospital was visible just beyond a warehouse that fronted the pier.

He retrieved the glass bottle from his coat pocket and turned it in his hands. In the growing daylight, he could see the parchment note inside. He hoped the heavily waxed cork stopper that sealed the bottle would protect it from the sea. For a moment, he wondered what the young sailor must think of his pointless gesture. But it didn't matter, the sailor was more than happy to make a little extra money and he kept his thoughts to himself.

June 30, 1787
Pennsylvania State House

John Oliver shook his head and took in his surroundings. His mind had wandered during Mr. Martin's long-winded speech, but he hoped he hadn't actually fallen asleep. If so, no one seemed to have taken notice. A quick check of the room told him most other minds had wandered too.

He shook his head again, hoping to somehow remember the gist of what Martin had been saying, but it was a blank. All he could remember was his own thoughts of the day he sent his symbolic farewell note to Becky and Caleb. The war was essentially over, and it was obvious the colonists, together with their French allies, would prevail. But, the shaky peace likely to emerge would not bring his wife and son back to America.

At first, Oliver thought his wife and child would return soon since the British had maintained control of New York. But months passed with no word from her until the letter came. It was the last communication he would receive from her and it stated categorically that she would not return. Her father forbade it. Lord Black had never approved of Becky's choice of husband, and once he got word that Oliver had joined the forces of the rebellion, he was adamant that she must never go back.

During the war, regular mail service between England and the colonies had ceased, and Oliver had feared it would be many years before communications returned to normal. He had no illusions that Becky would ever receive his message-in-a-bottle, but that wasn't the point. It was a ceremonial release of that part of his past, his acceptance of what was no longer deniable.

For nearly three weeks, the convention had been stuck on one issue: How would the two branches of the federal legislature be selected. Under the current system, the Articles of Confederation, there was only one legislative body, and each state got a single vote on legislative matters. The Virginia Plan provided for two legislative bodies, with each state's representation determined by the population of the state.

The Plan also envisioned the larger legislative body being selected by the people according to the rules of suffrage in place in the states. But such closeness to democracy still frightened many delegates.

"The first branch ought to be selected by the state legislatures and not by the people," Charles Pinckney had insisted several days earlier.

"Much depends on the mode of election," Elbridge Gerry insisted. "In England, the people's liberty is at risk because so few enjoy the right of voting. But, in Massachusetts our danger arises from the opposite extreme and the worst men get into the legislature."

"There is no danger of improper elections if the districts are large enough," James Wilson had stated. "Bad elections proceed from the smallness of districts which give bad men the opportunity for intrigue."

For many delegates from the smaller states, this concept was an unacceptable shift of power to the larger states. If they acted in concert, Massachusetts, Pennsylvania, and Virginia could force unfavorable legislation onto the smaller states. Mr. Brearley even suggested General Washington compose a letter to Rhode Island insisting they finally send representatives to the convention. He hoped to have another small state to support their positions.

But, after days of heated debate, motions and counter motions, there was finally progress and great hope for this Saturday session. Oliver directed his attention onto the convention floor when his Connecticut colleague, Mr. Ellsworth, rose from his chair to speak.

"Gentlemen," Ellsworth began. "As all here know, I voted in opposition to the motion which was yesterday approved by this body. On the whole, however, I am not opposed to the principle embodied in it, that representation should be allotted to people rather than to states. But I attend this gathering as a representative of a small state, one that will have little power in a federation designed as we have so far done."

"Especially with the slaves counted as is proposed," John Oliver heard his own voice speak in support of his Connecticut friend. The smaller Southern states had no problem with representation based on population, even though they would, in theory, suffer the same disadvantages as the small Northern states. The difference was in the way the Virginia Plan defined population for determining the number of legislative members for each state. A census would be taken every few years as the basis for allocating representation as determined by the total free population, plus three-fifths of the total slave population. The Confederation had used the same formula as the basis of allocating cost sharing to the states, but each state had only one vote in legislative matters.

"My colleague from Connecticut is correct," Ellsworth continued. "If this body should be determined to make the second chamber of the legislature in the same way it has made the first chamber, then the small Northern states will see the disadvantage and will not agree to join this union."

"Only Massachusetts would join," Dr. Johnson, also of Connecticut commented.

"Dr. Johnson is correct," Ellsworth said, "and it is Dr. Johnson who has given us the solution to this conundrum. He has already, some days past, proposed the first chamber be comprised of men elected by the people and the second chamber be composed of men of high character selected by the leaders of their state, an equal number for each state."

"Equal representation in the second chamber would allow states holding a small minority of the populace to blunt the wishes of the majority," James Wilson of Pennsylvania protested. "On what grounds should Delaware have equal standing with Pennsylvania?"

"The power of equality is necessary to protect the small states, such as Delaware, from being destroyed by the larger states."

Mr. Madison rose to speak, but instead of standing next to his chair, as the others had done, he strode to the podium near the dais.

"Gentlemen," Madison began. "I have heard expressed here much concern over the matter of size, which, in my opinion, is of no importance. For what divides the states is not their size, but their circumstances, which derive partly from climate, but mostly from their having or not having slaves. The great division of interest in the Confederation, and in the union we propose to form, does not lie between the large and small states; it lays between Northern and Southern states, and if any defensive power is to be given, it ought to be given to these two interests."

John Oliver's head nodded agreement with the course of Madison's speech, and as he glanced around the room, he saw that many others were also nodding. Madison had finally addressed the true issue that would divide America for many generations, possibly forever.

Madison had suggested they should balance the defensive capability between the two interests, but such a balancing seemed impossible to John Oliver. The union, if they could form one, would surely split apart in time as each faction found the other's position unacceptable. And if they could somehow balance these interests at the outset, the superiority of one over the other would be bound to occur at some future time.

Madison went on to suggest they could achieve this balancing by mandating that the number of representatives to one chamber should be determined by a count of all the free citizens of a state. And the number of representatives to the other chamber should be determined by a count of all people residing in the state, including slaves.

Oliver considered the ramifications of Madison's proposal. The slave states would control one house of the congress and the free states would control the other. Any legislation to expand or restrict slavery would be blocked from passage by one chamber or the other, thus containing slavery to the Southern region, but perpetuating it forever.

Still, Madison's speech had finally forced the convention to face its ultimate challenge. For Oliver, and some of the other Northern delegates, the codification of slavery into perpetual existence was a bridge they would not cross to find compromise. He was equally sure that many of the Southern delegates would not agree to form a nation which did not recognize slavery as a perpetual right.

Oliver looked across the room to where Hugh Marlow sat among a contingent of delegates from South and North Carolina. He tried to decipher the wry smile on Marlow's face. Certainly, Madison's proposal would please South Carolina as it provided a path to joining the union under favorable terms, without which the state, along with the other slave states would likely form a separate union. Marlow had said as much in their last conversation at Sullivan House. At that moment, it appeared the Southern states held a winning hand. They would not be convinced to accept a compromise that did not perpetuate the practice of slavery. The Northern states had little to offer in exchange for giving up, or limiting, the practice.

*****

Sullivan House

Susannah leaned over Simon and listened to his slow, soft breathing. Satisfied that her keeper was asleep, she tested the door of their attic chamber. Locked, as always. The key would be in the place Simon always put it when he felt like going to sleep, inside the crotch of his pants.

She knew she couldn't retrieve the key without waking Simon, but now she didn't need to. With her eyes still locked on Simon, she stepped quietly to the row of bells on the wall near the door and gave the wire above the second bell a gentle tug.

She continued to watch the sleeping Simon for any signs of awakening, but his slumber only deepened. He was oblivious to the sound of soft footsteps on the stairs and to three light taps on the door of the attic room. She tapped the door three times in response and watched Simon sleep through the sound of a key turning in the lock.

"Took 'im longer to fall asleep this time," Susannah told Ned once they were in the hall.

"Hennie said the powder doesn't work as fast in tea as it does in liquor," Ned Foster informed her.

"How long he gonna sleep?" Susannah asked as Ned guided her into the other attic sleeping quarter.

"Hennie says he'll be out for an hour at least; could be as much as two hours."

They sat facing each other on the two small beds in the unoccupied servant's room. Susannah reached across the small space between their knees and laid her hand over Ned's. He placed his other hand over hers and squeezed.

Simon had been wary when Henrietta Washington brought tea to the attic for them the first time. But he relaxed and enjoyed her wild stories of life as a slave in the islands. He was smiling when he drifted off into a deep sleep. While he slept, Hennie showed her how the bell system would work. They had replaced the wooden handle on the other end of the wire in Ned Foster's room with a tiny bell. The system worked in reverse.

She knew that Mrs. Sullivan and Henrietta had set up the arrangement so Ned Foster could help her escape if that was what she wanted to do. She had dreamt of escape many times in her young life, but never thought of it as a real possibility. For one thing, she had no idea where an escaped slave could go, and for another, she knew Simon and the slave hunters would chase her down and take her back to Hallow Hill or kill her.

Now, for the first time since Marlow had shipped her mother away, Susannah felt kindness from other humans. At Hallow Hill, the household slaves were friendly, but wary, knowing of the private time she spent with the master.

What she felt for Ned Foster was another new sensation. At Hallow Hill, she had overheard the young white girls talk about love at holiday parties, but she hadn't understood what they meant. The life of a slave at Hallow Hill was one of everyday struggle, even for those who lived in the house. None of them knew when they might be sold, fall ill, or worked to death, so long-term relationships among them were rare. They had sex when there was enough energy left at the end of the day, but all knew that every sensation was fleeting. Ned Foster was offering her freedom, but all she could think of was *would he go with her*.

"Have you decided?" Ned asked her.

"I want to, but I'm scared," she said.

"You're right to be scared, Susannah," Ned said. "Mr. Marlow won't be happy about you leaving. He'll come looking for you with Simon. They'll put up pictures of you all around, too, and somebody might tell where you are."

Susannah said nothing, but her lips began to quiver, and a tear formed at the corner of her eye. Ned gently smoothed her hair with his hand. "You tryin' to scare me outta doin' it?" she asked.

"No," Ned said. "But I don't want you to think this will be easy because it won't. But, if we make it, you got a chance for a good life."

"You said 'we'," Susannah observed. "You goin' with me?"

"I'm going to take you to Boston," Ned said. "We can decide what to do after that."

Susannah stood and pulled Ned to his feet. She threw her arms around him and kissed him. "When we goin'?"

Chapter 14

July 12, 1787
Pennsylvania Statehouse

"Aye," Roger Sherman announced the Connecticut delegation's decision on the proposed terms of Article I, Section 2, regarding election of members of the House of Representatives by the people, and allocation of representation among the states.

For John Oliver, the vote was a bittersweet moment. He had abstained from participation in the delegation's choice because he felt it was unfair to Connecticut on principle and unfair to slaves on moral grounds. Still, he understood Ellsworth's plea for compromise, knowing that it was the only path leading to a unified, if somewhat fragile, nation.

"Nay," Richard Bassett of Delaware announced

that small state's opposition to the amended proposition.

The revised proposal espoused the three-fifths principle, which the Articles of Confederation had used to allocate funding requests to the various states, as the ultimate means for allocating representation among the states. Under this principle, the population of the states would be calculated as the total number of free persons — not including Indians — and three-fifths of all black slaves residing there.

Supporters of the formula justified it as a measure of wealth since the slaves were property. And since they believed that a principal responsibility of any government was to protect wealth and property, the formula gave them property protection in the form of added representation in the government. Those arguments didn't resonate with John Oliver, though. Why were slaves deemed to be "property" worthy of representation in the congress, but the land, buildings, and investments he owned were not considered property worthy of such representation? He knew the answer and didn't like it. They intended to give the slaves states protections from a future congress that might outlaw the practice.

The roll call of the states continued in alphabetical order, with Georgia answering "yes", then a "Yea" vote from Maryland. That small state's delegation had said little during the debate and other delegates had wondered whether they would align with other small states against the measure, or if they would align with their predominant trading partner, Virginia.

Mr. Gerry then reported that the Massachusetts delegation was split. As James Madison had predicted, the interests of the various states went beyond the question of size. Even though they might enjoy a powerful alignment with Virginia and Pennsylvania, the Commonwealth was fiercely anti-slavery and opposed the notion of counting the slaves to determine representation, but then denying them the opportunity to vote.

North Carolina, Pennsylvania and Virginia voted "Yea" and New Jersey voted "Nay", just as John Oliver had expected. Pennsylvania's acquiescence to the compromise may have surprised some in the room, but John Oliver was not surprised. Despite Gouverneur Morris' protestations during the debate, most of the delegation agreed with Connecticut that there was more to be gained by forming a single union rather than breaking away into two or more nations.

South Carolina, like Massachusetts, reported a split vote, but for an different reason. While the Commonwealth of Massachusetts opposed counting the slaves at all, half of the South Carolina delegation insisted all the slaves be counted.

The final tally was six "Yea", two "Nay", and two divided. Three states — Rhode Island, New York, and New Hampshire — did not have a delegation present for the vote. Even though the proposal did not use the word "slavery", Oliver viewed it as a tacit acknowledgement and approval of the practice. The compromise had paved the way to form a nation, but it left in place the rot that would undermine the noble principles espoused in the rest of the document.

Oliver expected the rot would only worsen with time and when Madison stood to proclaim that the union they would form could last for a century, he couldn't suppress a sarcastic laugh. The compromise would allow both sides to ignore the rot for a time, but it would do nothing to prevent the festering growth of animosity and resentment. The contest of money versus morality would expand as the nation grew westward. In the end, perhaps, a dispute of such magnitude can't be resolved by compromise. One side will impose its views on the other.

Once General Washington gaveled the session to a close, the delegates gathered into smaller groups to discuss the activity of the day. Some were celebratory and others more subdued. John Oliver sat alone in his chair for several minutes, not particularly drawn to any of the groups. Some of the groupings were odd: an anti-slavery delegate from Massachusetts and a pro-slavery delegate from North Carolina. Both had opposed the measure, but for different reasons.

Only minutes earlier, the most momentous question for the convention had been decided. It was now a virtual certainty that they would form a union. It would almost certainly be a union with dangerous fissures in its structure, and one that would face an uncertain future from the first moment of its existence. But at that moment, the only emotion John Oliver saw on the faces of the delegates was relief. They would form a union. Their successors would have to figure out how to hold the union together.

*****

The sun had just dipped below the rooftops of the buildings on the opposite side of Chestnut Street when John Oliver emerged from the Statehouse. He shaded his eyes with one hand for a moment until the structures began to take shape out of the bright yellow light. When his eyes adjusted to the bright backdrop, he turned right and walked toward Fifth Street. But before he'd taken a half-dozen steps, he noticed two men on the corner of Chestnut and Fifth Street talking to each other animatedly.

When he was a few steps closer, he realized the two men were Hugh Marlow and his slave, Simon. He took a few slow steps, hoping the two men would start walking toward Sullivan House and he could lag quietly behind. Of course, he would come face-to-face with Marlow eventually and would have to discuss the compromise vote, but right now, he wanted none of it.

But Marlow spotted him and immediately started walking in his direction with Simon a few paces behind. "I warned you," Marlow said as he neared Oliver, his face flush with anger.

"Warned me?" Oliver questioned.

"My Susannah has run off with your man," Marlow bellowed.

"What?"

"You heard me," Marlow protested. "My slave, Susannah, has run off with your man, whatever his name is."

"Ned," Simon assisted his boss with the name.

"That's impossible," Oliver said. "Ned wouldn't leave without telling me."

"Whether he told you is neither here nor there," Marlow said, his voice trembling. "He is gone with the girl and I shall hold both you and he responsible for assisting a runaway."

"Perhaps the girl ran away on her own," Oliver insisted. "Who could blame her for wanting her freedom?" Even as he said it, he realized it wasn't true. The girl might truly want her freedom, but he doubted she possessed the strength or courage to run on her own. And he'd seen the way Ned looked at her over these several weeks, and he knew the man sometimes longed for the company of a woman. In Hartford there were no more than half-a-dozen black women and all of those were old and bossy, a condition Ned would not take kindly to.

"Your man is gone, too," Marlow spit out. "He's the one who's been putting ideas in her head. Simon here caught them talking once."

"I'm sure Ned had nothing to do with this," Oliver said. "He will be back by evening I'm sure."

"You should hope so, Oliver," Marlow said, "for I intend to arrange a party of slave hunters to go after them. Simon will go with the hunters and he can be quite brutal when he feels like it."

Before Oliver could respond, Marlow spun around and walked back toward the Pennsylvania Statehouse, with Simon two paces behind again.

*****

The front door of Sullivan House was unlocked as usual and when John Oliver stepped inside, he didn't encounter Sara Sullivan or Henrietta Washington, which was unusual. One of them was usually near the main entrance to greet him.

He hurried up the stairs to the two rooms he and Ned had occupied. He knocked on the door to Ned's room and waited for a response, but there was none. Oliver twisted the knob and heard the latch lift on the inside. He pushed the door open and examined the room in the dim late afternoon light that came through the window. In seconds, he realized that Ned Foster's faded brown carpet bag was gone.

He hurried back down the stairs and into the kitchen where he found Sara Sullivan and Henrietta Washington sipping from teacups at the small table in the kitchen.

"Have you seen Ned?" he asked them both.

"I haven't seen him since this morning," they both said simultaneously.

"Hugh Marlow believes Ned has run off with his slave girl," Oliver told them. He watched for a reaction but saw none. "It's true then, isn't it?"

He waited again for an answer, but neither of the woman said anything. "Very well," he finally said. "What time did they leave?"

"John, that girl deserves her freedom," Sara said.

"I know she deserves her freedom, but Marlow doesn't think so and if he finds out you two had a hand in helping them, he will be mighty angry."

"Well, I don't plan on telling him," Sara said.

"Good," Oliver said. "But you better learn to act more surprised than you were when I asked about Ned."

"We been rehearsin' dot all day, Mr. Oliver," Hennie offered.

"When did they leave?" Oliver asked.

"Four hours ago," Sara told him.

"Any idea where they're going?"

"They went north in a caravan of Quaker wagons," Sara said. "That's all I know."

"Did they have horses?"

"Yes."

"Do they have money?"

"They have enough."

Chapter 15

July 12, 1787
Near Philadelphia

Heavy clouds gathered in the western sky, masking the sunset on Susannah's first day of freedom. It would only be real freedom if their escape succeeded, but the sensation she felt was like nothing in her short lifetime. Ned was a free man with a piece of paper that proved it. She had a paper too, but it wasn't real, and she doubted anyone would believe it.

She'd stared at the odd markings on the paper Ned and Mrs. Sullivan had shown her, but it meant nothing if Simon found them. She shuddered remembering the time two young lovers ran away from Hallow Hill. Simon and two of the white boys found them and brought them back. Jonje died under the lash of the whip while Little Sue had been strapped in a chair and forced to watch.

The ride in the back of the wagon was much rougher than she expected. The cobblestones of the city made for a constant vibration, but the ruts and rocks on the rural road to the north caused unexpected shudders and jolts. Finally, the little caravan of wagons halted on the south bank of a creek and the Quakers began setting up a camp for the night.

Besides Susannah and Ned, the party included four Quaker men and two women. One of the men had explained to Ned that their land was north and west of Philadelphia about three days ride by wagon. They came to the city from time to time to sell their honey and other produce to local merchants or private buyers. That was how Henrietta Washington met them and learned of their disgust for slavery.

She watched as the Quakers moved about in a well-practiced process of setting up camp for the night. There was little need for talking as each one knew their role and went about it without hesitation. When they did speak to each other, it was in a language Susannah had never heard before. She wondered if the Quakers were some strange Indian tribe unlike the Edistos and Stonos who passed by Hallow Hill from time to time. But their skin was too fair to be Indians. Whatever they were, Ned trusted them, and she would have to, as well.

As darkness fell, the clouds in the western sky

broke up and a quarter moon appeared just above the horizon. The Quakers built a fire in the center of the camp, surrounded by the three wagons. Susannah and Ned sat on the tailgate of one wagon, finishing off plates of beans and ham prepared by the Quaker women.

"Will ye be havin' more to eat?" one woman asked them when she saw their plates near empty.

"No more for me," Ned said. "It was mighty good, ma'am," he added.

"What about for you, ma'am?" the woman then asked Susannah. "There's plenty."

The question confused her at first. In her short lifetime, no one, but especially no white person, had ever called her "ma'am". "No thank you," she finally said.

"Well, I'll take them plates then," the woman said.

As the woman took the plates and utensils, Susannah felt a tear form in the corner of her eye. Until a few weeks before, no white person had ever spoken to her as just another human being. But Sara Sullivan had cared about her, and now this stranger treated her with respect. Maybe they respected her because Ned had told them she was his wife. The way he carried himself, the way he spoke, made it easy to believe Ned was a free man and should be respected.

A man called Joseph approached their perch on the back of the wagon. "I looked at your horse and your mule, Mr. Foster," he said to Ned. "They both be in fair condition but appear to be of too much girth."

"You mean they're fat?" Ned smiled.

"Yes," Joseph said.

"That's not surprising," Ned said. "They've had no work for six weeks."

"They be getting some work soon," Joseph said. "Tomorrow we get to Kintnersville. You can cross the river there. You'll be on your own after that."

"I figure three or four days and we'll be in Connecticut," Ned said. "Folks know me there and they don't care much for the slave hunters."

"You both got papers," Joseph said. "Maybe the slave hunters'll leave ye alone."

"Maybe," Ned Foster said. "But I've known of men with papers who got taken away, regardless. The slave hunters just figure they get the full price of selling a grown man rather than a reward for catchin' a runaway."

"I have heard that truth myself," Joseph said. "Such men are evil in the sight of god, and god will pass judgement on them. But that don't make them any less dangerous tomorrow or the next day and New Jersey might be a dangerous crossing for ye."

"I expect some frightful moments, friend," Ned said in response.

"Well, your animals will do fine for a short run, but don't ye count on them to run all day," Joseph advised.

Ned looked at Susannah, who'd fallen asleep leaning against the side of the wagon. "I ain't so worried about the animals," he said. "The girl hasn't been on a horse much in her life."

*****

Sullivan House

John Oliver and Sara Sullivan dined on day old bread and hard cheese, with a bit of peach wine to wash it down. They sat across the table from one another, but said little during the sparse meal, each expecting Hugh Marlow to appear at any moment. After the meal, they took glasses of the wine to the parlor where they waited for Marlow's inevitable arrival.

"You should have told me what you were planning," John Oliver finally said to her.

"Would you have tried to stop us?"

"I don't know," he admitted.

"You wouldn't have stopped us," Sara said. "I know you that well. But you're an honest man and lying to Marlow wouldn't have come easy for you."

"I admit I've not practiced it much," Oliver said.

"For women, it is a necessary skill," Sara said with a smile.

"And men are hopelessly deceived," Oliver

conceded.

"I rather think the deception makes men hopeful rather than hopeless," Sara laughed.

"Hopelessly hopeful, I suppose," he suggested.

"Very clever," Sara said.

As Oliver nodded his acceptance of the compliment, the front door swung open and Hugh Marlow stormed in along with Simon and a stout white man. He strode into the parlor and stood directly in front of Sara and Oliver.

"These two know what happened," he said to the white man with him.

"What are you talking about?" Sara asked.

"You know what I'm talking about," Marlow fumed. "My girl, Susannah, has run off with Oliver's man, Ned."

"That can't be," Oliver insisted. "Ned has gone to make arrangements for a shipment of tobacco from my farm in Connecticut."

"You better hope your man ain't gone with that girl," Marlow said.

"I seen the way he been lookin' at her, Mista Marlow," Simon interjected. "They gone together."

"Maybe the girl just went on her own," Sara Sullivan suggested.

"Naw," Simon said. "Girl need a key to get outta dat room, and she ain't used dis one." He held up a key to the attic room.

"You sleeping all the time helped them plenty, too," Marlow said to Simon.

"Yeah, I been wonderin' bout that too," Simon defended himself. "Maybe dey been puttin' somethin' in my tea."

"That don't matter none right now, boys," the stout white man said to Marlow and Simon. Then he turned to Oliver. "My name's Ben Eldon and I been catchin' runaway niggers for a long time. I'm gonna get Mr. Marlow's property back for him, but I can't promise your man will still be alive when I do."

"Ned Foster is a free man," John Oliver said. "If he is harmed, I will hold you legally responsible."

"If your man is in possession of property stolen from Mr. Marlow, I have a right to recover that property by whatever means necessary," Ben Eldon said. "But I'll make a deal with you, mister. If you tell us where they're headed, I'll go easy on your man."

"I'm sure Ned didn't take the girl," Oliver said.

"Oliver is from Hartford, Connecticut," Marlow informed Ben Eldon. "That's probably where Foster will take Susannah."

"OK," Eldon said. "Simon and I will start in that direction in the morning. People along the way will tell us if they've seen 'em."

"Please tell me, Mr. Marlow," Sara interjected. "What would be your price to sell the girl to me?"

Marlow stared at Sara for several seconds. "The girl is not for sale," he finally said. "Now, if you will excuse us, we have come to gather some of my things. The governor of South Carolina has arranged new living quarters for me. I will have someone collect the rest of my things tomorrow."

"Goodbye, then," Sara said. "I shall not be sorry to see you go." She rose and walked away toward the kitchen without looking back.

Marlow turned his attention back to Oliver. "South Carolina is satisfied with the direction the constitutional gathering has taken these last few weeks, Mr. Oliver," he said. "I was prepared to return to South Carolina immediately to see to my estate. However, now I shall remain in Philadelphia until Susannah, my property, is returned to me."

*****

Sara didn't go to the kitchen. Instead, she climbed the stairs to her room, where she sat on the edge of the bed and tried to calm her anger. She knew from the moment she, Hennie, and Ned concocted the plan that Hugh Marlow would be immensely angry if Susannah did indeed run away.

What she hadn't expected was for Marlow's appearance in her parlor to resurrect all the old fear and hatred she felt for Alfred Carlisle. She too had been a possession. She'd worn nice clothes and jewelry because that was the way Carlisle envisioned her. But none of it was hers. At least, not until she took it.

She heard the main door slam and then the

tromp of boots on the front porch. She hurried to the open window and watched as Marlow, Simon, and Ben Eldon walked out into the night, Simon carrying two bags of Marlow's belongings. *Good riddance*, she thought. But then she wondered about John Oliver. He was a good man, maybe too good to be blindsided by what they had done, but it couldn't be helped. It was just like John said: He might not be very good at lying to Marlow.

But Oliver did lie to Marlow. He made up a story that Ned was off making arrangements to ship their tobacco. Marlow didn't buy the story, but at least John Oliver had made the effort. But, if Oliver was now part of their plot, what should be the next step?

She tried to remember if she had heard him come up the stairs to his room and decided she hadn't. She slipped out of the single petticoat she was wearing under her skirt and examined herself in the mirror. It might not be fashionable to forego the undergarment, but the night was warm, and it certainly was more comfortable. It was more becoming, too.

She slipped out the door and into the upstairs hallway which was dimly illuminated by two oil lamps. Her soft shoes made little noise as she made her way down the stairs and to the main parlor where John Oliver still sat on the settee in his stocking feet, his boots on the floor next to the couch.

"I thought you had retired for the evening,"

Oliver said to her.

"No," she said. "I simply couldn't be in the room with Hugh Marlow for another minute."

"He's gone now," Oliver said. "With luck, you will never see him again."

"I hope that's true," she said, "but, I don't think this business with Susannah is finished."

Sara's eyes scanned the scene. She could sit in the chair opposite Oliver, as she had earlier, or she could take the place next to him on the couch. A second later, she made her decision. She sank into the softness of the couch and curled her feet underneath her. With no petticoat, her thin summer skirt conformed to the shape of her thighs and exposed several inches of hairless calves. She wondered if he noticed that she shaved her legs. It was a rare practice in the colonies, but more common in France, where Paul Barré had given her a straight razor and some intimate lessons in its use.

John Oliver twisted to his left to face her. He propped his elbow on the back of the couch and rested his head against his hand. The dim light from the lamp cast a glow on the side of his face and illuminated strands of his brown hair that had escaped his usually pristine ponytail.

"Ned is brave and smart," Oliver said to her. "It's quite likely that they will make it to wherever he has decided to go."

"Will he go to Hartford?" she asked.

"I doubt it," Oliver said, "but, he will go in that

direction, which means Ben Eldon and Simon are on the right track."

"What can we do to help them?" She twisted a little to her left so she could face Oliver.

"I haven't ridden at night since the war, and I didn't like it much then," Oliver said. "But those Quakers wouldn't have gone far today, and I need to find that camp before morning."

"I've ridden at night a few times," she said. "I'm all right with it."

"You're a good horsewoman, Sara, and you know your way around here," Oliver said, "but it could be dangerous."

"I know where to find the Quakers," Sara said, "so, I'm going with you."

Chapter 16

July 12, 1787
Philadelphia, Pennsylvania

A sleepy young stable hand looked quite puzzled when Sara Sullivan and John Oliver appeared at the stable door at just past ten PM. The horses had all been fed and most were sleeping in their stalls by that time.

"You're Dave, aren't you?" Sara asked the young man. He had assisted her on a few previous visits to the livery.

"Yes'am," Dave said, rubbing his eyes and still looking confused.

"We need our horses tacked up and ready as soon as possible," Sara said.

"Yes'am," Dave said again, this time looking

away from Sara toward John Oliver.

"This is Mr. Oliver," Sara told him. "You've got his horse boarded here too."

"Yes'am," Dave said once again. "I know Mr. Oliver's horse. It's just that folks don't go out much at this time of night."

"I'm sure they don't," Sara agreed. "But it is urgent that Mr. Oliver and I go out tonight."

"Yes'am," Dave conceded. "I'll get 'em right up for you."

A few minutes later, Dave reappeared leading the two horses, her own dapple-gray mare and Oliver's bay gelding. The glazed look in their eyes told Sara the animals were just as confused as Dave had been.

"They don't seem par'ticlar happy 'bout gettin' rigged up after supper, ma'am," Dave said as he handed the reins to them.

"They'll get over it," Sara assured him.

"Yes'am, I'll swing the big door open for ya," Dave said. "When ya bring 'em back, ya might have to yell purty loud. I'm a hard sleeper."

The two riders clopped along the Philadelphia streets until they reached the northern edge of the city where the road split, with the main artery going northeast along the Delaware River and a smaller road going north into the countryside. Sara brought her mount to a halt and Oliver stopped his bay alongside her.

"We'll take the left fork here," she told Oliver. "With any luck, Eldon will go to the right toward Trenton."

"We came into Philadelphia from Trenton," Oliver said. "Why wouldn't Ned go that way?"

"If they're still with the Quakers, I'm sure they would go this way," she said, pointing toward the left fork. "I've seen them setting up a camp by the creek near Abbington. That's about as far as they would get today."

John Oliver took out his pocket watch and checked the time by the dim light of an oil streetlamp. "It's a little after eleven," he announced. "How long to reach Abbington?"

"If we keep a steady pace, we should be there in an hour and a half," she said, "maybe a little less."

"Let's get going then."

"I hope the Quakers don't mind strangers riding into their camp in the small hours of the night," Sara observed.

"I met a few during the war. They're peaceful folks," Oliver said, "but they're not careless folks."

Sara nudged her mare into a walk and started up the dark northern road. Oliver glanced back at the last streetlight of Philadelphia before falling in behind her. A moment later, she increased the pace to a faster walk, which they had decided would be the best speed to navigate through the woods in the dark. Darkness wasn't their only concern. Highwaymen patrolled these woods and though those men would be sleeping at this hour, the sound of galloping hooves echoing through the woods would surely wake them.

They proceeded along the heavily wooded road for some time until finally the forest gave way to a broad open field. Even though the quarter moon provided little illumination, the absence of the heavy oak and hickory canopy gave Sara a sense of relief. In the dim light, she discerned a small creek a few yards to the right of the road. If she had guessed right, the Quaker campsite wouldn't be far away.

"I think the camp will be over that hillock," she said to Oliver.

"How far beyond the hill?"

"Not far," Sara said. "There is a grassy spot with some trees about a hundred yards on."

"OK, we'll stop at the top of the hill and let them know we're friendly."

Sara tapped her mount on the flank and started a slow walk to the crest of the hill. Oliver followed close behind until they neared the summit, then passed in front of her. They needn't have concerned themselves about how to alert the Quakers to their presence because as soon as Oliver's horse crested the hill, the Quaker's dogs began to bark and circle the camp. Within seconds, two oil lanterns came to life near the remains of a small fire.

The two riders stood as still as possible and held their arms in the air to signal they meant no harm. Finally, Oliver shouted down to the camp. "We come in peace," he announced.

"That may be," a deep voice came back to them from the creek bank to their right. "But, ye have come at a time when good intentions are not so common."

"I need to speak with a man who may be traveling with your party," Oliver said. "His name is Ned Foster."

"Keep your hands in the air," the voice commanded. The shape of a large man appeared out of the shadows by the creek. The shape included a long rifle pointed in their direction.

"Is Mr. Foster with you?" Oliver asked the shape.

"Who are ye?" the shape asked back.

"My name is John Oliver. Mr. Foster has been in my employ for many years."

"It's all right, Joseph," another voice came out of the darkness. Oliver recognized the second voice as that of Ned Foster.

They led the horses into the camp and secured them to one of the wagons alongside Ned's horse and the pack mule that had come with them from Hartford.

"Who's going to ride the mule?" Oliver asked Ned.

"Me I guess," Ned said. "Susannah doesn't have much experience riding anything, and that mule can be ornery sometimes."

"Susannah needs to hear what we have to say," Oliver said.

Ned retreated to one of the wagons and then returned minutes later with the frightened looking girl. The Quakers added a few pieces of wood to the fire before leaving the four of them to set down to talk.

"I did what I had to do, John," Ned Foster said once they were all seated.

"I know you did, Ned," Oliver said, "and I don't blame you for it. But you need to know that Marlow came to Sullivan House earlier tonight, and he is furious. He plans to send his man Simon and a white slave hunter named Ben Eldon after you first thing in the morning."

"I figured he'd send Simon, and he would have to find a white tracker who's familiar with this part of the country," Ned acknowledged. "I thought it would take a couple of days, though, and we'd have a pretty good lead on them."

"You'll only have a few hours lead on them in the morning," Oliver said, "and they will be traveling faster than these wagons."

"They may take the river road first," Sara offered. "That could give you a little more time."

"We were planning to cross the river at Kintner's Crossing," Ned said. "Does the river road go that far?"

"I think so," Sara said, "but it's more likely they figure out you didn't take the river road and they make their way back to this one."

"How far to Kintner's Crossing?" Oliver asked.

"Thirty miles according to Joseph," Ned said. "A full day in the wagons."

"You won't have that much time," Oliver pointed out.

"If we leave at dawn on horseback, we could be there in six hours," Ned said. "Maybe less."

"Can Susannah handle the ride?" Sara asked.

"She'll have to," Ned said. They all looked at the girl who nodded nervously.

"What's your plan once you're across the river?" Oliver asked.

"Get across New Jersey as fast as we can and cross the Hudson at West Point. From there we were going through Connecticut to Holyoke. I know some folks there who can help."

"You should stay away from Connecticut," Oliver said. "Ben Eldon has already guessed that's where you're headed."

"Where then?"

"Don't cross the Hudson," Oliver instructed. "Instead, follow the river north. When you get to the town of Kingston, ask around for Colonel Gabriel Riley."

"You know this man?"

"We were together in the war. He's half Indian. He can help you get north into the Iroquois

Federation lands. You should be safe there."

"What do I tell Riley?"

"There's a letter of introduction in this packet," Oliver said, passing a brown oilcloth package to Ned. "It's all you'll need with Gabriel."

"You sure Colonel Riley is still in Kingston?" Ned asked.

"He was still there three years ago," Oliver said. "That's the last letter I had from him."

"A lot can happen in three years," Ned Foster observed.

"Yeah, I know," Oliver conceded. "If you can't connect with Riley, keep heading north. There are some Iroquois camps around Great Bear Lake."

"Friendly camps?"

"Sometimes."

*****

The silhouette of Sullivan House took shape as Sara and John approached it in the early morning darkness. As promised, the stable hand, Dave, had been difficult to rouse at almost four AM, but finally he had responded and taken the two tired horses back to their stalls for a little hay and sleep.

Hennie had left a low-burning lamp in the parlor for when they returned, and Sara went straight to the older woman's door and tapped twice. She pushed the door open a crack and said, "We're back." An indecipherable response told Sara the woman was sleeping well, so she made her way back to the parlor where John Oliver stood near one of the large windows overlooking the front porch. He had removed his boots and laid them in the hallway.

"I don't know whether to go to bed, or stay up the rest of the night," Oliver said.

"I've got a better idea," Sara said. She walked straight to him, put her arms around his neck and pulled his lips down to hers. She felt a flash of resistance — or maybe it was surprise — before he relaxed into the kiss. One hand slid down her back to her rump, drawing her body firmly against his own, his arousal growing by the second.

"That was quite a surprise," he said when their lips parted.

"I hope you don't mind surprises."

"I don't mind this surprise."

She had recognized his attraction to her that first night at dinner when his eyes kept wandering to her cleavage. He would look away every time she looked up, but never quite fast enough. But she was hesitant to show interest in return. She wanted to love again, ached to love again, but trust did not come easy. One man had hurt her physically and another emotionally. But John Oliver had shown himself to be a good man. That didn't mean he wouldn't hurt her, but he was worth the chance.

She kissed him again, then pulled away, "Now

it's time for bed," she said as she took his hand and led him toward the stairway. She picked up the lamp from the hall table and climbed the stairs, Oliver a step behind.

Sara pushed open the door to her bedroom and began to walk slowly backward inside, leading Oliver by the hand. He pushed the door closed behind himself and pulled her to him again. This time the kiss was softer, more relaxed, more sensual.

Sara walked to the window and drew the curtain closed, then turned back to face Oliver. She stood a few feet away from him and lifted each foot to remove the riding boots she'd worn. Her hands drifted to the top button of the white shirt she'd worn on the night ride. She watched Oliver's eyes widen as the button gave way and popped open. As she began working on the next button, he cocked his head a little to the right. Maybe he wanted her to hurry, but she wouldn't do that. When the third button released, the top of the blouse spread open, revealing a little cleavage above the thin undershirt she wore underneath. The corners of his mouth turned up as she began to work on the last button, his exhaustion of a few minutes earlier now replaced by spring-loaded energy. He let out a soft moan as the blouse slipped off her shoulders and onto the floor.

With one foot, she kicked the shirt to the corner of the room while she loosened the belt of her breeches with her hands. She hooked her thumbs into the waistband and pushed the breeches down until they fell to the floor. As the breeches descended, the long tail of the undershirt fell to cover her naked womanhood. She raised her arms and removed two silver clips that had secured her mass of red hair. When she shook her head, the curls spilled about her face and shoulders, catching and reflecting the light of the lamp.

Sara kicked the breeches toward the corner where the discarded shirt lay. She stepped to him and put her left hand behind his head and pulled him into another kiss. She felt his hands lift the back of the undershirt and caress her naked buttocks. As she explored his lips and teeth with her tongue, she deftly loosened his waistband with her right hand. When the trousers slipped to the floor, she led him to the bed.

"I haven't done this in a long time," he said.

"I haven't either," she responded, "but, I think we'll remember the basics."

Sara turned and drew the bed covers back before removing her undershirt. She looked back at Oliver who had pulled his shirt off over his head and tossed it on top of his discarded trousers. One look confirmed he was ready.

They lay on their sides, facing each other. With a hand on her buttocks, Oliver pulled her closer until she felt his erection throbbing against her belly. She willed herself to slow down, to let passion grow into pleasure. John Oliver must have felt the same because he pushed himself back from her. He rolled her onto her back and began to lightly trace his fingertips around her right nipple, then slowly down to her navel and back to the left nipple. Again, his fingertips traced the centerline of her abdomen, this time traveling to the soft hairs at the apex of her thighs before moving back to her right breast. She sensed her body warm to his touch. Sara reciprocated with her own fingers, tracing his nipples, then his abdomen. Then, with her fingertips, she gently stroked his erection.

Sara rolled him onto his back and pushed herself on top of him. She raised her hips a few inches and guided him into the cleft between her thighs, then lowered herself onto him until he was fully inside her. They each began to move, slowly at first, and then quickening as they found their rhythm. Oliver's hands explored her breast with tender squeezes, then gripped her buttocks as his pleasure peaked. Sara's body trembled with the pleasure of it as she felt the explosion of his orgasm inside her.

Exhausted, Sara rolled herself onto the bed beside him, both of them still panting. She lay her head on his shoulder and rested her thigh across his midsection. "I think I can sleep now," she said.

"Should I go to my room?"

"Absolutely not," Sara said. "I expect a repeat performance in the morning."

Chapter 17

July 13, 1787
Abbington, Pennsylvania

Susannah slept little after the meeting by the campfire. She hadn't really lied to Ned Foster when she told him she'd ridden a horse a few times. What she hadn't told him was that she was no more than seven or eight years old at the time, and the ancient horse was connected to a heavy plow controlled by her father.

Daylight was coming on quickly as a thin line of yellow sunlight peaked above the horizon. Ned's horse and the mule were both saddled, and Ned was busy distributing their supplies between two sets of saddlebags.

Even though the morning was warm, Susannah was shivering from fear and anticipation. A day earlier, she had breathed free air for the first time in her life, and the emotion had been pure exhilaration. Then, Mr. Oliver and Mrs. Sullivan had come during the night, bringing with them the realization that real freedom was just an illusion unless they made it to a safe place, if such a place even existed.

In the pale light, she looked at her tiny feet clad in the thin cloth shoes she wore in the manor house at Hallow Hill. They weren't intended for the kind of day that was about to begin. Her thin cotton dress wasn't much better, but it would have to do for now.

"You ready, Susannah?" Ned Foster said to her once he was satisfied with the animals.

"I guess so," her voice trembled.

"Did you eat something?" he asked.

"I can't eat nothin' right now," she said.

"Well, I got some dried meat and apples in the bag on the mule," Ned said. "When you get hungry, eat some of that."

"I will," Susannah assured him.

He led her to his old mare, "I'll help you up," he said, his hands cupped beneath the stirrup.

She tentatively put her foot in his cupped hands and allowed him to lift her up until she was high enough to swing her leg over the horse. As she settled into the saddle, the cotton dress rode up several inches above her knees and her bare bottom sensed the cold hard leather of the saddle. Perhaps she should have worn the pants Mrs. Sullivan had offered, although the breeches had been too large for her.

Ned Foster mounted the mule and walked it up beside her. "Give her a little tap on the side with your foot," he instructed.

Susannah took a deep breath to calm her nerves, then did as he instructed. She expected the mare to begin walking, but nothing happened.

"Tap her harder," Ned suggested.

She did and immediately felt the rear end of the animal drop several inches. Then, its head and neck went up and its body lurched forward into a gallop. Terror swept through Susannah. She released the reins and gripped the front edge of the saddle with both hands. She tried to wrap her legs around the animal's midsection, but it was too large for her petite frame. She looked at the ground to her left, then to her right. The animal's huge strides grew longer and higher with each step. She clinched her knees against its sides and tightened her grip on the saddle.

Her panic began to subside when she realized Ned Foster was alongside her on the mule. The mare must have realized it as well because she glanced sideways at the mule beside her and flicked her ears around to hear the familiar voice of her master.

"Whoa, Annie," Ned shouted to the mare. It slowed enough for Ned to catch the dangling rein. "Hold on tight," he instructed Susannah.

He pulled the rein lightly at first, then in a series of short tugs until the mare understood what was expected and slowed to a walk before finally stopping. Susannah relaxed her knees from the horse's side and loosened her grip on the saddle. Annie sensed the episode was over and bent her head to rip a mouthful of grass from the sod next to the road.

"Are you all right, Susannah?" Ned asked.

"I don't know how to ride a horse, Ned," Susannah said.

"Yeah, I figured that out," Ned smiled. "But you did all right there. Most folks would've been laying on the ground back there."

"What we gonna do?"

"Oh, we've still got to get to Kintner's Crossing as soon as we can, so you've got to ride something," Ned told her, as he dismounted from the mule. "Now, slide down off Annie," he added, placing his hands under the stirrup for her to step into.

Her spirits rose significantly once her feet touched solid earth again. "Maybe we could walk real fast," she suggested.

"I don't think those shoes of yours will be much good walking on this rough trail," Ned said. "Besides, Simon and that hunter will catch us in no time if we're on foot."

"Bloody hell," Susannah said.

"Bloody hell is right," Ned agreed. "Where did you learn to say that?"

"Mr. Marlow say it sometimes," she explained.

"Well, it don't matter now what Mr. Marlow says."

Ned took a lead rope from one of the bags hanging over the mule's back and clipped one end to its bridle, then unrolled the rope to its full length.

"Come on, girl," he said. "You're going to ride the mule. He'll follow Annie on the lead rope. You don't have to touch the reins."

*****

Sullivan House

John Oliver opened his eyes to a stream of bright sunshine coming through a window near the bed. Once his eyes adjusted to the light, he took in his surroundings, confirming that he was in a different bedroom from the one in which he was accustomed to waking.

The clock beside the bed showed it was almost nine o'clock. No doubt, a few of the delegates were already gathering at the statehouse to argue details of the compromise they had settled on the day before, but Oliver saw little urgency to be there. He viewed the "compromise" more as capitulation than middle ground, and the convention would spend the day attempting to attach a pleasant smell to the pig they had birthed the day before.

He rolled over onto his left shoulder and felt the

warmth of Sara's naked thigh against his own as she lay with her back to him. His right hand slid up her thigh to her abdomen and pulled her buttocks into his midsection. Sara's hips oscillated slowly from side-to-side against his growing erection. She gave out a pleased sigh before lifting herself to her knees and elbows. "Let's not waste that mood you're in," she said.

*****

"Sit down right dar whilst I pour ya a coop o' tea," Hennie instructed Sara when she came into the kitchen. The clock by her bed had informed her it was after nine o'clock.

"Thank you, Hennie," Sara said. As she took a seat at the small table near the kitchen stove, she heard the front door close as John Oliver left for the convention.

"Dat mus' be Mr. Oliver goin' to his meetin'," Hennie observed.

"Yes, I suppose so," Sara offered.

"I find his boots in da hallway dis mornin', but Mr. Oliver not in his room."

"Oh," Sara feigned surprise. "Where do you suppose he slept?"

"I s'pose Mr. Oliver slept in da only room up dar with da door closed," Hennie casually observed.

"I guess he was so tired he fell asleep in the first bed he came to," Sara suggested with a smile.

"If dat's goin' be your story, you better do somethin' 'bout that squeaky bed o' yours," Hennie laughed.

"All right, it wasn't all sleep," Sara conceded.

"Bout time you had some fun, Missy," the older woman said. "Men been comin' round here for years and nothin' happen."

"It's been a long time since I trusted a man," Sara said.

"Mr. Oliver be a goot man," Hennie observed.

"Yes, he is a good man."

*****

Trenton Crossing

Simon shaded his eyes with a hand and squinted toward the yellow reflection of late morning sun on the Delaware River. They'd ridden along the river road for nearly two hours since the fork in the road where Ben Eldon had calculated their options.

"I'm guessing they took the river road," Eldon had said. "They don't know the lay of the land around here, but they know they gotta cross this river somewhere to get where they goin'," he added.

"Where you spectin' they cross?" Simon asked.

"Trenton's the closest place," Ben Eldon said. "I know the ferryman there. He'll tell us if two niggers crossed."

Two and a half hours later they reached the crossing. Simon watched as the flat raft made its way across the slow-moving river, guided toward the near shore by a rope connected to a pully. A man at the rear of the vessel controlled a long tiller which kept the bow aligned with the dock on the riverbank. On board, a small, mule-drawn wagon and two horsemen were readying to make their way onto the western shore.

As the raft clattered into the wooden dock, a young man in ragged clothes and a broad-brimmed hat secured it with ropes, pulling it snug against the wooden facing. After the horsemen and the wagon clattered onto the dock and started off on the road toward Philadelphia, Ben Eldon boarded the ferry and talked to the tillerman for a few seconds before walking back toward Simon.

"They didn't come this way," he said. He mounted his horse and turned back in the direction they had come from.

"Dat's it?" Simon asked. "We jus' give up and go back?"

Eldon stopped his mount and turned to Simon, "We ain't goin' back," he said. "There's a trail up ahead to cut over to the other road."

"You said dey gotta cross da river," Simon reminded him.

"The western road goes to Kintner's Crossing," Eldon said. "That's where they'll cross."

"We gon' lose time goin' back," Simon said.

"Why don't we cross da river here and go up to this Kintner Crossin' on da other side?"

Eldon adjusted his hat to better shield his eyes from the sun. He looked to his left, then to his right before again facing Simon. "I been huntin' down niggers since the war ended," he said, "and I ain't never needed a nigger to tell me how to do it. Now, if you goin' to be part of this hunt, let's go."

Simon stared at the back of Ben Eldon for several seconds as he turned back to the road and started off at a slow trot. *You ain't never seen a nigger like me*, he thought, before giving his animal a tap to follow Eldon.

Chapter 18

July 14, 1787
Western New Jersey

Susannah felt the earth shake. Her eyes sprang open and after a moment of confusion, she realized the earth wasn't shaking, but Ned Foster was trying to wake her for another day of travel. For the second night in a row, she had slept very little. The night before, Mrs. Sullivan and Mr. Oliver appeared in the middle of the night with an ominous warning. And on this night, her aching behind had not found comfort on the hard ground.

They crossed the Delaware River just before sunset. The ride from Abbington had taken longer than Ned had hoped, but there had been no sign of Simon and hunter. The ferryman was suspicious, but Ned's Spanish coins and the freedom documents had been enough to convince him to take them across the river. Once on the New Jersey side of the river, Ned crouched low in a small Alder grove and watched the ferryman pull his way back to the Pennsylvania shore.

"What ya doin'?" Susannah asked.

"I just want to make sure he doesn't come back this way," Ned said.

"He seen de paper, Ned," Susannah said. "He think we be free folk."

"He didn't read those papers because the man can't read," Ned said, "but he saw a bag of Spanish money."

They surveyed the river for half an hour until Ned was satisfied the ferryman wouldn't return to rob them or worse. When the ferryman secured the raft for the night and walked away toward some nearby village for the night, Ned relaxed. Once the ferryman disappeared around a bend in the road, Ned led Susannah and the animals to a small clearing surrounded by Alder and Red Oak trees. Still cautious though, he decided against having a fire.

Susannah hadn't slept outside since she was a child and sweltering South Carolina nights forced the whole family to opt for sleeping under the stars. Not that it was any cooler outside, but at least the air moved around, and hungry starlings plucked a few of the mosquitoes from the air. Her only memory of those nights was the time she woke to find a large snake staring at her from a few inches away. Susannah had screamed causing the frightened snake to back away before her father chased it into a nearby cornfield. When her father returned, he assured her the snake wasn't poisonous, but the fact did little to relieve Susannah's anxiety.

She sat up and stretched her arms over her head, hoping the bones of her back and shoulders would slide back into place. Finally, she found the willpower to come to her feet and when she did so, her body informed her of its urgent need to pee.

Ned Foster must have anticipated her need. He took a sheet of newspaper from a rolled-up bundle and held it toward her. "You'll want to take care of your morning needs," he said. "Over behind those Alders is as good a spot as any."

When she returned to the campsite, Ned Foster had rolled and stowed the mat she had slept on and was waiting to lift her onto the mule. She hesitated for a moment, as she dreaded what another day in the saddle would do to her already aching behind. But her course was set. Freedom was ahead. She took a deep breath and stepped a foot into Ned Foster's waiting hands.

Ned Foster connected the mule's lead rope to a hook on the back of his saddle before mounting the mare. "We made thirty miles or so yesterday," he said to Susannah once he was settled on his horse. "We need to do fifty miles today," he added.

"I ain't sure I can do it," Susannah said, her

aching buttocks protesting.

"We'll rest some along the way," Ned said.

*****

The morning sun was well into the sky and passengers were gathering on both sides of the river when the Kintner's Crossing ferryman arrived for work. Simon and Ben Eldon had reached the crossing too late the night before and camped in the woods near the river. They approached the ferryman as he began preparing the vessel for its day's work. "You work this crossing yesterday?" Eldon asked.

"I work this crossin' every day, mister," the man responded. "I own this boat and the permit to operate it," he added.

"Did you take a coupla niggers across yesterday?" Eldon asked.

"Matter of fact, I did," the man answered. He stopped his work and faced Eldon. "What of it?"

"They're runaways," Eldon said. "Me and this one aim to catch 'em," he added with a nod toward Simon.

"Them two had papers sayin' they was free," the ferryman insisted.

"Dat girl the property o' Mr. Hugh Marlow o' South Carolina," Simon said.

Both men turned to Simon in surprise, "They had papers," the ferryman said again.

"Dem papers ain't real," Simon said. "Dat girl's papers ain't real for sure."

"Did you read the papers?" Ben Eldon asked.

"I ain't learnt much readin'," the ferryman confessed.

"Then how come you assumed the papers was real?" Eldon pressed.

"They had money," the man explained, "good money, Spanish money. Runaways don't got money like that."

"Dey pro'ly stole money from Mr. Marlow," Simon suggested. He knew it wasn't true, but he could sense the ferryman's fear and wanted to press the advantage. Ben Eldon must have sensed it too.

"Look here, man," Eldon said. "I believe you when you say you thought the papers was real. We ain't goin' to tell nobody you was aidin' and abbettin' runaways. Now, where you suppose those folks was headed?"

"That fella said the papers was from Connecticut," the man said. "That's probably where they headed."

"Yep, that's what we thought too," Ben Eldon said. "Now tell me, if folks are goin' to Connecticut from here, what's the best way to go?"

"From here, you cross the Hudson at the West Point narrows," the ferryman explained. "You go directly East from there and you in Conncticut."

"Is there any chance they'd be goin' to New

York City?" Eldon asked.

"It ain't likely," the ferryman said. "Folks goin' to the city generally cross the river at Trenton."

"That makes sense. Now, what time was it you took those two across the river?"

"Must o' been nigh-on six o'clock," the man said. "It was the last crossin' o' the day."

"Thank you, sir," Eldon said. "Now, if you don't mind, we'll pay our fare to the other side and be on our way."

Simon led the horses onto the raft while Ben settled the fare with the ferrymen. He secured the reins to a hitching post and leaned against the ferry's siderail to wait for Eldon.

"Dey cross de riva las' night," Simon said, once Eldon joined him. "Dey got several hours start on us."

"No, they ain't that far ahead," Eldon said. "They crossed the river late, maybe an hour of daylight left before they made camp."

"How far ahead be dey?"

"Two, three hours at the most," Eldon said.

Simon stewed over the three hours they had spent backtracking from the Trenton Crossing to get here, but decided it wasn't the best time to mention it to Ben Eldon. Instead, he said, "We gon' catch 'em today den. Dat girl ain't no rider."

"We'll catch 'em today if we get lucky," Eldon said.

"What you mean?"

"There's half-a-dozen trails that can get a person from here to West Point Crossing. We could get lucky and take the same trail they do, but we pro'ly won't."

"So, we gon' lose 'em again," Simon observed.

"Naw, we ain't," Ben Eldon said. "We gonna ride like hell to West Point Crossing and be there waitin' for 'em."

*****

Susannah hoped Ned Foster would soon stop to make camp for the night. They rode much further than the day before and not only did her behind ache, but her feet hurt from standing in the hard metal stirrups to relieve the pressure on her buttocks. Once again, she questioned her decision to reject the sturdy boots Mrs. Sullivan had offered.

Finally, Ned brought his mare to a halt, and the mule stopped just behind her. Ned pointed to a small clearing on a hillock a short distance away from the trail. "That looks like a good place to camp for the night," he said to Susannah.

From the site Ned chose, they could see some distance back along the trail they had just ridden, yet two large bushes provided cover from being seen.

"I'll watch the trail till dark," Ned said.

"We gonna have a fire tonight?" Susannah

asked. She wasn't chilled. In fact, the air was muggy, even for July. Still, a fire would be a comfort, as if it could keep the night away.

"No fire," Ned said.

"You think Simon be back dar?" Susannah asked, staring toward the trail.

"I don't know," Ned said. "But if they are back there, I want to see them before they see us."

"Simon don' know nothin' 'bout these parts," Susannah said. "He might not find us at all."

"Simon ain't the one I'm worried about finding us," Ned said. "That slave hunter will know there ain't but two or three places where we can cross the Hudson."

"Mr. Oliver say we don' 'pose to cross dat river."

"That's right," Ned agreed, "but the road to the north is next to the river so we've still got to get to West Point."

Chapter 19

July 15, 1787
Philadelphia, Pennsylvania

It was a short walk from Sullivan House to the Indian Queen Tavern on Fourth Street. Luther Moore's invitation to dine with he and Stephen McGrew surprised John Oliver. Both men were, like himself, minor delegates from Northern states, Moore from Pennsylvania and McGrew from Massachusetts. Neither had been vocal participants in the proceedings to that point.

His first inclination had been to decline the invitation. His mind was preoccupied with the plight of Ned Foster and Susannah. He doubted he would be particularly engaging in a social setting, or insightful as to matters involving the new nation's emerging constitution.

But Sara Sullivan had insisted. "There's nothing you can do for Ned and Susannah, now," she said.

"I suppose not," Oliver had answered.

And it was true. There was nothing he could do at that moment to help his friend and long-time companion. Ned understood the risks of helping a slave escape from her owner and he had taken those risks. Now, he and Susannah were somewhere to the north trying to outrun a pair of dangerous slave hunters. If the hunters captured them, they would haul Susannah back to Hugh Marlow and might force Ned into slavery as well, his freedom papers notwithstanding.

Oliver turned off Market and onto Fourth Street, then angled across the lane to the Indian Queen. Despite its disheveled appearance from the outside, the Queen, as it was known, was considered one of the finer establishments in Philadelphia. It was a frequent dining and gathering spot for convention delegates and Oliver had been there many times. But, since it was a Sunday afternoon, he doubted the tavern would be crowded with other delegates.

His eyes adjusted to the artificial light inside the windowless tavern and he spotted Moore and McGrew at a table in the far corner of the room. A few other patrons were scattered about the establishment, but none at tables near them.

The two men stood to shake hands with John Oliver, "Please sit down, Mr. Oliver," Arthur Moore said, with a wave toward one of the empty chairs. "Mr. McGrew and I were just discussing the merits of the mutton stew in this establishment. Have you had it?"

"Yes, it's excellent," Oliver said as he positioned himself in the chair. "Please, call me John," he added. "I get enough of formality in the conference room."

"Yes," Moore said, "and call us Arthur and Stephen."

A waiter delivered three bowls of mutton stew, a loaf of crusty bread and a pitcher of ale to the table and then disappeared into the kitchen. Oliver tore a piece of bread from the loaf and dipped it into the soup, then took a swallow of the ale. Next, he scooped up a large spoonful of the stew and plunged it into his mouth. The others were doing the same.

"The food is delicious, as always," Oliver said when all three men were between scoops, "but, I sense there is more to this meeting than a simple repast."

"Yes sir, there is more to it," Arthur Moore said. He placed his spoon on the table next to his bowl and leaned forward. "What is your sense of the success of our gathering so far, John?"

Oliver hesitated before answering. He didn't know these men well but believed both opposed slavery. "I believe we are poised to surrender too much to the Southern states in the manner of counting people for representation," Oliver finally offered.

"We are disappointed, too," Stephen McGrew interjected. "It appears that all compromise will favor the slave owner."

"It is unfortunate, but many among those who don't hold with the practice of slavery are so determined to form a union that they concede their morality," Arthur Moore suggested.

"Mr. Ellsworth from your own state is one who comes to mind," McGrew said.

"Ellsworth is determined that joining all the states in a single union is the only way to avoid war among the states, or their European allies," Oliver offered.

"Regardless of whether we form a union, it may one day come to war as a means of resolving the question," Moore suggested.

"I have had similar thoughts, Arthur," Oliver said. "But, what can we do? The pudding seems to be baked at this point."

"The pudding isn't completely baked, John," McGrew suggested. "There is still a chance to adjoin provisions to the document that will lead to a gradual elimination of slavery."

"How would it be done?" Oliver asked.

"There are matters of taxation that have not been resolved," McGrew said.

"The Southern states will never agree to the taxation of exports," Oliver said.

"No, nor should they," Moore offered. "If we

are to be a union, the export of goods will benefit all."

"It is a tax on imports we favor, John," Stephen McGrew said. "Specifically, we wish to tax the importation of slaves."

"The Southern states won't accept such a tax," Oliver said.

"I believe the Southern states will be divided on the matter," Moore said. "Already, Virginia has banned importation of new slaves and North Carolina taxes them."

"Yes, but the three-fifths compromise means that each new slave imported adds to the political power of the state," Oliver suggested. "It would benefit Virginia to reinstate importation."

"Perhaps, but I don't think so," Moore stated. "Conditions in Virginia are quite gentle on the slaves when compared to the low country of South Carolina and Georgia. They have an excess of slaves simply through breeding."

"Slaveholders in Virginia already make a tidy profit from selling their excess to the lowland plantations," McGrew interjected. "If importation is restricted, the value of their stock will rise."

"Yes," John Oliver mused. "I can see the possibility of it. How do you plan to raise the proposal?"

"We believe Mr. Hamilton will forward the idea with General Washington," Moore said.

"I don't know Hamilton well," John Oliver said.

"He has a reputation as an abolitionist."

"That is his reputation," Moore said, "but ambition is Hamilton's north star. He shapes his beliefs to the mold of the man whom he believes will help his career the most, and he believes that man is General Washington at the moment."

"Washington has had little to say during the convention," Oliver pointed out.

"No, he hasn't," McGrew agreed. "But the reality of it is that this convention will produce a document which provides for an executive officer and everyone here understands that the first such executive officer will be General Washington."

"Washington owns many slaves," Oliver pointed out.

"That is true," McGrew countered, "but, Washington is also a Virginian and an astute businessman."

"John, we know that abolition is not possible at this time," Moore put in. "However, a limitation of imports is a good beginning."

"Have you spoken of this to Hamilton?" Oliver asked.

"No."

"I don't know what to make of Hamilton," Oliver said. "He fought against the English monarchy but has recently proposed an American monarchy — an elected monarchy to be sure, but a monarchy none the less."

"We are of a mind that his proposal was a ruse intended to make the Virginia Plan more appealing," Moore said.

"If such was his aim, he certainly succeeded."

"Yes," Moore said. "Hamilton and Madison are a bit of a pair. Along with a few others, including perhaps General Washington, they make a powerful political league. They call themselves Federalists."

"We have come together to form a federal government," Oliver said, "so I suppose we are all Federalists."

"It is true all of us wish to form a federal alliance, but some differ as to the purpose of such an alliance," Moore explained.

"Differ in what way?"

"The Federalists would make the rights of property superior to the rights of man," McGrew explained.

"As exemplified by the three-fifths compromise," Oliver noted. "It awards the slave holders representation on the basis of property owned rather than ballots cast."

"Exactly," Moore agreed.

"If property is to be represented in the new congress, then why shouldn't my acreage and forest land be represented alongside the slaves?" Oliver asked.

"The whole of it is a concoction devised to protect the slave trade," Moore said. "If your, and my, property were treated equally, their advantage would disappear. But, if we succeed in limiting importation of new slaves, the slave states advantage in representation will be reduced in time."

"Should we not organize a similar cabal to oppose the Federalists?" Oliver asked.

"Just such a cabal is soon to be realized," McGrew said. "However, our leader, Mr. Jefferson, is in Paris and cannot take part in these proceedings."

John Oliver gulped down the last of his ale. "Then we must do what we can and solicit all who will listen in favor of limiting importation."

"Agreed," Arthur Moore said.

Chapter 20

July 15, 1787
West Point, New York

Ned Foster brought the mare to a halt and dismounted. He helped Susannah down from the mule and then led the animals into a grove of cedar trees twenty yards off the road.

"What's happenin'?" Susannah asked as Ned secured the mare's rein to a low limb.

"I saw the ferry landing when we came over that hill there," Ned explained.

"West Point?"

"Yep."

"Ain't that where we goin'?" Susannah asked.

"I saw some men there by the dock," Ned said.

"What men?"

"I don't know for sure, but one of them was a tall black man."

"Simon?"

"Could be, I don't want to take a chance."

"How dey get here 'fore we do?" Susannah asked.

"They guessed we'd come to West Point, and they rode faster than we did."

"Dey see us?"

"I don't think so," Ned said. "The setting sun was behind us."

"What we gon' do?"

"The trail runs north along the river," Ned said. "We'll walk the animals through the woods for a ways. We'll camp tonight and join the trail somewhere upriver in the morning."

Ned Foster led the mare through the dense forest, the shady canopy further reducing the waning daylight. Susannah sat atop the mule which Ned had tethered behind the mare. As the light continued to fade, Ned's walk slowed to avoid exposed roots and downed tree trunks. Before long, they reached a clearing that sloped toward the river and was bounded by a creek on the west side. The daylight was almost gone when Ned stopped and lashed the mare's rein to a tree limb next to the creek.

"This looks like a good place," he said as he

helped Susannah dismount from the mule.

"We far 'nough away from Simon?" Susannah asked.

"It's a mile or so back to the ferry landing," Ned said. "I don't think they'll come looking for us at night."

"It's gon' be a full moon," Susannah observed.

"Yep," Ned confirmed. "Plenty of light if they were going to come looking, but I don't think they will."

"I hope you right."

"If they'd seen us back there, we'd already know about it," Ned said. "No, they still think we're coming to West Point, and it'll probably be a day or two before they realize we ain't."

"Maybe we get to Kingston 'fore they realize," Susannah suggested.

"Yeah, I think so." He had removed the saddles and supplies from the animals and begun arranging the camp site.

"We gon' have a fire tonight?" Susannah asked. Despite the warm summer nights, she'd felt a chill each night since they had left the Quakers at Abbington.

"Yeah," Ned said. "We can make a little fire down by the creek. The creekbank will hide it if anybody comes by along the road below."

"Thank ya," she said. Susannah looked over her shoulder in the direction Ned Foster was looking.

She couldn't see a road through the trees below them, but Ned would be sure it was safe.

"You go gather some wood — anything that looks like it'll burn good — while I get the camp set up and stake the horses out where they can reach some grass."

Susannah didn't need any instruction to gather firewood. It had been part of her family chores since she was old enough to walk. But she didn't mind if Ned Foster thought she might be a delicate girl unaccustomed to hard tasks. The corners of her mouth turned up as she skipped off into the surrounding trees. Ned Foster had kissed her once, and she had expected him to do it again. But he hadn't. In fact, he had barely touched her since they left Philadelphia, and then only to help her onto the mule.

An hour later, they sat next to the small fire under bright moonlight. Besides the potatoes and carrots Ned roasted over the fire, he had caught two trout in the little stream. Along with dark tea from their supplies, the simple meal was a great feast to Susannah.

"Dis water's warm," Susannah exclaimed as she dipped the two tin plates into the creek to wash them.

"Yeah," Ned Foster said. "It must bubble up from a warm spring around here."

"What make it warm?"

"I don't know," Ned admitted. "Some are hot,

some are warm, and some are cold."

"How deep is it?" Susannah asked.

"It's about waist deep in the middle."

She brought the cleaned plates back to the fire and laid them by Ned's saddle bags. "Dey any snakes in dis creek?" she asked.

"I don't imagine so," Ned said. "Leastwise, no snakes like you'd have in South Carolina."

Susannah walked back to the waterline and stared at the creek for several seconds. Then, she began to pull the cotton dress over her head. A moment later, she threw the dress to the ground behind her and stood by the water completely naked.

"I gon' have myself a bath," she said and began wading into the creek. When the water was just knee deep, she turned to face Ned Foster and laughed as she watched his eyes travel up and down her torso. She dipped a hand into the creek and splashed the warm water over her thighs and abdomen. Then, she lowered herself to sit cross-legged on the warm stone creek bottom.

"You want some privacy?" Ned Foster asked.

"For what?"

"For your bathing."

"Haha," Susannah laughed. "You ain' never been a slave have ya?" She splashed the warm water over her breasts. The droplets glistened from the moonlight on her smooth brown skin. She sensed her nipples swell as the night air cooled her wet skin.

"I was a slave, but it was a long time ago," Ned said. "Most of that time, I lived in a fine house in England or New York," he added.

"If ya was a slave at Hallow Hill, you wouldn't know nothin' 'bout privacy," Susannah said. "Ya jus' do what ya gotta do and if somebody watchin' ya do it, then that's jus' the way it is."

"You're not a slave now," he pointed out.

"No, I'm not," Susannah laughed. "Now, I get to 'cide if I want privacy or not."

"That's why I asked if you want it," Ned said.

"I don't," she told him. "What I want is you in dis warm water with me."

Susannah held her lower lip between her teeth while she waited for Ned Foster to respond. She did not understand how a free woman told a free man that she was interested in making love. She had watched the young white girls bat their eyelashes and throw half-smiles and side-glances toward the boys at Hallow Hill parties. But Susannah didn't have time for coy flirting. She'd been free for two days. It might last forever or it could end in a few hours.

Finally, Ned Foster stood and removed his shirt. He took something from the bag that lay by the fire and walked to the creek bank before removing his boots and stockings. He loosened his belt and let his trousers fall to the sandy ground, then stepped into the warm stream.

Her heart sped up as she watched him come toward her. His legs were lean, but well-formed with long, smooth muscles from belly to knees. His torso was lean and firm. As he got closer, she saw a thin strip of curly black hair running along his torso from the center of his chest to his navel. Below his navel, thick, dark hair surrounded his manhood, which was already signaling his arousal.

He stood next to her for several seconds before slowly sinking to his haunches on the creek bottom, knees bent in front of him. "The warm water feels good," Ned said.

"Yeah," Susannah said. She nudged herself closer to him so that their thighs touched under the water.

Ned lifted a hand from the water and showed her a chunk of gray substance. "What dat?" Susannah asked.

"Soap, for your bath," Ned said.

"Oh."

"Yep," Ned said. "Turn around now, so I can wash your back."

Susannah did as he instructed and soon felt the gentle stroke of his hands as they made little circles on her back, the soap in one hand and scoops of warm water in the other. He slid his hands beneath her arms and propped her back against his chest. With the same circular motion, he slid the smooth soap over her breasts and abdomen. She closed her eyes, trying to capture the moment in her forever memory.

"Stand up now, Susannah," Ned instructed.

She stood naked with her back to Ned. A moment later, a sweet shiver of pleasure ran through her body as the soap and his hands moved across her buttocks and down her hamstrings to her knees, paying special attention to the sensitive places at the top of her inner thighs. The afternoon's heat had dissipated, but a surge of warmth ran through her entire body.

Susannah turned around and took hold of Ned's right hand, guiding him to his feet. She took the soap from him and used it in the same way he had, making little circles, then larger ones, on his chest and abdomen. Twice she stopped to dip water from the creek to rinse the soap away.

She gently washed his most private parts. She had never seen an erection quite like the one Ned Foster was now displaying. Certainly not Hugh Marlow.

After she scooped up a double handful of water and rinsed Ned's midsection, he bent over, put one arm behind her knees and swept her into his arms. He carried her to the sleeping blankets he'd laid out by the creekbank and laid her on one of the blankets. He took the other blanket and dried her feet and legs, before lying next to her.

Ned kissed her and stroked her side, buttocks and thighs before rolling her onto her back. As he mounted her, she guided his erection into her, then grasped his buttocks as he began to thrust. She thought of Miss Hattie, a kitchen slave at Hallow Hill, who had told her about the "spot", a place inside her that a man could stroke to bring a woman pleasure. Ned had found the spot. She wrapped her feet around his buttocks and willed him to continue stroking the spot.

Susannah closed her eyes and let the sensations of her body take over her mind, her pleasure growing with each movement Ned made. His strokes became shorter and faster. She opened her eyes and saw Ned's face clinch tight as he neared his climax. Then, her own climax took over her body.

Afterward, Ned put fresh fuel on the little fire, and they lay near it under the second blanket, still naked. The sensation she had just experienced still coursed through her body. "Ya know somethin', Mr. Ned Foster," Susannah said.

"What?"

"I am a free woman now."

"What do you mean?"

"I jus' did somethin' 'cause I wanted to do it," Susannah said. "Nobody made me do it."

Chapter 21

July 16, 1787
West Point, New York

Ben Eldon sat on a stack of freshly cut firewood left to season for the coming winter when the little ferryman's shack would be freezing. But in mid-July, the morning was warm and moist, with clouds gathering over the forest northwest of the landing. He sipped tea from a tin cup and surveyed the approaches to the landing.

Simon leaned against the shack and watched Eldon. They had reached West Point not long after noon the day before. By Simon's calculations, Ned Foster and Susannah should have gotten there as well.

Some tracker, Simon thought. Eldon was a fool. First, he'd taken the wrong road at the fork outside

Philadelphia. Then, when Simon suggested they cross the river at Trenton to get to Kintner's Crossing before the fugitives, Eldon insulted him and wasted hours going back to the other road.

Now, he was wasting time again — sipping tea — while it was obvious Foster and the girl had avoided West Point. It was already mid-morning. Even if they had camped before crossing the river, the fugitives should have arrived by then. No, something was definitely wrong.

He was about to say as much to Eldon when he saw two riders approaching them from the north. Simon stood tall as the riders got closer. At first, he thought maybe Ned and Susannah had finally arrived, but he quickly surmised they wouldn't be coming from the north. When the riders were close enough, he realized they were both white men in dirty, tattered military uniforms.

"Mornin' to ya," one of the men said to Eldon as he dismounted in front of the landing.

"Mornin' to you, soldier," Eldon replied. "Where ya comin' from?"

"Patrolin' up around Albany," the soldier replied. "Just to keep an eye on the savages."

"Trouble up that way?" Eldon asked.

"Naw, but you never know with savages," the soldier said. "They can be friendly for years and then just start burnin' down cabins."

Both soldiers led their horses to the hitching rail where Simon was standing. The man who had been doing the talking turned to Ben Eldon. "This your nigger?" he asked.

"We're riding together," Eldon said.

"Where you headed?"

"Might get our business done right here," Eldon said. "Might have to go to Connecticut, though."

"What business?" the soldier asked.

"Catchin' runaways," Eldon answered.

The soldier looked at Simon again. "You use a nigger to catch niggers?" he asked Eldon.

"Weren't my idea," Eldon said.

"You lookin' for a man and a woman?" the soldier asked.

Ben Eldon stood up. "You seen 'em?"

"Seen a nigger man and woman up the road a way," he said.

"Why didn't you stop 'em?" Ben Eldon asked.

"My job is Indians, mister," the soldier said. "Your job is niggers. Besides, they had papers."

"Where were they headed?"

"Ain't nothin' up that way but Kingston and Albany," the soldier said.

"How far up did you see 'em?"

"Coupla hours, could be a little less."

"How're they travelin'?"

"Horse and a mule," the soldier said.

"Get our horses, Simon," Ben Eldon said. "If

they're two hours ahead of us, we'll catch 'em before nightfall."

*****

"Stop Ned," Susannah shouted from the back of the mule. "I gotta pee."

Ned Foster halted the mare and the mule stopped behind it. He dismounted and then helped Susannah get off the mule. "We can rest for a while," he said.

Susannah stepped to the side of the road where she lifted her dress and squatted to pee. When she finished, she joined Ned who was leaning against a tree by the road.

"How much farther to Kingston?" she asked.

"An hour if the rain holds off," Ned said.

Susannah looked up through the trees to the clouds that had been thickening since morning. The wind had grown as well, now bringing a steady showering of leaves from the Maple and Pin Oak trees that lined the trail.

"How we gon' find Mr. Riley once we get to Kingston?" she asked.

"I don't know that yet," he said, "but we're gonna be careful about who we ask."

"Dem soldiers didn't have no problem with da papers," Susannah said.

"The soldiers didn't want to mess with us," Ned

said. "They just wanted to go home to their barracks at West Point."

"Dem soldiers goin' to West Point?" Susannah asked.

"I imagine so," Ned said. "There's a fort down river from the ferry crossing."

Susannah closed her eyes and shook her head. "I sure hope dem soldiers don't talk to Simon and that hunter," she said.

"Yep, I been thinking the same thing," Ned said. "If those soldiers stopped at the landing, there's a good chance that slave hunter knows we headed north."

"What we gon' do?"

"We're gonna get to Kingston before they catch up to us," Ned said. "I figure we got a couple of hours start on them, but they can go faster than we can. Now, let's get back in the saddle and go."

Again, they traveled north along the rutted trail, making a better pace now. A half an hour later, the rain started, at first, a few large, cold drops, but soon it became a downpour. The canopy above provided little shelter as the weight of the rain bent the leaves down. Lightening streaked across the sky, followed by loud claps of thunder. Wind whistled through the big trees.

Their pace slowed. The bare ground of the trail softened as the rain continued to pelt them. Ned moved the animals to the edge of the trail looking for more solid footing, but tree branches made that part of the path unpassable. Finally, at the crest of a good size hill, Ned stopped and dismounted.

"We'll walk the horses down this slope," he said, then assisted Susannah off the mule.

Susannah looked back at the trail they had just passed through, then toward the descent ahead of them. She wanted to get to Kingston as fast as possible, but her instincts told her Ned was right. They needed to get to the bottom of the hill. It would be slippery, and, on the right, the landscape dropped sharply toward the river. If one of their mounts slipped over the edge, they might not get it out until the mud dried.

The rain had soaked her thin cotton dress, and it clung to her body as if it had melted. Within a few steps, the muddy earth had sucked the soft shoes off her feet. She bent and retrieved them but didn't put them on again. The mud squished between her toes as they slowly made their way to the bottom of the slope.

When they neared the bottom of the hill, the rain stopped as suddenly as it had begun. The wind, which had howled a moment earlier, was quiet.

Ned Foster stopped. "We can ride again now," he said. "The road looks safe up ahead."

He helped Susannah into the saddle on the mule before mounting his mare. As Ned settled into the saddle, a musket blast rang out and leaves and acorns showered them from the trees above. Susannah looked backward to where the blast had come from and saw two riders at the top of the hill they had just come down. One of them was Simon.

Ned Foster saw them as well. "Hold on tight, girl," he said.

Ned dug a heel into the flanks of the mare and the horse sprung forward. The lead rope tightened instantly, and the mule jumped into a fast trot behind the mare. Susannah leaned forward with both hands gripping the edge of the saddle. She turned her head enough to see the two men descending the slope. The slippery surface forced them to go slow, but she realized they would come fast when they reached the flat.

She tried to judge their pace against what she thought the two horsemen could do on the flat. While she knew little about the speed of the animals; instinctively, she realized that Ned Foster had moderated their pace because their mounts were tethered together.

Susannah made a decision. She edged as far forward in the saddle as she could, her bare feet pressed hard against the metal stirrups. She laid her torso against the mule's neck, and with one arm wrapped around its neck, she reached forward with the other. Her fingertips barely reached the metal hook that connected the lead rope to the mule's bridle, but she managed to disconnect it and throw it to the side.

She straightened and took the rein in both hands. When she leaned to the left, she found that the mule moved in that direction. She tapped its side with the stirrup and soon the mule was alongside Ned Foster on the mare.

"What are you doing?" Ned asked.

"We can go faster dis way," she yelled back to him.

"All right," Ned said. He turned in the saddle and began to reel in the lead rope. "Don't want this thing to get hung up on a tree."

As their pace quickened, Susannah turned in the saddle, hoping Simon and the hunter were no longer in sight. They weren't in view, but she knew they wouldn't be far behind. The mule was steady, but not fast, and she doubted it had much more speed to offer. Also, she wasn't sure she could stay on the animal if it went any faster. Its awkward stride threw her from side to side and up and down. Her legs already ached from pressing hard against the stirrups.

As they crested a small hill, Ned's mare slowed suddenly, walked a few steps and stopped. The mule did the same without any instruction from Susannah. A glance forward told her the reason for stopping. A large branch from a nearby tree lay across the path, obviously a victim of the earlier storm.

"Can't we go 'round dis thing?" Susannah asked.

"It's gonna be slippery if we go down toward the river," Ned said. "Probably better to go up the hill a little and around that way," he added, pointing to their left.

Susannah nodded and watched the way Ned handled the reins to turn the mare to the left. But, before Ned could get his mount started up the hill, she heard hoofbeats on the trail behind them. When she turned around again, Simon and the hunter had come to a halt some forty yards back.

"Don't go no further," the white man yelled. He was pointing a muzzle load pistol in their direction.

Ned stopped still. Simon and the hunter began walking their horses toward them. Bile churned in her gut as Susannah sensed her freedom slip away. If she kicked the mule in the flanks with the metal stirrups, it would bolt up the hill, but what then. She would surely fall or lose her way. Ned would try to follow, but the hunter was close enough now that even a pistol shot could be accurate enough to take Ned out of the saddle before he got off the road.

The hunter stopped when he was a few yards away. "This nigger girl is a runaway slave from the estate of Mr. Hugh Marlow, and I have the legal authority to return the runaway to Mr. Marlow," he announced. "I don't have no claim on you, Ned Foster, but you are committing a criminal act of helpin' this girl run away."

Before they could react to this demand, Susannah heard a swish sound and saw an arrow bury itself deep into the hunter's shoulder. He dropped the pistol from his right hand and reached for the wounded shoulder. For a second, he tugged at the arrow, but it wouldn't budge.

Now, Ned Foster had his own pistol in hand and aimed it at the two men. Simon grasped the direness of the situation and quickly turned his mount around and rode fast toward the hill behind them. The hunter got hold of his reins with his right hand and turned to follow Simon up the hill.

"Shoot 'em," Susannah said.

"The pistol is useless at this range," Ned said. "Besides, I don't know who shot that arrow and I don't want to have to reload."

"I think we gon' find out right now who shot it," Susannah said with a nod toward the woods behind Ned.

Two native men were approaching them from the woods to her right. A snap of brush caused her to look to her left where she saw two more bare-chested men moving in their direction.

Ned Foster had seen them too, "We mean no harm," he said.

The men were silent but continued their approach. "Any of you speak any English?" Ned asked.

The four natives stopped their advance. All were tall and naked from the waist up, except for elaborate leather collars suspending brightly painted wooden or metal carvings that hung over their chests. Each had long, dark hair cinched in the back with beaded leather straps, and spikes of colored feathers circled the crowns of each head. Soft looking deerskin trousers covered them from the waist down.

"I speak your language," the tallest of the men said.

Ned returned the pistol to his saddle bag. "Thank you for helping us," he said.

"My father does not approve of these slave hunters," the Indian said.

"We have come to find a man named Gabriel Riley," Ned said. "He is supposed to be living somewhere near Kingston."

"I know Riley," the Indian replied.

"Can you take us to him?"

"What business do you have with him?"

"I bring a letter from an old friend of his," Ned said.

The native pondered Ned's answer for a short time before he spoke again. "Very well," he said. "We will take you to him."

*****

Simon squatted low behind a moss-covered ditch bank and watched the road. So far, neither Ned Foster nor the Indians had followed them in their retreat, but these local savages might track them. He doubted they had horses — none of the tribes in South Carolina did — but, if they did, they would certainly outrun he and Eldon. He looked down at Ben Eldon on the ground beside him still trying to work the arrow out of his shoulder.

"Help me with this thing," Eldon said to him.

"What you wan' me to do?"

"Get it out."

"Den what?"

"Get me back to that army post at West Point."

"So, now you wan' help from a nigger," Simon said. He paused for a long moment, "Naw, I think dis is da place you goin' spend eternity."

Simon drew a long knife from his belt. Ben Eldon's eyes widened with realization just before Simon plunged the blade deep into his chest.

Chapter 22

July 16, 1787
Near Kingston, New York

The deference the Indians showed to her and Ned Foster surprised Susannah. She had only seen a few indigenous people during her years at Hallow Hill. Those had come to trade for supplies. Occasionally, they came to steal unattended livestock or goods. They were civil, but had no love for the white man, believing their land had been stolen and defiled.

But perhaps because she and Ned weren't white, these Indians had shared their fresh water and dried venison before helping Susannah onto the mule, then walked alongside them towards Kingston. One man trailed behind by a quarter mile distance to guard against the return of the hunters, although that was unlikely given the wound delivered to the white man.

As dusk neared, the party stopped at a clearing and waited for the rear guard to catch up. When he did, they turned off the main trail and proceeded onto a barely visible footpath through a thicket of ash and maple trees. The fading sunlight made it hard for Susannah to see the little trail, but the Indians obviously knew where they were going.

Their destination appeared before them sooner than she expected. After cresting a hill, they came upon a large clearing in the trees. In the center of the clearing was a sizable building with a gabled roof and built of mature timbers. A dim light emitted from an open wooden window on the front. Next to the cabin, a corral surrounded by a fence built of small timbers enclosed a cow at one end and several pigs at the other end. Beyond the log cabin was an oblong building made from limbs and branches. A large fire burned between the cabin and the other structure.

The troop stopped in front of the cabin and Ned Foster dismounted from the mare while one of the Indians assisted Susannah down from the mule. When her bare feet touched the ground, the earth was cool and still wet from the rain. She brushed the wrinkles from her thin dress. At least it was now dry.

"What have you found, Natani?" a question came from the porch of the cabin.

"We found them running from slave hunters,

father," the tall Indian replied. "This man said he was looking for you. He has a letter."

A man — Gabriel Riley — stepped off the porch into the fading light. He was tall, like his son, the Indian he'd called Natani. He wore the same deerskin trousers as the others, but also a deerskin shirt with long buttons made from bone. Instead of the moccasins the others wore, Gabriel Riley wore knee-length boots.

"Name's Ned Foster," Ned said, extending the letter to Riley.

"We'll go in the cabin," Riley said. Then to Natani, he said, "Take care of their horses, Natani."

The inside of the cabin was warm and dry, with woven grass mats covering a dirt floor. Several candles threw a golden glow over the space which was one large room, with living quarters on one side and stacks of hardgoods on the other. The living area was sparsely furnished with a table, two chairs, a rocking chair, a narrow bed, and a small bedside table. A low fire glowed in a fireplace on the wall opposite the entrance.

Riley pointed to chairs for Susannah and Ned while he seated himself on a stool next to the fireplace and opened the letter. In the light from a candle on the mantle, Susannah noted deep lines on his tanned face. She had expected Mr. Oliver's friend to be of a similar age, but she could tell Gabriel Riley was older. He smiled as he read the message.

"It has been a few years since I have had correspondence with Captain Oliver," Riley said. "I am very pleased to hear from him."

"He said you could help us," Ned said.

"And I shall help you," Riley said. "But first, tell me how my friend is faring. I see he has addressed this letter from Philadelphia."

Ned Foster told Riley about the constitutional convention going on in Philadelphia. He told him about their stay at Sullivan House and Hugh Marlow's arrival with his slaves. Finally, he told him about the plot to get Susannah free and Oliver's early morning visit to the Quaker camp with the letter of introduction.

"I know just the place for you if you and the girl don't mind living in the wilderness for some time," Riley said.

Ned looked at Susannah, "Does that sound all right with you, Susannah?" he asked her.

"I'll go anywhere Simon can't find me," she said.

"Where is this place?" Ned asked Riley.

"There's a Mohawk village on the northern end of Lake Champlain. It's very near the British territory of Quebec," Riley said. "The chieftain is Odonida."

"Do you know this chieftain?"

"I know him well," Riley said. "He was a great help to me during the war against the British."

"Mr. Oliver said you were a colonel in the Continental army," Ned noted.

"Not really," Riley said. "General Washington called me 'colonel', but I wasn't in the army. I kept a watch on the Iroquois Confederation to see who was helping the British. I passed that information along through Captain Oliver."

"The Indians mostly stayed out of it, didn't they?" Ned asked.

"A good many sided with the British thinking they would grant the land to them. A few supported the colonists, remembering that the British had never been fair with them," Riley said. "Most stayed out of it altogether. The Iroquois don't care for the white man's kind of war where a lot of folks are killed."

"The white people down in the cities think the Indians are fierce warriors," Ned observed.

"They can be fierce, true enough," Riley said. "But they don't seek death when fighting. Captives is what they want. If a warrior is killed in a fight, they think his spirit becomes an unruly ghost."

"John said you're half Indian," Ned observed.

"Yes," Riley confirmed. "My mother was Algonquin. The Algonquin and Mohawk are traditional enemies. The Mohawk took her as a captive. They treated her well and eventually they made her part of their tribe. My father was a Catholic priest, and he taught many of the children to speak English, including Odonida."

"Is Odonida a Catholic?"

"My father wasn't much good at converting the Mohawk," Riley said. "In the end, he gave up and converted to their religion."

"What is the Mohawk religion?" Ned asked.

"It's hard to describe," Riley said. "I guess I would have to say they worship nature. They believe everything in the universe has a force within it — they call it the Orenda. The force can be good, or it can be evil. The Mohawk's task is to help good defeat evil."

"It's a mighty task," Ned said. "There's plenty of evil in the world."

"They don't expect to win, Ned," Riley said. "But they must put up the fight."

"How long to get to Odonida's camp?"

"Five- or six-days hard ride on horseback," Riley said. "Natani will go with you along with his wife and a couple of the other men. The Mohawk walk most of the time, but we have good horses for when we need them."

"When can we go?"

"You will leave tomorrow," Riley said. "Now, tell me more about this new nation the colonies wish to make."

Ned told him everything he could remember from his conversations with Oliver. Even though, the meetings were supposed to be secret, Oliver would often express frustration to his longtime companion. When he told Riley of the three-fifths compromise, the man shook his head.

"They must deal with the matter of slavery once and for all," Riley said. "Else, it will poison any union they form."

"John said much the same thing," Ned Foster said.

*****

Simon leaned against the trunk of a large maple tree and stared at the dead man. His pockets had yielded a few gold Spanish coins and a wad of the nearly worthless Continental dollar notes. But the dead man's pants and boots were a nice fit and better quality than the ones Simon had just discarded. He had hoped to find another shirt in Eldon's saddle bag, but it only contained dried meat, gun powder, and musket balls.

The ammunition reminded him that Eldon's pistol lay somewhere on the trail nearby and it would soon be too dark to find it. He took the dead man's feet and dragged him twenty yards further down the hill toward the river. He doubted Ben Eldon had any friends or relatives who would care enough to look for his body, but at least it wouldn't be easy to find if they did. In any event, wolves, bears, and vultures would take care of it within a few days.

He debated whether to take Eldon's horse with him but decided against it. A black man with one horse would raise enough questions. His letter from Hugh Marlow explained that both Simon and the horse he rode were the property of Marlow and that Simon was on a mission for his master. He hadn't needed to show it to anyone as long as he was riding with Ben Eldon, but the situation would be very different now.

He led Eldon's horse back to the trail, pointed it to the north and gave it a hard slap on the rump. Maybe the Indians would find it and accept it as tribute instead of coming after him.

When the animal disappeared around a bend in the trail, Simon trotted slowly toward the place where the Indian's arrow struck Eldon. He dismounted and walked along the road until he spotted the distinctive shape of the weapon. Simon picked it up and stowed it in his saddle bag along with the ammunition. He glimpsed the horizon through a break in the trees and judged he could travel for a half hour or so before it was too dark. He got back on his horse and turned it toward the south, glad to be away from this place.

*****

As darkness engulfed Gabriel Riley's little compound, the Indians began adding fuel to the small fire burning between the cabin and the oblong structure, which they had learned was called a longhouse. Before long, the fire roared, the flames rising above Susannah's head. When they were satisfied with the fire, the Indians arranged chairs around a long table.

"The feast is ready," Gabriel Riley said to Ned and Susannah.

"Feast?" Ned asked.

"Yes," Riley replied. "It's in your honor, but to tell you the truth, the Mohawk will take any excuse for a feast."

"A feast sounds good right now," Ned said. "Sound good to you, Susannah?"

"I be hungry for somethin' 'sides that dry meat we been eatin'," Susannah said.

They followed Riley to the long table and took the seats he indicated for them. Once Gabriel Riley had taken his place at the head of the table, Natani, and the other Mohawk men took their own places around the big table.

Once everyone was settled into place, two women emerged from the longhouse carrying trays of food. They circled the long table, placing a wooden plate laden with hot food in front of the guests first, then Gabriel Riley, then the young Mohawk. Finally, they laid their own plates on the table and took the two empty chairs that remained.

"My wife, Emma, prepared this feast," Riley said with a nod toward the older of the two women, "along with Natani's wife, Tabita," indicating the younger woman.

Susannah leaned forward to smell the aromas coming from the plate in front of her, a medley of vegetables and a pile of meat sliced very thin. She picked up a short knife from next to the plate and stabbed a chunk of the squash.

"Venison?" Ned asked their host about the meat on the plate.

"Yes," Riley said. "Natani brought it in this morning."

"Are the deer plentiful around here?"

"It looks like a good year," Riley answered. "Natani and the rest of the Mohawk here are doing the annual survey of the deer population."

"Annual survey?"

"Yes. Every year, the tribes send out teams to check the deer population. That way, they know how many they can take in a season."

"What happens if the population is down?" Ned asked.

"Then they eat more turkey, rabbits, and squirrels, and less venison."

"Good planning," Ned said.

"The Iroquois tribes rely on the land," Riley said. "They know it has to serve not only themselves but their children and their children's children."

"A lot of folks in those cities on the coast could learn from the Iroquois," Ned offered.

Riley nodded his agreement, then turned to Susannah, "You want some salt on that, Susannah?" he asked, passing a small bowl in her direction.

Susannah took a pinch of the salt between her thumb and forefinger and sprinkled it on the beans, corn, and squash. She liked salt. Hugh Marlow never distributed salt in the slave quarters at Hallow Hill, so the only times she had it was when Hattie sometimes pilfered a small amount from the kitchen in the big house. "Dis is real good," she said after a mouthful of the salted vegetables.

"Where do you get the salt out here?" Ned Foster asked. Salt had been a major factor in the war of independence because of its importance in preserving food. Before the war, most salt was imported from England. When that salt was no longer available, the colonists began setting up their own saltworks, but were subject to continual raids by British patrols. Even after the war ended, the former colonies still struggled to produce enough to meet demand. As a result, salt was quite expensive.

"The tribes have been trading salt for hundreds of years," Riley said. "They take it from the ground."

"Mines?"

"I suppose you could call them that," Riley said.

"They could make a bit of gold selling salt in Hartford or Philadelphia," Ned suggested.

"They could I'm sure," Riley agreed. "But they won't."

"Why not?"

"They won't because once the white man realizes the salt is there, they will take the land away."

Susannah devoured the plate of food quickly, then glanced around the table and realized that all the others were finishing as well. As each person finished their meal, they laid the short knife on the table beside their plate. Once everyone had laid down their knives, Emma and Tabita removed the plates and replaced them with bowls of roasted apples.

"These are delicious," Ned Foster said after the first bite.

"They're roasted in goose fat and honey," Riley said.

Despite thinking her hunger was satisfied after the venison and vegetables, Susannah ate all of her roasted apples too. When they walked away from the table, Gabriel Riley guided them into the cabin.

"Sleep well tonight, my friends," he said. "Tomorrow will be a long day."

"We can sleep on the porch," Ned suggested.

"No, you won't," Riley said. "There is a fine bed in the cabin. Emma and I will sleep in the longhouse."

Chapter 23

July 17, 1787
Hudson River, New York

Simon led the horse along a narrow trail to the edge of the Hudson River. He stepped carefully as the rocky surface of the trail turned to bare earth before turning to mud at the water's edge. Once the animal began to drink, Simon squatted next to it and scooped handfuls of the cool water into his own mouth. He splashed his face with the refreshing water and washed the dust of travel away from his eyes. Finally, he refilled his gourd canteen and hung it back in its place behind the saddle.

He had found a campsite for the night which had provided forage for the horse, but little comfort for himself. He was reluctant to make a fire and had attempted to sleep with his back propped against an elm tree. Ben Eldon wasn't the first man Simon had killed. But Eldon was the first white man he'd killed, and if anyone found out he delivered the fatal wound, he would be a dead man himself. Hugh Marlow could not protect him.

He tugged the horse's rein to signal the time had come to finish its drink and begin their journey, but the animal was reluctant to leave the soothing water. Though he had ridden horses for years, Simon had little training in their maintenance and care. Mostly, he had ridden alongside one of the white bosses in search of a stray slave or a troublesome boar.

Simon didn't have to be an expert to realize how tired the animal was, though. At the stable, it normally made short rides into the countryside or to small towns near Philadelphia. Even after resting all night, the aging gelding walked stiffly as they began the long trek back to the city.

Simon felt it too. The four-day chase was nothing new, but he feared the trek alone back to Philadelphia through country he didn't know. White man's country. It occurred to him that the safest thing he could do was to turn around and ride back north. Canada lay in that direction, and many of the slaves talked of Canada as a land where slavery didn't exist. Freedom might appeal to most slaves, but not to Simon. Hugh Marlow understood Simon's peculiar needs and provided the means to satisfy them. A man of his taste would likely end up dead in an ally if he tried to live among free men.

No, the safest place for Simon was Hallow Hill.

He rode south along the same road he and Ben Eldon had taken north the previous day in their chase of the two fugitives. At West Point he would turn southwest toward Philadelphia. He wasn't sure he could find the same route they had ridden through New Jersey, but if he continued going southwest, he would eventually come to the Delaware River.

*****

Susannah watched from the cabin's porch as Natani and another of the Indians readied Ned's mare and the mule for their journey. Not far away, two other horses and a pack mule stood ready.

She turned at the sound of the cabin door and saw Ned Foster in the same clothing the Indians were wearing, buckskin shirt, trousers, and knee-high boots. Strings of colorful beads hung over his chest.

"How do I Look?" he asked her.

"Damn good," Susannah answered.

"Well, now it's your turn," Ned said.

Ned led her into the storage room of the cabin and pointed to a stack of clothing folded on a rustic table. "These will be a lot better to travel in," Ned told her. He held up a deerskin dress for her to examine, "There's boots too."

Susannah didn't hesitate. She pulled her cotton

dress off over her head and discarded it on the floor of the cabin. She took the deerskin from Ned Foster and slipped it over her head. She smiled when she saw Ned's eyes following the hem of the garment over her breast and down her torso. The soft leather caressed her skin with luxurious comfort.

Next, he handed her a collar of darker leather and fur which she slipped over her head. "Is this right?" she asked Ned.

"I think so," he said. He smoothed the collar so it lay flat on her shoulders.

"Put this around your middle," he said, handing her a beaded two-inch wide leather strap.

She took the strap and wrapped it around her midsection before tying it in the front. There was no mirror in the cabin, but Susannah could tell the belt accentuated her shape and Ned's smile confirmed it.

"Now the boots," Ned said.

She stepped into the calf-high deerskin boots one at a time. The leather around her calves and ankles was as soft and warm as the dress, but a hard leather sole would protect her feet from the rocky ground.

"Dey just da right size," she proclaimed.

"These things belonged to Natani's wife, Tabita," Ned said. "You two looked to be about the same size."

"Tabita don't mind me wearin' em?"

"Tabita brought this stuff to me," Ned said.

"She said you needed to wear it."

Susannah extended her arms to the side and made a full turn, "I feel like a Indian princess," she said.

"You look like an Indian princess, too," Ned said.

"Be sure to call 'em Iroquois or Mohawk when you get amongst them," Gabriel Riley said as he entered the room. "They think 'Indian' is a white man's word that don't mean nothing to them."

"I'll remember that," Ned Foster said.

"Good," Riley said. "Natani is ready to leave, so you folks need to get mounted. You got a long journey ahead of you."

"Thanks for all your help, Colonel," Ned offered.

"You can call me Gabriel," Riley said. "I never was a soldier, just a spy."

*****

Although he wanted to get back to Philadelphia as soon as possible, Simon knew he must preserve his own strength and that of the horse. He let the animal walk as slow as it wanted. After an hour in the saddle, he got off and led the horse on foot for another hour before finding a shady place for them both to rest. He took an apple from his saddle bag and cut it in half. He gave one part to the horse and ate the other half along with a chunk of dried beef.

He rested with his back against an alder tree until the sun was at its midday zenith.

It was well past noon when he threw himself astride the horse again and began a slow walk toward West Point. If he knew these woods, he would have avoided the trail altogether, preferring a longer, but safer, journey back to Philadelphia. But he didn't know the woods, so the road was his only choice. So far, he had encountered no other travelers, but the trail was a busy thoroughfare between civilization and the wilderness. He was certain to meet other travelers, but he hoped to avoid soldiers from the stockade at West Point.

Simon had traveled less than a mile when the first of the travelers appeared. He saw them from a fair distance. A wagon. A man and a woman. The line of sight was unobstructed, so they had probably seen him too. He took both pistols from his saddle bag, checked them, and stuck them in his belt. As the distance between himself and the wagon closed, Simon sensed his heartbeat accelerate. At Hallow Hill, he feared no one as long as Hugh Marlow supported him. But in this wilderness, he was just an out-of-place black man with a strange explanation for his presence.

Simon slowed his mount even further. The wagon slowed. Now, they were only twenty-five yards apart. The man in the wagon pulled his long gun closer to his side. Simon brushed a hand near the pistol on his right hip. One step at a time, Simon drew closer to the wagon. Then, when they were less than ten yards apart, Simon and the wagon stopped. Simon turned his horse to the left to make sure the man saw the pistols in his belt.

"Where ya headed, mister?" the man in the wagon asked Simon. He was small and wiry. Not an old man, but a man worn down by years of labor in the fields.

"Philadelphia," Simon answered.

"We don't see your kind around here much," the man said, his hand still on the long gun.

"I be on business fo' my masta'," Simon said.

"What kind o' business?" the man asked with the same arrogance any slave owner might assume.

"I reckon it don't matter none to you what bi'niss Mr. Marlow got here," Simon said, his hand poised just above the pistol.

Simon realized his bravado was having the desired effect. The man's face flushed red. He moved his hand away from the gun. "We don't want no trouble, mister," the man said. "We'll be on our way to Albany and you can be on your way to wherever you're going."

Simon nodded to the man, then rubbed his heels against the horse's flanks. The animal lowered its backside and sprang forward in a slow trot. When he passed the wagon, Simon breathed a sigh of relief. The farmer from Albany had been easy to intimidate. The soldiers would be a different matter.

Chapter 24

July 21, 1787
Philadelphia, Pennsylvania

John Oliver loosened his collar and pushed his shirt sleeves up above his elbows, but these adjustments had little impact on the withering heat in the room. Madison and Washington had insisted the windows of the convention hall be nailed shut to prevent eavesdroppers from overhearing the deliberations. But that was May, when a fine spring day might draw an occasional trickle of sweat. In mid-July, strong men withered in their chairs as oppressive heat bore down on them.

In fairness to the two Virginians, no one expected the gathering to continue deep into the summer. Oliver supposed his own expectations were lower than most. He believed the divide between those who favored slavery and those who opposed it would cause even the most determined to give up within a few weeks. Success would only be possible if both sides agreed to compromises they once thought unconscionable.

But the delegates had continued to trudge forward through June and now more than halfway through July. And, they had compromised. In Oliver's view, the compromises largely favored the slave states. Even his own delegation from Connecticut had agreed to things he could not abide. The thought of it anguished John Oliver, but it didn't surprise him.

At some point — perhaps in mid-June — he had felt the momentum shift. One-by-one, delegates from the Northern states began to soften their rhetoric. They feared the South would align with Spain, or even Britain. France would dominate the Western territories and parts of the Northeast. The only path to security lay with forming a strong unified nation. The cancer of slavery would continue to rot away the new nation's innards, but outwardly, it would be strong. That was their hope anyway. *No, the problem won't go away,* they reasoned, *"but we'll figure it out before there's trouble."*

Only a few days earlier — on July 12th — the convention accepted the three-fifths compromise. Oliver was so dejected that he considered packing his things and going back to Hartford immediately.

Then, everything changed. Ned Foster ran away

with Hugh Marlow's slave girl, Susannah. He and Sara Sullivan had ridden much of the night to warn Ned and Susannah that Marlow had secured an experienced slave hunter to come after them. Finally, he and Sara fell into bed together.

He'd slept in her bed every night since then, too, often languishing there until the sun was well into the sky. They made love often and with a passion he had never known with Becky. Suddenly, Philadelphia was the only place he wanted to be. He was physically present in the convention hall each day, but his mind was with Sara Sullivan in the house on Third Street.

He worried for his friend's safety. But Ned Foster was smart and resourceful. Eight days had passed since Simon and Ben Eldon left Philadelphia to hunt down Ned and Susannah. As each day passed without the return of the hunters dragging their prize back to the city, Oliver's confidence of their escape grew. More than likely, they were now under the care and protection of Gabriel Riley.

A large grandfather clock stood against the wall to General Washington's right. Oliver studied it for a moment, wondering how much longer the afternoon session would last. The momentous decisions of July 12th virtually assured the conclave would produce a proposed constitution to replace the failing Articles of Confederation. Now, the delegates faced sorting out details of items they had deferred in earlier deliberations. While these were important decisions, none of the participants were likely to fall on their sword for or against anything at this point.

After an extended debate, the delegates reversed an earlier decision that provided for the legislature to select the executive. Now, they feared this arrangement would make the executive too deferential to legislators in order to secure his reappointment. Still, they feared the alternative of having an executive selected by the people at large.

"The extent of the country renders it impossible that the people can have the requisite capacity to judge the respective pretensions of the candidates," Colonel Mason of Virginia insisted.

A short time later, Gouverneur Morris took the floor and spoke passionately in favor of direct election by the people. "A great objective of the executive is to control the legislature," he said, "for they will seek to aggrandize and perpetuate themselves."

Morris continued with this line of thought. "It is necessary then that the executive magistrate should be the guardian of the people, even of the lower classes, against legislative tyranny, against the great and the wealthy who, in the course of things, will necessarily compose the legislative body," he said. "Wealth tends to corrupt the mind and to nourish its love of power and to stimulate it to oppression."

"There is grave danger in too much democracy," Hugh Marlow exclaimed from his seat among a group of southerners. It was no surprise that the Southern states opposed direct election since the much larger populations in the Northern states meant northerners would likely prevail in such contests.

"Too much democracy seems an unlikely outcome," John Oliver argued back to Marlow. "This gathering has already decreed the limitation of voting to owners of property. As is, only a fraction of citizens may vote. Women, slaves, Indians, farm tenets, and ordinary merchants are denied. Hardly democracy."

"It seems that Mr. Oliver would have the rabble of the streets decide the fate of the nation," Marlow sneered.

"The rabble, as you call them, will be the first you would send into battle should the English return to reclaim their colonies; or if the Spanish should decide to claim our Western territories," Oliver countered.

"Thus, their purpose will have been served," Marlow responded. He turned away from Oliver, as if signaling an end to their row.

But Oliver wasn't ready to concede the argument. "We have recently thrown off the trappings of English aristocracy," he said. "Yet, you would create a new aristocracy on this continent."

Marlow turned again to face Oliver. "The greatness of nations results from the qualities of their aristocracies," he said. "It matters not that no titles are handed out, this must be a nation guided by its aristocratic elite."

Oliver's eyes scanned the room, hoping to see heads shaking in disagreement with Marlow. Instead, he saw a dozen or more nodding their approval of Marlow's declaration. Why should it surprise him? He knew quite a few of the men here already fancied themselves the landed gentry of the new nation. For some, the revolution was as much about putting themselves in the place of English nobles as it was about freedom from tyranny. Many already viewed themselves as members of the future Senate of the United States, where landed elites would control the vulgar impulses of the elected House of Representatives.

The noble words of the Declaration of Independence spurred many thousands of farmers, merchants, and tradesmen to join the continental army to fight for their "freedom". But without suffrage, their lives would change little under the proposal now before the convention. They must count on the good graces of the gentry to assure justice.

Mr. Shays rebellion had shown Oliver that the people's patience with the ruling class was not infinite. A day would come when they would demand justice or take to the streets. Yet the Federalists, who now seemed to dominate the convention, saw only danger in the faces of the people, and the need for stronger, more forceful response to protests.

But, while they were bent on avoiding the pitfalls of too much democracy, many of the delegates now realized that their initial solution to the question of selecting the executive was also folly. A few days earlier, they had voted to have the executive selected by the national legislature, as it was outlined in the Virginia Plan. But having considered that notion for some time, they now felt the idea opened the door to political intrigue as well as breaking down the separation of powers they had strived for in other parts of the plan.

Then Mr. Wilson of Pennsylvania offered a middle-ground solution. Under his notion, a college of electors would choose the executive. Each state's legislature would choose the states electors. The response to this idea was quick and positive, and after a short debate, the convention approved the idea, with the details to be sorted out by the Committee of Detail.

John Oliver made a note to himself to insist on certain details in the committee deliberations. First, allow the states to choose between having electors selected by the legislature, or by direct election. Second — and most critical — how many electors would each state have?

*****

Even the mid-afternoon sun was a relief from the stifling heat of the sealed meeting hall. When his eyes adjusted to the brightness, Oliver noticed Sara Sullivan on the other side of Chestnut Street walking toward Fifth. He hurried across the street and caught up to her just before she reached the corner.

"Are you on your way home?" he asked when she realized he was beside her.

"Yes," Sara said.

"I'll walk with you," Oliver said. "We have finished for the day."

"Good," Sara said. "I wanted to talk to you as soon as you got to Sullivan House."

"Oh?"

"Yes," she said. "I encountered Mrs. Bache at the cheese shop just now."

"Mrs. Bache?" The name was familiar, but he couldn't place it at that moment.

"Mr. Franklin's daughter," Sara informed him. "She arranged your stay at Sullivan House."

"I should send her a bouquet of flowers in thanks," Oliver said.

Sara smiled briefly, then she was serious again. "She said Mr. Marlow has filed a complaint with her father, as governor of Pennsylvania, claiming that you and I incited Ned Foster to steal Susannah."

"Technically, he is the President of the Commonwealth Council," Oliver pointed out, "but, that is much the same as governor."

"Whatever he's called, it's a serious accusation."

"Yes, it is," Oliver conceded. "Did Mrs. Bache say how her father reacted to Marlow's complaint?"

"He promised Marlow he would look into it," Sara said.

"I wonder what that means?"

"I asked Mrs. Bache the same question," Sara said.

"And?"

"She told me her father will put off Marlow as long as he can."

"I suspect Ned and Susannah may have made it to safety by now," Oliver told her.

"I hope so," Sara said.

"If Simon and Ben Eldon come back without Susannah, Marlow will put more pressure on Franklin."

"What should we do?" Sara asked.

"Nothing yet," Oliver said. "I think Mr. Franklin will protect us at least until the convention finishes its work."

"What then?"

"Keep a travel bag ready."

Chapter 25

July 21, 1787
Lake Champlain, New York

Susannah sat as high in the saddle as possible, trying to see over the scrub brush near the trail. Occasionally, she saw glimpses of bluish water through gaps in the foliage, but she had yet to see the giant lake Natani had promised the evening before.

The ride from Kingston had been long, just as Gabriel Riley had assured them, but was not as difficult as Susannah imagined. For one thing, the terrain was mostly flat from near Kingston to north of Fort Saratoga, followed by several miles of low, lush hills. The other thing was that Natani knew the way. Each time the trail forked, Natani didn't hesitate, but followed a path that would get them to their destination safely without encountering white settlements such as Albany or Fort Saratoga.

Each night, Natani led them to ideal camp sites with lush forage for the horses. Susannah helped Tabita prepare and serve a tasty mix of corn, beans, okra and peppers, along with fish, rabbit, squirrel, or venison taken by the hunters. They drank a mildly fermented wine made from native plum trees.

After supper, she would lie with Ned on a down-filled blanket Tabita gave them. Unlike Philadelphia, the air cooled quickly after sunset. Susannah would pull Ned's blanket around her shoulders and slide her hand under his deerskin shirt, then lay her head on his chest and absorb his warmth.

Since that first time by the creek near West Point, they had had sex only once, in Gabriel Riley's cabin the night before beginning the journey north. She ached to have him inside her again, but Natani had insisted the camp area be small and easily defended if necessary. The five nations of the Iroquois Confederation were generally peaceful with one another, but occasional squabbles emerged over hunting territory. The journey had been uneventful, though, except for a mother bear with two cubs passing near the camp on the third night out. Later today, they would reach Odonida's village where she hoped the sleeping arrangements would be more conducive.

She wondered how life would be in the Mohawk

village, but the unknown didn't bother her. For most of her life, Susannah hadn't dared dream of freedom. Tabita, who spoke English almost as well as Natani, told her stories of Indian life: of children's games in the forests, and of swimming naked in the great lake. At Hallow Hill, children played their games under the watchful eye of white masters and Hugh Marlow strictly forbade swimming in the snake and alligator infested ponds. After all, a healthy slave child was valuable property.

Ned Foster interrupted her thoughts. "Look over there," he said, pointing ahead to the right.

Her eyes followed the direction of his arm where a break in the thick line of trees provided a view of the lake. There it was. The big lake Natani had described. "Da water so blue," Susannah said.

"The French called it Lake Champlain," Ned said. "I don't know what the Indians — I mean the Mohawk — call it."

As they proceeded nearer the lake's edge, the full expanse of the blue water opened up to Susannah. Lake Champlain wasn't wide — a dim outline of the far shore was visible from where they stood — but it was long, stretching beyond her field of vision in both directions.

Natani halted the procession so everyone could take in the vista. The Mohawk all dismounted and walked to a high mound overlooking the lake. Ned and Susannah soon did the same.

"What a beautiful site," Ned said when he was beside Natani.

"Yes," Natani agreed. "The waters of the lake have quenched our thirst for a thousand years."

Ned slowly scanned the surrounding landscape. "This land, this lake, it's too perfect," he said to Natani. "Eventually, the white man will want it for himself."

"During the war, white men passed through these lands — both English and American," Natani said. "There eyes were full of greed for our land, but they were busy killing one another then. They were few at that time, and we were many, but I fear they will return one day."

"They will return," Ned Foster said. "And when they do, they'll be in great numbers."

"Some who claim to speak for the Iroquois nations signed a paper that gave this land to the Americans," Natani said. "They agreed to move across the river into Quebec."

"I guess Odonida didn't agree to that," Ned conjectured.

"He did not."

An hour after they had stopped to admire the lake, Natani's party topped a small ridge to find Odonida's village spread before them. It was larger than Susannah had expected, and the structures differed greatly from the little longhouse behind Gabriel Riley's house near Kingston. There, the building looked more like a small log cabin, except the logs were arranged upright instead of lengthwise. The buildings in this camp were huge by comparison. One, she guessed, was about the size of the stable at Hallow Hill. And they weren't constructed of logs either, except for the framework. A solid material filled the spaces between the log frame timbers. Each of the longhouses had an arched roof with several square holes along its peak. A small portico overhung an animal hide doorway at the end of each longhouse.

At the edge of the village, Natani halted the party and waited as two tribesmen walked toward them from the camp. They were young, probably younger than Susannah, and might have been twins as they were strikingly similar in appearance. They wore buckskin trousers and were naked from the waist up, except for several strands of colorful beads over their chests. Their skin, probably darkened by the summer sun, glowed bronze, and was accentuated by long black hair cinched by each ear with colored ribbon. They were as tall as Ned Foster — who was taller than most men she'd known — but with broader shoulders.

When the two men stopped a few feet from the travelers, Tabita dismounted from her horse and approached the twins, who spoke to her with animated gestures.

"What's happening," she heard Ned ask Natani.

"They bid welcome to their cousin Tabita," Natani informed Ned and Susannah. "They inquire if we are tired and hungry."

"Well, I am tired and hungry," Ned said.

"Yes," Natani said. "But it wouldn't matter if we were not hungry. We would say we are."

"Why?"

"It is the manner of greeting guests," Natani said. "A kindness is offered and excepted."

"So, those two are Tabita's cousins?" Ned asked.

"Everyone in the village calls each other cousin," Natani said. "But, in this case, Tabita and Odonida's sons really are cousins."

"Those boys are the chief's sons?"

"Yes, and Tabita is his niece. Their grandmother's sister is the leader of the clan."

"A woman leader?"

"It is the way of the Mohawk and the other Iroquois tribes," Natani said. "The female elders are the clan leaders and make most major decisions for the tribe."

"What about the chief?" Ned asked.

"The chief is the leader of warriors and hunters. He decides where to hunt and how much game to take, and he chooses tactics in battle."

After a short conversation with the two young Mohawk, Tabita motioned Natani to follow and turned to walk with her cousins into the village. Natani and the rest of the party dismounted and followed a short distance behind them, leading the horses.

"I thought there'd be mo people 'round," Susannah said to Ned as they reached the center of the village.

"The men are out hunting," Natani said, having overheard Susannah's observations, "and the women are working their gardens."

"Oh," Susannah said.

"Odonida will send out messengers to announce our arrival," Natani told them. "In a few hours, everyone will be here ready for a feast."

Three young boys approached the group and spoke to Natani. "The boys will take the horses to a paddock," he told Ned.

They handed their reins to the boys, then Ned and Susannah followed Natani and Tabita into the largest of the longhouses. Susannah expected the space inside the building would be large and open, but instead, the interior consisted of a long hallway with walls of small timbers, cloth and hides on each side. As they moved down the hallway, she realized the large space was divided into smaller rooms on each side of a central hallway. Each compartment featured a doorway covered with animal skins that opened onto a firepit in the center of the hall. The scent of long-burning fires and constant cooking permeated the air, yet Susannah didn't find the smell unpleasant.

When they reached the last of the doorways, Tabita turned to them. "This will be your room," she said, pointing to the hide covered passages on the right side of the hallway.

"Whose house is dis?" Susannah asked.

"This is our clan house," Tabita said. "We have extra room now. Natani and I are in the next room."

"It will be some hours until the feast is ready," Natani said, "but we can eat from the pot now to keep the hunger away until then."

"The pot?" Ned asked.

"Yes, the Mohawk don't have regular mealtimes," Natani said. "They eat when they're hungry, so every house keeps a pot of stew warm all the time. When someone takes some of it, we add more."

*****

Simon squatted behind a broad Alder tree and watched as the ferry crossed the river toward the Pennsylvania side. His knees ached from the awkward position he had held for more than an hour as he'd watched the ferry crisscross the river twice before. He had hoped to see the ferry ready to leave the New Jersey dock with no passengers already aboard. Then he would rush down to the pier and force the ferryman to take him across with his horse. But each time, other passengers had appeared before he could make his move.

The sun was already disappearing behind the tall trees on the far shore, which might mean the ferry service was finished for the day. Typically, the ferryman waited about half an hour on each bank before crossing to the other side. By then, it would be too dark to begin another crossing.

Ten minutes later, the ferryman tied the vessel up to the dock on the far side of the river and began securing it for the night. The passengers clamored off toward their destinations in Pennsylvania. There would not be another opportunity for Simon to commandeer the ferry on this evening.

Tomorrow might present a better opportunity, but it might not. He could be bold and ride up to the pier to wait the same as white folks did. The ferryman might not remember him from his last visit when Ben Eldon had discovered that the fugitives had not crossed here. He might realize Simon's white traveling companion was no longer with him. If the ferryman was alone, Simon's physical presence would be intimidation enough to fend off awkward questions, but he had no wish to face more than one man.

He stood up to search for a suitable campsite for the night when he noticed a small rowboat moving slowly toward the little town of Trenton a quarter of a mile up the river from the ferry landing. A lone man tugged at the oars, struggling against the current to keep the small craft pointed toward the eastern shore.

A new idea started forming in Simon's mind. If he could get the horse across the river in the morning, the ride to Philadelphia would take about four hours. But after watching the ferry for nearly two hours, he doubted such a crossing would be possible. On the other hand, he could leave the horse and cross the river in a small boat like the one nearing the eastern shore. Then he would have a ten to twelve hour walk to the city. Now he saw a third choice.

His mind raced through several scenarios while the man in the little boat finally disappeared behind a short wharf at the river's edge. The appearance of the Indians easily explained Ben Eldon's death. But if he abandoned the horse, it would be the same as horse theft, and if he stole a boat, that would be serious too. He imagined that either offense might lead to his hanging. But, once he was in Philadelphia, he would have Hugh Marlow's protection.

Simon walked the horse a short way closer to the town where he found a secluded place with enough forage for the animal. From this vantage point, he had a clear view of most of the town. He ate half an apple along with some dried turkey, gave the other half of the apple to the horse, and settled back against a tree to sort out his plan.

*****

Simon guessed it must be near midnight. He'd watched for hours as the lanterns and candles of the little town gradually went dark. Near the town pier, a single tavern was still illuminated, but few customers entered or left the establishment. If he waited another hour, perhaps the tavern would close, but it might mean arriving in Philadelphia after sunrise. Besides, his legs ached from squatting behind the bushes of his hideout.

He stood and stretched his legs. "You be quiet now," he said to the horse as he began leading it into the town.

Strangely, his fear subsided upon entering Trenton. A musket ball might strike him down in the next second, but Simon knew his best chance of surviving lay in reaching Philadelphia as soon as possible and as secretly as possible. Besides, a musket ball might not be the worst thing. *I done some real evil things in my life*, Simon thought. *And if I live through this night, I'll do more of those things.*

His confidence grew each time he passed one of the clapboard houses seeing no sign of life. Then, at the fifth house along the right side of the street, a man lay on the front stoop, his booted feet pointing toward the ceiling. Simon halted the horse and eyed the porch, one hand on his pistol. But the man still didn't move. Finally, Simon decided the man could not get into the house, probably because of an angry wife, and had passed out on the stoop from too much rum.

The horse let out a loud snort when Simon tugged the rein to start it moving again. He stopped and again looked at the man on the stoop. Still nothing. The drunk was sleeping soundly.

They passed a few more houses without incident

before Simon saw his first objective, a livery stable. It was a large barn with a hayloft on the upper level. The main door was closed, but it was so misaligned that large spaces were open around its top and below the latch. No light emitted from inside the barn. In front of the stable, a single hitching post stood empty.

Simon led the animal to the hitching post and tied the rein around it. Once again, he examined the metal plate on the back of the saddle. Although he didn't read, he was certain the plate would inform the stable man as to the ownership of the saddle. And since the emblem on the saddle matched the brand on the animal's rump, he would assume the horse and saddle belonged to the same owner, a livery operator in Philadelphia.

Satisfied that he had done everything possible to avoid being accused of stealing the horse, Simon removed the saddle bags and walked in the direction of the pier where the little rowboat had landed.

Chapter 26

July 22, 1787
Philadelphia, Pennsylvania

John Oliver listened to Sara Sullivan's soft breath. The steady rhythm of it told him she was still sleeping, and he would not wake her. He often wished he slept that soundly, but it would never be. Even as a child, he frequently woke long before daylight, even after reading by candlelight well into the night. As he grew older, books on history and the law replaced the novels he read as a boy. Courtship, marriage, a young child, and a burgeoning law practice became priorities ahead of rest and recuperation.

The fact that Becky's father never approved of him added to his stress. His own father owned a sizable tobacco farm near Hartford, but in the

English nobleman's eyes, a man who worked his own land was the equivalent of a tenant, regardless of his wealth. In retrospect, he often wondered if the war had only been a convenient excuse for Lord Black to spirit Becky and Caleb away from him and back to England.

Before Becky left, Oliver had kept his distance from those who advocated for the rebellion, even close friends. He didn't consider himself a loyalist, but he was no revolutionary either. Then, within the space of a few days, his wife and child were gone, and the British falsely accused his best friend of spying. The crash of the trapdoor in the gallows floor still vibrated through his head as John Oliver left New York to find his father's friend, Benjamin Stevenson, whom he knew to be a senior officer in George Washington's army.

He knew nothing of soldiering, but his years of managing labor crews in the tobacco fields had taught him the art of leading men. Stevenson saw potential in the young lawyer and sent him to train in Massachusetts. Later, he was assigned to General Schuyler's forces near Albany, New York.

In the beginning, the Continental Army was a ragtag bunch of merchants and farmers, most with no fighting experience except for an occasional tavern brawl. Even so, there were early successes in upstate New York, most under the leadership of General Benedict Arnold and Schuyler. Oliver himself deserved some credit as well for helping to keep the Iroquois mostly neutral.

After those initial successes, the British resolved to bring the fight to the colonists, resulting in huge losses for the Americans at Long Island, Fort Washington, and Philadelphia. But despite their superior arsenal and career military leadership, the British often failed to capitalize on their victories and allowed the beleaguered colonials to escape.

Then, on Christmas Day 1776, Washington sneaked his ragtag army across the Delaware and routed a Hessian garrison at Trenton, taking nearly a thousand prisoners. When the British counterattacked, Washington held firm. A few months later, the Americans in upstate New York soundly defeated a British invasion force from Quebec, taking over six thousand prisoners.

The series of victories proved to the French and Spanish that joining the fight on the side of the Americans would likely be a worthwhile venture. Now, the English faced a worldwide conflict against naval and ground forces comparable to their own. Although it would be many months before the French could fully deploy their forces on the continent — and the British took some advantage of that time — the overall course of the war had changed to favor the rebels.

A light breeze stirred the curtains by the bedroom window as early morning light began to stream across the room. A storm during the night had cooled things a little, but Oliver expected another warm day.

The bed shook with the motion of Sara rolling

onto her stomach and sidling next to Oliver. She was breathing deeper now, almost awake. He rolled onto his side and let his hand trace slowly up her thigh until it rested on her bare bottom. Her skin was smooth and warm to his touch.

He needed her, and that need was growing by the second. Yet, he didn't want to rush. He wanted to savor the smoothness of her skin beneath his hands, the smell of her hair beneath his face. These were the moments he had come to treasure each morning.

He moved his hand slowly up her back where he brushed away the curly locks of red hair. He kissed her bare shoulder, then the back of her neck.

Sara raised her head from the pillow. "You're up early this morning," she said.

"Too early?"

"Nope," Sara said. She rolled to her side facing him and slid as close as possible. She pushed a thigh between his legs and nestled it into his crotch. His hand slid down her back and pulled her even closer, his erection growing stronger by the second.

After a lingering kiss, Sara rolled him onto his back. Oliver let out a long breath as she began to kiss his chest, teasing his nipples with her tongue. As her kiss drifted down his torso, her tousled red locks tickled his belly while her lips explored his naval. John Oliver gasped when her lips closed around his erection.

He groaned as the sensation took hold of him.

He'd heard other men talk about such things but had never experienced it himself. Oliver felt his juices rise within him and wondered as to the etiquette expected.

But Sara must have sensed he was losing what little control he had. She pulled away, turned and sat astraddle his thighs. With both hands, she lightly gripped his member and began to stroke slowly up and down. Seconds later, his body shuddered, and he sensed a warm wetness on his abdomen.

He felt powerless even to move as Sara looked down on him with a wide smile. She rolled off the bed and walked to the washstand where she took a cloth and dipped it into the basin. She washed her hands, then returned to the bed to rinse his belly and private parts. The cold water brought him out of his stupor.

"That wasn't what I expected," he said.

"You didn't like it?" she asked as she sat on the edge of the bed.

"Oh, I liked it a lot," Oliver said.

"Good," she said. "It may be the way for the next few days."

"Why?" Oliver asked.

"My 'monthly' is due," Sara told him. "It hasn't started yet, but I thought it might."

"Monthly?"

"The woman's curse," she informed him.

"Oh, sure," he said. "I hadn't thought about that

for years."

"It would be nice not to think about, but I must," Sara said.

Oliver sat up on the edge of the bed and glanced at the clock on the bedside table. Not quite eight o'clock. Over the past few days, they had often lingered in bed until after eight-thirty, but the early morning activity had filled him with energy.

Even though it was Sunday, he expected a busy day of meetings with Luther Moore, Stephen McGrew, and probably a few others. They were certain the convention would start work on the details of the document in the next few days and realized there could never be enough preparation for the arguments that lay ahead.

*****

Simon awakened to a bright morning sun in his eyes. He didn't know how long he'd slept, but he was still exhausted as he lay on the bank of the Delaware River just south of Philadelphia's main port. He'd pulled the little rowboat far enough up the bank he was relatively sure it wouldn't slide back into the river and drift away. Not that he intended to use the boat ever again, but he hoped Mr. Marlow could return it to its owner to keep Simon from the hangman's noose.

Besides planning to return the vessel, Simon had tied a small bag containing two Spanish dollars to a post on the pier next to where the little boat had been secured. While Simon knew little about commerce, he was confident that the two pieces-of-eight constituted a sufficient rental payment for the little craft.

That was the beginning of a night of terror. Simon was accustomed to facing down danger with his intimidating physical presence and his seeming lack of fear. But the wide, fast-moving river didn't care about that. No sooner had he maneuvered the little craft away from the pier when the river reminded him that he didn't know how to swim or how to guide the boat where he intended it to go.

At first, he tried sitting in the center and facing forward to work the oars, but each time he moved, the craft tilted so that water nearly came over the side. He realized he should turn his back to the front in order to gain more leverage on the oars but the idea of going down the river backwards was too terrifying. Finally, he decided that the current alone was enough to carry him to Philadelphia. He would use the oars only to steer.

When the stronger current further from shore grabbed the vessel and propelled it faster down the river, Simon panicked and tried to steer it nearer to shore. But downed limbs and floating debris made the going slow nearer the bank, so he steeled himself and steered back into the main current.

A quarter-moon provided only dim light, but it reflected off the little wavelets at the center of the channel providing Simon a bit of guidance. But sometime well after midnight, clouds rolled across the sky and the comforting light vanished. Then light rain began to fall. The warm night air suddenly turned much cooler.

Thunder — distant at first — drew his attention to the southwestern sky where he saw the first bolt of lightning. Storms rarely scared Simon. Then again, he'd never been on a river in a boat he barely knew how to control during a storm.

Within half an hour, the storm was right over him. Simon looked to the bank on each side and wondered which one he should steer toward. He tried to guide the craft toward the Pennsylvania side, but the current had strengthened, and he made little progress. *If I lives through dis night, I gon kill dat Ned Foster*, Simon thought.

The rain pelted him hard now. Within minutes, he saw that it was accumulating in the bottom of the rowboat. Simon tried to scoop the water out with his hands but each time he released the oar, the craft drifted back toward the center of the river. He quickly realized he couldn't bail water fast enough to keep up with the accumulating rainfall. He must reach the shore, or he would surely drown.

Instinctively, Simon knew he must turn his back to the bow to get enough leverage on the oars to drive the vessel out of the main current. As he began to lift himself off the seat, the boat rocked — first to the right, then to the left. A small amount of water came over the left gunwale. He froze. Finally, the motion subsided.

The wind diminished a bit and the hard rain

suddenly slowed to a drizzle. Simon moved again, this time more slowly. Eventually, he would have to release his hold on the gunwale and trust his own balance. He closed his eyes and envisioned the movements he was about to make. Finally, he released his grip on the sidewall and stood. He steeled himself again, lifted his right leg and slowly placed it behind the bench. He sat on the bench with one leg in front of it and the other behind. Now, as he faced the western shore of the river, he realized he was drifting past the darkened shapes of the city of Philadelphia.

With renewed urgency, he leaned backward and brought his left leg over the bench. The boat rocked again but now he hardly gave it a thought. He slipped an oar into the metal hooks on each gunwale and began to row in the way he'd seen its owner do it.

With the first stroke of the oars, Simon realized he now had power over the vessel. Enough power, at least, to guide it out of the main current and to the western shore. He would wind up south of his intended destination, but he would get there soon. The main thing was, he would not drown.

Faint light was turning the eastern sky light gray when he finally jumped out of the rowboat and pulled its bow onto the muddy riverbank. As he tugged the vessel further up the beach, the last vestiges of the adrenalin rush that had powered him to the shore slipped away. He found a relatively dry spot a few feet away where he leaned against a small tree and fell asleep.

He shook himself awake and stood to stretch. After relieving himself in the muddy river, he began to access his situation. He recognized the Philadelphia docks from his position and guessed them to be at least a half-mile upriver. The current close to shore was lighter than mid-river. Now that he had learned to row properly, he figured he could make it to the nearest pier in less than an hour. But then there would be a lot of explaining to do until someone fetched Hugh Marlow to confirm his story. On the other hand, he could walk to the city in half the time.

A distant voice interrupted his thoughts. *Da lord be waitin' for me…*, the voice sang. Simon crouched behind the bush and watched the path above the riverbank. *When my time do come…*, the voice sang, much closer now.

Then the source of the song appeared on the path only a few yards from where Simon crouched; a black man carrying a cane pole and a wooden pail. He was small and looked old, probably well beyond midlife; his thin body naked from the waist up, with ragged pants and bare feet below.

Simon waited until the man was almost alongside the bush before he emerged to stop him. The old man was startled and dropped the pail. "I ain' got nothin' mista," the frightened man said.

"What you doin' here?" Simon asked.

"I come to catch a fish, so we got sumpin' to

eat," the man said. "Is you a runaway?"

"I ain't no runaway," Simon assured him.

"We's freedmen here," the man said. "Don' wan' no trouble."

"I ain't gonna cause ya no trouble," Simon told him. "I be a slave and I been on bi'nes for my masta' Mr. Hugh Marlow. Now, I needs to get into Phil'delphia to see Mr. Marlow."

"We's freedmen here," the frightened man repeated.

"See dat boat there?" Simon pointed to the rowboat. "I wan' you to take dat boat up to dem docks yonder," he added with a finger indicating the city piers.

"I gotta catch some fish," the man said. "I don' catch no fish, we ain' got nutin' ta eat."

Simon stuck a hand into one of the leather bags on the ground beside him and came out with two of the silver Spanish dollars. "Dis'll buy ya all da fish ya need," he said.

The man stared at the coins for several seconds. "Folks'll be askin' where I get that money," he finally said. "Dey be thinkin' I stole it somewhere."

"You tell'em Mr. Hugh Marlow give ya dat money to deliver the boat."

The man stared at the coins again, then slowly reached out to take them.

Chapter 27

July 26, 1787
Philadelphia, Pennsylvania

Colonel Mason's face flushed with exasperation, "The charter to be brought forth from this conclave must certainly be approved by the people of the various states," he insisted.

The question of how the new constitution might be put to the states for ratification had been raised several times since they began work in May and had been the primary point of discussion for the past four days. Now, the delegates considered the two proposals before them. Under one proposal, each state would convene a convention of citizens to consider ratification. Under the other idea, the legislatures of each state would decide the question of ratification.

Many — like Colonel Mason — believed that only a referral to the people would give the new system broad acceptability and relieve the public's fear of a new aristocracy. Others believed the public too ill-informed to judge properly the question put before them.

"The people will bring too many of their own notions to the gatherings," Elbridge Gerry of Massachusetts suggested. "Great confusion would be the result as they will never agree on anything."

Edmund Randolph, the young Virginia governor countered, "Whose opposition will be most likely to be excited against the system?" he questioned. Then he suggested his own answer, "The local demagogues who will be degraded by it from the importance they now hold."

Oliver Ellsworth disagreed. "A new set of ideas seems to have crept in since the Articles of Confederation were established. Conventions of the people, or with power derived expressly from the people, were not then thought of. The legislatures were considered as competent."

Randolph had proven to be a surprising ally through the course of the convention. While he hadn't spoken a great deal, when he had he was usually in tune with Oliver and the rest of the more progressive delegates. In fact, it was the young governor who pushed hardest for a limitation on the importation of slaves, making it unnecessary to seek Hamilton's help. Randolph also believed — as did Oliver — that the Senate had too much power in the proposed organization. He feared collusion between the president and the Senate would frustrate the checks and balances they sought.

Through the course of the deliberations, Oliver had learned a little of the man's history and was impressed. The son of a successful lawyer from Williamsburg, he graduated from the College of William and Mary and began studying law with his father and uncle. But in the tumultuous year of 1775, his father, a British loyalist, abandoned the colony for England, and Edmund — against his father's wishes — joined the fledgling Colonial Army.

The discussion of the means of ratification continued for some time. Elbridge Gerry suggested the first step should be approval by the Confederation Congress, reminding the gathering that the last section of the Articles of Confederation required approval by the congress which was tantamount to unanimous approval of the states.

Finally, late in the afternoon, General Washington brought the matter to a vote. First, the president asked the delegates, voting by state, to decide on Ellsworth's motion that ratification be referred to the state legislatures. Ellsworth was a strong advocate of that approach and led the Connecticut delegation to vote in favor of it despite John Oliver's objections. But in the end, the measure failed by a count of seven states opposed to three in favor.

The convention approved the second proposal

quickly. It called for submission to the Confederation Congress followed by submission to statewide conventions of delegates chosen by the people in each state. Of the ten states voting, only Delaware gave a nay vote. While he was relieved the delegates had chosen that method, Oliver realized that there were still many open questions as to what the document they would present to the states for ratification would contain. Still, small victories were better than no victories.

After a short conference among Washington, Madison, and Franklin which Oliver couldn't hear, Washington signaled for quiet in the room. He announced that the convention would adjourn for ten days to allow a committee of detail to construct a draft document to reflect the proceedings to date.

After some deliberation, the delegates selected the men to make up the Committee of Detail and Oliver was generally pleased with the choices, especially Edmund Randolph. In addition to Randolph, John Rutledge of South Carolina would chair the committee. The rest of the five-person committee consisted of Oliver Ellsworth of Connecticut, Nathaniel Gorham of Massachusetts, and James Wilson of Pennsylvania.

As the assembly quietened and awaited Washington's declaration of adjournment, General Pinckney of South Carolina stood. He reminded the delegates — particularly those on the Committee of Detail — if the committee should fail to insert some security to the Southern states against an emancipation of slaves and taxes on exports, he should be bound by duty to his state to vote against their report.

Without comment on Pinckney's statement, General Washington adjourned the convention and set the date of the next meeting to be Tuesday, August 7. In seconds, the delegates were mostly on their feet; some talking in small groups; others looking to escape the heat of the room.

Oliver sat back in his chair. For two months, he had witnessed every important decision of the convention. But most of those decisions had been intentionally vague, leaving many details to be worked out as the final document emerged. Ten days would pass before he saw the committee's interpretation of those vague details. That would be the beginning of negotiations in earnest.

On the one hand, he regretted not being involved in the committee's work. On the other hand, he would spend ten uninterrupted days with Sara Sullivan. He smiled as an image of her red curls laying against the soft white skin of her breast passed through his mind.

As he stood to make a hasty walk to Sullivan House, Oliver came face-to-face with Hugh Marlow. The two had not spoken since the night Marlow moved out of Sullivan House, but Oliver had sensed a new malevolence in Marlow's glare over the last few days.

Marlow's angry glare was now just inches away from Oliver's face. "I have instructed my solicitor to draw up a claim against you, Mr. Oliver," Marlow said.

"A claim for what?"

"A claim for ten thousand Spanish dollars as compensation for the loss of my slave girl, Susannah."

"I suppose that means your henchman, and the paid hunter were unsuccessful in their attempt to recover the girl," Oliver observed. "I am delighted to learn of that eventuality, but I assure you, I am not responsible for your loss."

"Simon and Ben Eldon were ambushed by Indians," Marlow said. "They killed Mr. Eldon."

John Oliver couldn't repress a smile at learning that his friend and the girl had apparently made it to safety. "That's certainly unfortunate," he offered, "but as I have already said, I am not responsible for your loss."

"We shall see what the magistrate has to say," Marlow said. He turned to walk away but stopped and faced Oliver again. "I understand your relationship with Mrs. Sullivan has blossomed," he said.

"It's none of your business," Oliver replied.

"Perhaps not," Marlow said. "On the other hand, she is a woman with a mysterious past. Perhaps she is a spy. Or a thief. Or a murderess."

"She is none of those things," Oliver insisted.

"Perhaps not," Marlow said again. "However, I

have instructed my associates in Britain to conduct a thorough investigation of the lady."

"Your investigation will find nothing," Oliver said, hoping his voice was steady.

"We shall see," Marlow said, as he turned and walked toward the door.

*****

Lake Champlain, New York

Odonida sat on a short wooden stool and smiled as Tabita led Ned Foster and Susannah to stools facing him. Next to the chief, a woman sat on a larger stool, her wrinkled hands folded in her lap. Her hair was gray, but still thick and shiny in the braids that hung to her chest on each side of a deeply tanned and wrinkled face. She was slim, with thin legs extending from beneath a buckskin skirt, and slender arms exposed by a sleeveless white cloth blouse. Her dark eyes followed every step as the two newcomers entered the room and sat on the two stools across from her and Odonida.

The four of them sat in a small clearing next to a little creek that fed into the lake. Susannah had seen the woman at the feast the night they arrived in the camp, but they did not speak to her.

"Happy morning to you, Ned Foster," Odonida said, "and to you Susannah."

"Thank you for welcoming us to your village,"

Ned replied.

"Osieta is the most revered and respected elder of our village," Odonida said with a nod toward the woman next to him. "She is also my mother," he added.

"Greetings Osieta," Ned said to the woman. Susannah only nodded in her direction.

"Osieta does not speak English," Odonida said, "but she asked me to express her welcome to the village."

"Tell her we appreciate the hospitality and that we will strive to be no bother to anyone," Ned said.

Odonida relayed Ned's statement to the woman who then offered a statement for Odonida to translate. "Osieta says that you will not be a bother, but also, she wishes to know if you plan to stay with us or move on to Canada?"

"They say Canada is a safe place for Susannah," Ned said.

"Susannah is safe with us too," Odonida said. "Perhaps I didn't interpret mother's statement well enough. She wishes to know if you want to join our village as a member of the community."

"I didn't know we could do that," Ned said.

Susannah's eyes drifted from Ned Foster to Odonida, to Osieta, and back to Ned. Joining the tribe had never occurred to her, nor did she imagine it had occurred to Ned. In fact, they hadn't talked at all about their future lives; there would be time for that when they were safe. She had only a vague understanding of the word "community", but it appealed to her. Until now, the only community she had been part of was the ever-changing troop of slaves at Hallow Hill, where uncertainty and fear always overshadowed loyalty and communal love.

"It is not uncommon," Odonida replied. "Many of the people you see in the village are descended from Algonquins captured in war."

"You mean your captives joined the tribe that captured them?" Ned asked.

"Yes, if they wished to."

"What happens if they didn't want to join?"

"If they refused to join us, they were tortured to death," Odonida said.

"I guess most joined."

"Yes."

"How do you know they will stay loyal?" Ned asked.

"This has been the way of all the people since the beginning of time," Odonida explained. "The people of all the nations understand this."

"What about us?" Ned asked.

"You are our guest," Odonida said. "If you don't wish to join us, you may continue to stay as our guest until you decide you wish to go somewhere else."

"Why should we join?"

"As a member of our tribe, Susannah will have

the protections of the treaties the Iroquois have signed with whites."

"I don't know if that will carry much weight with Hugh Marlow," Ned offered.

"I doubt the state of New York will come to Mr. Marlow's aide."

"You're probably right about that," Ned said, "but the white men will break your treaty one day."

"We have seen white men nearby drawing pictures on paper," Odonida said.

"Surveyors," Ned suggested.

"Our friend, Colonel Riley, says first they draw the pictures, then the farmers come for the land."

"Sounds right," Ned Foster agreed.

"Our way of life will not be the same for much longer," the Mohawk chief said. "We will learn new ways if we have to, but until then, stay with us."

Ned looked at Susannah who had said nothing but was following the conversation closely. "I think we should stay," Ned said to her.

Susannah nodded.

Ned turned to Odonida, "If we join the tribe, can you perform a wedding ceremony?" he asked.

Susannah stared at Ned Foster, a tear forming in the corner of her eye. Her lips quivered as she tried to smile. She should say something, but nothing would come out. A few moments earlier, she was a runaway slave with an uncertain future. Now, she was about to be part of a community that wanted to protect her, and the wife of a man she loved.

Odonida turned to Osieta and spoke in the Iroquois language. Osieta nodded, then spoke to Odonida for several seconds.

Finally, Odonida turned back to Ned and Susannah. "It is customary in our culture for the mothers of the man and woman to decide if a marriage between them is proper," he said.

"I haven't seen my mother since I was five-years-old," Ned said to Odonida, "and Hugh Marlow sold Susannah's mother away to another plantation years ago."

"Don't worry," Odonida said. "Osieta will be your mother and Tabita will be Susannah's mother."

"When can we get married?"

"In a few days," Odonida said. "Osieta needs time to arrange a feast."

"We really gon' get married?" Susannah asked Ned as they walked back toward their lodge.

"If you'll have me as a husband," Ned responded.

Susannah stopped and took Ned's arm. She turned him toward her and pulled his head down so their lips met. "You know the answer to that," she said.

Chapter 28

August 1, 1787
Philadelphia, Pennsylvania

The morning sun streamed brightly through the bedroom window. Sara had drifted in and out of sleep for the last hour. She rolled from one side to the other in concert with the movements of John Oliver, always being sure to keep her thigh in contact with his body.

She wondered what the time might be, but it wasn't of such importance for her to get up to look at the clock on the bedside table. Instead, she snuggled closer to Oliver and felt his warmth surge through her body. Mornings had become a progression of sensual escalation since the convention adjourned for several days. They lingered in bed, often until mid-morning, only rising when hunger or thirst forced them downstairs to find the tea and breakfast Hennie had prepared for them.

The sound of the heavy door knocker against its iron plate on the front entrance of Sullivan House interrupted her thoughts. Mr. Martin was due back in Philadelphia any day to arrange receipt of another shipment of British goods from Trinidad. Through the open window she heard snippets of a short conversation between Hennie and the visitor. Momentarily, she wondered how Mr. Martin could arrive so early in the day, unless he had camped very near the city last night.

The sounds of the front door closing and of a man's boots walking away told her the visitor wasn't Mr. Martin. Perhaps a delivery from the vegetable market near the dock. She decided she should go downstairs and see if Hennie needed any help.

She slipped out of bed quietly, trying not to wake Oliver. But as she stood near the bed peering into the armoire, his hand slid up the inside of her thigh, "Trying to sneak away?" he asked.

"I'm going downstairs to see if Hennie needs help," she answered.

"Hennie can wait a few minutes," Oliver said, tugging her toward the bed. "I have needs of my own."

"You're a needy man, Mr. Oliver," Sara laughed as she turned toward the bed.

As she pulled the cover back and began to slip into the bed, a knock on the bedroom door stopped her. "A letter done come for Mista Oliver," Hennie's voice came through the door.

"We'll be downstairs in a few minutes," Sara responded.

"Dat mon say it real important," Hennie said with emphasis.

Sara looked at John Oliver and sighed. "All right," she said to the woman on the other side of the bedroom door. "We'll come down right now."

Oliver was already out of the bed and pulling on his trousers. He smiled as she pulled a plain white cotton dress from the wardrobe and slipped it on over her head.

A few minutes later, they sipped tea at the small table in the kitchen while John Oliver read the document. "It's a summons to appear before the Magistrate Court in two days' time," he said.

"What on earth for?"

"Mr. Marlow has lodged a complaint against both of us," Oliver told her.

"Because Susannah ran away?"

"Yes."

"The girl had every right to run away," Sara said. "Marlow abused her badly."

"That won't be the issue before the Court," Oliver said. "The question before the Court is whether you and I assisted Susannah in running away."

"Oh?" Sara sounded surprised. "Hennie and I might have helped Ned some," she admitted.

"Not only that," Oliver said, "but you and I rode to the Quaker camp to warn them about the slave hunter."

"What will the magistrate do?" Sara asked.

"He'll investigate the charge," Oliver said. "I've been giving the matter a lot of thought, and I do not believe the magistrate will find enough evidence to rule that you and I assisted their escape."

"Are you sure?"

"No. But this is Pennsylvania and the magistrate may be prejudiced against slavery to begin with," Oliver said. "Also, the Quakers are the only ones who know we rode to their camp that night, and they won't betray us in favor of someone like Hugh Marlow."

"The stable boy knows," Sara suggested.

"The stable boy knows we rode out late at night," Oliver said, "but he doesn't know where we went."

"Still," Sara said, "I don't like the idea of being investigated."

"There is something else I should tell you," Oliver said.

"What?"

"Marlow spoke to me after the last meeting of the delegates," he explained. "That's when he told me that Simon had come back and that Indians had killed the slave hunter."

"Yes, that was wonderful news."

"That's also when he told me then that he intended to file an action."

"You didn't tell me that."

"I didn't think he would actually do it," Oliver said. "He wanted money."

"How much does he want?"

"Ten-thousand Spanish dollars."

"I have that much," Sara offered.

"It isn't necessary," he assured her. "Even if Marlow prevailed in court, the market value of a slave girl is far less than ten-thousand."

"We both understand why Marlow puts such a high value on Susannah," Sara said.

"The judge won't consider that in estimating Marlow's loss, if it should come to that."

"I don't like investigations," Sara said again.

"Then I should tell you there is more to Marlow's threats," Oliver said.

"What?"

Oliver took a deep breath before speaking again. "He said he had ordered his associates in Britain to investigate Sara Sullivan."

Sara leaned back in her chair and closed her eyes as a wave of fear gripped her body. Despite the passage of time and the distance she had covered, someone was bound to make the connection between Sara Sullivan and Sara Carlisle.

She opened her eyes and looked at John Oliver. Would he look at her the same way if he found out the truth behind her escape from Dublin? The truth about the death of Alfred Carlisle? She had told him only that she had stolen money from her husband before running away to France. How would Oliver react when she told him the rest of that ugly story?

"I assured him there was nothing to find," Oliver continued. "You took some money from your husband's safe, but the United States doesn't have an extradition treaty with England."

She decided to tell John Oliver everything. She needed him. Not just for the protection he might provide, but for the love she craved since the night of their ride to the Quaker camp. Certainly, there was risk. But in her mind, she had decided that Oliver perfectly combined Robert Murray's protective kindness and Paul Barré's loving passion.

"I didn't tell you everything," Sara whispered.

"Perhaps you should tell me everything, now," Oliver said.

"I will," Sara said, then sat silent for several seconds. "I love you, John," she began again. "You love me too, I think. But there is much I haven't told you yet. I hope you will still love me once you've heard my story."

"There is nothing you can tell me that will stop me loving you," Oliver assured her.

She could only hope what he said was true. "I told you my husband was dead," she began, "but I didn't tell you how he died."

"No."

She glanced into the hallway to be sure Hennie wasn't somewhere nearby. "I killed Alfred Carlisle with a kitchen knife," she said. Her voice sounded stronger than she expected. The image of Carlisle in her mind brought back the anger and pain that led to that night eight years before.

Oliver's shoulders slumped and he leaned back in his chair. "I'm sure you had to defend yourself," he offered.

"No, at least not in the way you're thinking," she said. "I plunged the knife into his back while he undressed for bed." She looked directly into Oliver's eyes, determined now to unburden herself of the past she had carried with her for years.

"Tell me everything," Oliver instructed.

"I told you once that I didn't choose Alfred Carlisle to be my husband," she continued. "My father and the parish priest forced me to marry him. Every time he touched me, I felt violated."

The expression on Oliver's face hardened. He sat upright in the chair and looked directly at Sara. "But murder?" he questioned.

"Please hear my story before you condemn me," Sara insisted.

"All right."

"I grew up in Dublin," she began. "We were poor and lived in a rough neighborhood — not the worst, but bad enough. It wasn't always that way. I remember as a little girl, we lived in a nicer house. But my mother died when I was five years old and my father was never the same after that. He drank a lot of whiskey on top of the ale he always drank."

"Did he abuse you?" Oliver asked.

"No," Sara said. "But when my brothers did, he looked the other way."

"How old were you then?"

"Twelve or thirteen," Sara answered. "It stopped when I gave one of them a nasty kick to his manhood."

"Good for you," Oliver smiled.

"About that time, my father started doing odd jobs for Alfred Carlisle. He was a skilled craftsman and Carlisle's big house needed a lot of maintenance. Father would go to the manor house almost every day — at least the days he was sober enough. Carlisle didn't seem to mind his drinking as long as he got the work done."

She poured more of the hot tea into her cup and took a long sip before resuming. "Not long after I turned sixteen, one of my brothers got hurt in a gang fight. I went to the manor house to get my father. That was the first time Alfred saw me and I guess he took a fancy to me. Anyway, after that, he found reasons to ask father to bring me along. I polished silver, or cut flowers, or many other jobs he already had servants to do. After a while, I realized he was infatuated with me."

"How old was Carlisle then?"

"He must have been about thirty," Sara said. "He never told me his age, but his brother was heir to the title and was only thirty-three."

"Go on."

"I didn't know it, but Carlisle offered my father a lot of money to marry me soon after I turned eighteen. Father thought I would be happy about it, but I hated Carlisle. I flatly refused to marry him, but father wouldn't accept my decision. He told Carlisle I had accepted. Father O'Malley gave his enthusiastic approval for everything. I only found out later that he got some of Carlisle's money too."

"What did Carlisle's family think? Wouldn't they object to him marrying an Irish Catholic?"

"Lord Carlisle is the most prominent Catholic in England so that wasn't a problem. But, being Irish was a problem to Lord Carlisle. He was furious when he found out about the plan. Alfred didn't care though. He hated his father."

"So, you married him?"

"Yes," Sara answered. "My father and the priest gave me a lot of wine. I barely remember the wedding. The effect of the wine wore off though, and when Carlisle wanted to consummate the marriage, I refused.

"For several days, I kept refusing his demands. Most of the time, I locked myself in a room. As each day passed, he got angrier and angrier. Finally, he snapped. He made my father hold me down while he raped me. Then he bloodied my face for good measure."

"I can see why you hated him," Oliver observed when Sara paused for a sip of the tea.

"The rape gave me a new understanding of what my marriage meant," Sara continued. "If I didn't comply with his desires, I would die. At that very moment, I started planning my escape.

"For the next six months, I pretended to be a compliant wife. Every time he touched me it was all I could do to keep my supper down. He disgusted me but I never let him see that. I watched everything he did during those months.

"That's when I realized he had been stuffing money into a strongbox in his study for years. At first, I assumed it was just part of running the family operations in Ireland. They owned so much land and factories as well. But when his brother, Dennison, came to review the operations, Alfred never showed him the strongbox. That's when I realized Alfred was stealing the money from the family."

"Why steal from the family?" Oliver asked. "Surely he would inherit the money anyway."

"Not really," Sara explained. "As the heir, Dennison would control the estate. Alfred would get whatever allowance Dennison gave him."

"And Alfred didn't trust Dennison," Oliver

concluded.

"I told you before that Alfred hated his father," Sara said. "But it was really Dennison that he hated. He thought Dennison a toadying fool — his words — and not fit to be heir, but his father wouldn't budge on it. I suppose Alfred assumed Dennison would take his revenge when the opportunity came."

"That makes sense."

"After the rape, my father started drinking even more than before," Sara said. "I thought he wouldn't live much longer. My brothers drifted away to their gangs. My ties to Dublin — such as they were — had mostly disappeared.

"I still had some of the ragged clothes I'd worn before I married Alfred Carlisle and I began exploring the docks in disguise. I met a man who said he could arrange a passage for me. He wanted money before making the arrangements, but I convinced him I would have the money when the time came. A couple of weeks later, he sent a message that everything was set. A Dutch freighter would sail shortly after midnight two days hence. I knew what I had to do.

"That night after the servants finished their duties and retired to their quarters, I flirted mercilessly with Alfred. I knew how he would respond, and it didn't take long before he insisted we go to the bedroom we shared for just those occasions. While he undressed, I took a ten-inch kitchen knife I'd hidden in the room and jammed it to the hilt in his back just below his shoulder blade.

"I didn't know if he was dead or not, but he was unconscious and that was the main thing. I hurried to the study and cleaned out the strongbox. Then I changed into my old clothes, took the trunk I'd already packed and left Carlisle Manor forever."

Chapter 29

August 1
Sullivan House

John Oliver eyed Sara as she poured fresh tea in their cups and spread the soft butter on a slice of crusty bread. He tried to sort through the emotions he felt. The woman he loved had just told him she had murdered her husband and stole his money before running away. Yet, Her story hadn't repulsed him. Perhaps he even admired her courage and her determination to escape an untenable situation. It wasn't so different from the rebellion he had so recently been a part of; they had achieved freedom through violence.

"As I said earlier, neither the Confederation or Pennsylvania has an extradition treaty with Britain," he reminded her.

"I suppose that means they won't send me back to Ireland," Sara said.

"That's right."

"Well," she said. "I've never worried much about Britain wanting me. It's Lord Carlisle I've always worried about."

"I understand," Oliver said. "But it's been eight years. Lord Carlisle probably has other things on his mind now." In particular, he considered England's struggles in recent years with war in the colonies and the almost continual conflicts with France and Spain. Also, an emerging middle class in Britain had eroded the power and influence of men like Lord Carlisle.

"People like Carlisle are accustomed to getting what they want," Sara observed. "As far as I know, he is still offering a reward for me."

"Reward?"

"Yes," Sara said. "I learned about it while in France. He offered a large amount to anyone who will deliver me to England or Ireland."

"A reward complicates matters," Oliver said. "If Marlow finds out about it, he could cause a lot of trouble."

"Yes," Sara said.

"Tell me about France."

"All right," she said. "The ship took four days to reach Brest on the French coast. I spent the first day retching in my cabin, but after that, I was fine.

Anyway, Brest turned out to be a good place for me. A lot of Scotch and Irish folks moved there to get away from the English. The captain of the freighter told me of a tavern where many of them gathered at the end of the day. I got a room above the tavern and tried to figure out what came next."

"What did you do with the money?"

"I hid it in the bottom of my trunk," she said. "Acting the part of a poor girl from Dublin came naturally of course. No one suspected I had a fortune in my possession."

"What happened next?" Oliver asked. Far from being shocked, her story fascinated him.

"A few days after I arrived in Brest, a girl in the tavern told me about a Scotsman who was looking for an English-speaking housemaid for his estate outside of the city. That's how I came to work for Robert Murray."

"Tell me about Murray."

"His family came to Brest when Robert was a small child. They left Scotland with almost nothing after the Jacobite uprising in 1745. But they were strong, resourceful people and built a successful shipping and trading business in Brest. By the time I arrived, Robert ran the whole operation. He understood French perfectly, but unfortunately, he never lost the Scottish brogue, so the French couldn't understand a word he said."

Oliver laughed. "I can't understand the Scottish when they're speaking English."

"That's true enough," Sara laughed too, but then got serious again. "But the situation made me uncomfortable at first. Here I was again with a wealthy older man — Robert was in his forties. Soon though, I realized he posed no danger. Robert preferred the company of men where bedroom matters were concerned. He was genuine and caring. I still think of him as the best friend I ever had. Until now, he is the only person I've told about my escape from Alfred Carlisle."

"And he taught you to ride," Oliver observed.

"He taught me the basic things about riding," she said. "I enjoyed it, but I learned the joy of riding from someone else."

"Oh?"

"Robert came to me one day after I'd worked in the house for about two years; he asked me to become the assistant for the new chef who had just come to the estate. By that time, my French was good, and the new chef didn't speak English. I agreed to do it.

"His name was Paul Barré. At first, I thought of him as just a brash young man with a very high opinion of himself. I was sure I would despise him before long, but, instead, I was in his bed within two weeks."

She cast her eyes down when she said this, apparently not wanting to make eye contact with Oliver. His own reaction surprised him. He tried to suppress the moment of jealousy that flooded his mind, realizing he had no claim on her then, and perhaps had no claim now. *Probably, I should thank Paul Barré*, Oliver thought. He had brought down the wall she'd built around herself.

"Did the romance continue?" Oliver asked.

"Yes," she said. "I was surprised by how easily I fell in love again given my experiences with men up until then. But, somewhere in my mind, I always knew being in love could be wonderful. For the first time, I understood the physical pleasure of sex, too. That part of me was free of Alfred Carlisle."

"I'm glad of that," Oliver said, "but I don't understand why you left France."

"Not all stories have happy endings," Sara said.

"What happened?"

"You said you would still love me," she reminded him.

"Yes," he said. He grinned and added, "Unless you murdered him too."

"No," she smiled back at him, "and I promise I'll never murder another husband."

"All right."

"Paul had a cozy little room next to the kitchen," she began. "Every day, we would find time to go there. It was a wonderful time. Often, I smelled fresh bread cooking nearby while we made love. Sometimes, we took long rides in the afternoons before we started preparing the evening meal. I'm sure others on the staff realized what was happening but no one said anything. I'm sure Robert Murray knew too, but he was glad to have a happy chef.

"We kept on that way for several months. I was deeply in love with Paul Barré and I thought he loved me too. I'm sure he did in a way. Then one day, I realized I was pregnant. I was thrilled, and I was sure Paul would be too."

"He wasn't?" Oliver guessed.

"No," she shook her head. "That's when he told me he already had a wife and child. I had no idea. He would sometimes be gone for several days and when I asked about it, he said he visited family in Paris. But he never mentioned a wife."

"What about divorce?"

"Divorce was next to impossible in France without permission from the Catholic church," Sara said. "If the church got involved, Lord Carlisle might hear of it. Besides, I realized Paul didn't want a divorce."

"Oh?"

"No. That's what hit the hardest."

"What did you do?"

"I didn't know what to do," she said. "I ran from the kitchen in tears. Robert Murray saw me in the hallway and spotted the tears. When he asked about it, I told him the entire story. He offered to send Paul away and allow me to have the baby at the estate, but I couldn't agree to that. A chef of Paul's reputation was invaluable to his business. He suggested a doctor who performed abortions on the side. That's what I decided to do."

"Was it legal in France?"

"No. The church considered it a cardinal sin. It was dangerous, too."

"Still, you went ahead with it," Oliver concluded, since Sara didn't have any children with her.

"Yes," she said. "For a brief moment, I saw myself marrying Paul, having a child, and living a normal life. But after Paul told me he was married, I realized I might need to hide from Lord Carlisle for years. My child could be an orphan at any moment."

"Do you think about it often?"

"No. Not often," she said. "But sometimes, I envision what might've been. A family of my own."

"You have another opportunity," Oliver said. "He is setting across the table from you right now." He saw the statement moved her. Her lower lip quivered, and a tear trickled from her eye.

"You would still have me after what I've told you?" she got the words out with a shaky voice.

"Well, you have promised not to murder your next husband," he pointed out.

"You have my solemn oath," she said. A small laugh came out as she wiped away the tears.

She explained how Robert Murray had arranged her stay in Martinique and provided passage on one of his ships. Oliver had already heard the rest of that story. She disliked Martinique from the beginning and had found a profitable passage to Philadelphia after only a few months on the island.

Chapter 30

August 3, 1787
Lake Champlain, New York

When Tabita slipped the wedding dress over her head, Susannah trembled as the soft leather slid over her naked body. The white deer skin was softer than any cloth she had ever worn and was so light she might still have been naked. She gazed down the front of the dress with approval. Colorful beads and tiny feathers outlined the deep v-neckline to accentuate the rise of her breasts. Thin strips of the white leather formed long fringes under each sleeve and along the hem just below her knees. Moccasins made of the same white leather and decorated with many colorful beads adorned her feet.

At Hallow Hill, if Susannah felt pretty it often meant danger was near. The looks from the white bosses and even some other slaves were a signal to move fast back to safety, if such a place existed. But this morning, she knew she was safe and being pretty made her joyful, an emotion she had never known until Ned Foster had led her away from Hugh Marlow.

The morning had begun when Tabita led her to a secluded place on a small creek that flowed into the giant lake. They had stripped off their clothes and sat in the chilly water on a creek bottom of smooth round stones. Tabita used a soft buckskin cloth to wash her back and shoulders, then Susannah stood and let Tabita wash her legs and buttocks.

The two women laid on a large rock beside the creek to let the sun dry them. Tabita was almost as dark-skinned as Susannah, the result of many days of living and working in the summer sun. Susannah noted the stretch marks on her lower abdomen and realized that she too might have such marks before long. That thought brought another new emotion. The concept of "family" was always tenuous at Hallow Hill. Children were marketable assets as soon as they were old enough to work in the fields. Families rarely stayed together as a unit.

"Beautiful," Tabita said, as she stepped back to admire the dress.

"It feel beautiful," Susannah responded.

"We go now," Tabita said. She held Susannah's hand and led her toward Osieta's longhouse.

As they approached Osieta's longhouse, the largest in the village, a large wreath made of small alder branches woven into a circle drew Susannah's eyes to the entrance. Strands of white leather and colored feathers plaited into the wreath signaled a celebration was to happen inside the longhouse.

"That's the wedding wheel," Tabita said. "It represents a happy future for the wedding couple."

"We gonna be happy," Susannah assured her.

The longhouse was cleaner than any Susannah had seen. The soft smells of herbs smoldering in little pots had replaced the usual scent of smoke from cooking fires. Rooms in the big building were opened up, so it resembled a large banquet hall rather than a collection of small living quarters. Near the center of the longhouse, Osieta and Odonida sat on a long bench. Ned Foster stood in front of them, his back to the entrance.

Ned Foster turned as she approached the group. He wore shiny new doe skin from head to toe. The soft tan leather was accented with a large bronze plate that hung over his chest suspended by several strands of beaded leather. A simple, round headdress of eagle feathers and beads adorned the crown of his head.

Susannah's entering the longhouse must have signaled to the tribe the ceremony was to begin. The members of the community began to stream in, first the older women, followed by younger women, and finally the men of the tribe came in.

A More Perfect Union

Odonida motioned for Susannah to join Ned at the center of the hall, then instructed them to sit on a bench facing him and Osieta. Tabita sat next to Susannah. Once Tabita was seated, the gathered crowd went quiet. Ned Foster took her hand in his own.

Osieta stood and spoke to the gathering in the Iroquois language. Susannah had learned a few words of the language in the days they had been in the camp, but she recognized nothing in Osieta's speech except for their names.

Instead of taking her seat on the bench by Odonida, Osieta sat on the facing bench and signaled to Ned Foster to sit next to her. Now, Odonida addressed the wedding party in English. "I will now ask the mothers of the bride and the groom a few questions," he said. "This is traditional."

Susannah and Ned nodded to him.

Odonida first addressed Tabita, who was acting as the mother of the bride, asking her a series of questions to which she answered "hen" after each. Next, he directed the same set of questions to Osieta as the mother of the groom. Osieta said "hen" after each of the questions.

Next, Odonida addressed Susannah and Ned. "Your mothers have consented to this marriage," he said. "I have asked them if you are suitable for this marriage and will fulfill the obligations of the marriage, and they have said yes. They have committed their clans to help you should the need for help arise."

Odonida shifted his weight on the bench and continued to speak to the couple. "Now, I will ask each of you the questions of your marriage," he said. "If you answer 'yes' to each question, then the ceremony will continue."

Susannah and Ned both nodded.

"Susannah," Odonida began the questions. "Are you prepared to be Ned's wife for the rest of your life?"

"Yes," she said without hesitation.

"Will you prepare food for your husband and children?"

"Yes," she said, then quickly added, "I don't know much 'bout cookin', but I gonna learn." There were a few snickers from the gathering, including from Ned Foster.

The rest of the questions dealt with parenting and social responsibilities and Susannah answered each in the affirmative.

Then, there was a final question. "Marriage is an equality of man and woman," Odonida said. "One does not dominate the other. Do you accept this?"

"Yes."

Odonida looked directly at Ned Foster. "Ned Foster, are you prepared to be Susannah's husband for the rest of your life?"

"Yes."

"Will you provide food and other necessary things for Susannah and your children?"

"Yes."

"Will you instruct your children in the ways of our people and help them become good members of the community?"

"Yes," Ned said.

"Marriage is an equality of man and woman," Odonida said. "One does not dominate the other. Do you accept this?"

"Yes."

Odonida instructed the couple to extend their arms, Ned's left and Susannah's right. From the bench, he took a long, beaded strap and wrapped it around their joined arms.

"The Wampum belt is a symbol of the authority of this tribe and of Osieta, our communal leader. The joining of your bodies together with the Wampum belt is notice to all present and to all you will meet in your life, that you, Ned, and you, Susannah, are married and belong together. All people will know that you have made these commitments to one another and that you will honor those commitments until death."

Odonida unwrapped the Wampum belt from their arms and instructed them to stand and face each other. He continued to hold the belt stretched in front of him. Two young women approached the benches, each carrying a woven straw basket. As she took her basket from the woman nearest her, Susannah hoped she could remember the lines she had rehearsed.

Susannah lifted the straw lid from the basket and showed the contents to Ned. "The cloth and clothing in this basket are a symbol of my commitment to keep my husband and family dressed in clean, mended clothing, and to keep a clean and warm home." She handed the basket to Ned, who bowed to her and placed the basket on the bench.

Ned then took the basket from the other young woman. He lifted the lid and showed the contents to Susannah. "This sweet cake is a symbol of my commitment to provide food and sustenance to my wife and children," he said. Susannah took the basket and placed it on the bench where she had been setting.

After the exchange of baskets, Odonida again picked up the Wampum belt and gave one end to Susannah and the other end to Ned Foster. He turned toward the gathered crowd in the longhouse and spoke to them in the Mohawk language. Susannah didn't understand what was being said, but she could see approving nods and smiles from the members of the community.

After his speech, Odonida took the Wampum belt and handed it to the person nearest the wedding party. That person then passed the belt on to the next, and they passed it to the next until every person present had touched the Wampum.

When the passing of the belt made its way back to Odonida, the chief spoke again. Tabita leaned near Susannah's ear, "Odonida says the wedding is completed and the feasting and dancing will begin soon."

While the men cleared away the benches where the wedding party and guests had sat, the members of the village came to Susannah and Ned to offer congratulations. Mostly, she didn't understand the words, but Susannah understood their meaning and was thankful for it. The only community she had been part of before now was the slaves of Hallow Hill, who rarely trusted one another and fought over scraps. Survival had always trumped love.

When the men finished clearing away the benches, a small group of boys and men sat on the floor in one corner and began to play their flutes and drums. This was the signal for Susannah to lead the women while Ned led the men in a dance to salute the Great Spirit.

The dance continued for several minutes. Susannah sometimes forgot the movements Tabita had taught her, but the other women followed her haphazard dancing as if it were the way they had done the dance for centuries. A glance at Ned told her he was having the same problem.

When the feather dance ended, Odonida and Osieta led the wedding party and guest outside to the large open area in the center of the village. Long tables laden with platters of venison, rabbit, fish, vegetables, and savory turtle soup awaited them. At the end of the table, an assortment of sweet cakes and nuts roasted in maple sugar would satisfy their sweet tooth. Wooden tubs of fresh lake water and sassafras tea were there to wash down the feast.

The feasting continued until after sunset. Then, a large fire in the center of the yard illuminated the area and kept the mosquitos away. Occasionally, small groups of men or women would dance near the fire. A group of young girls sang traditional songs in perfect harmony.

It was well after dark when Tabita whispered to Susannah that it was time for the happy couple to enjoy some time alone. As they rose to leave the festival, the crowd suddenly became much quieter. Susannah couldn't suppress a giggle as she and Ned passed through the smiling crowd and away from the circle of light from the fire.

At the edge of the circle of light, a young warrior handed a torch to Ned. He took Susannah's hand and led her toward the little cabin Odonida had arranged for them on the outskirts of the village.

The cabin stood next to corn and bean fields and was used by villagers who stayed there to protect the young crops from deer and other poachers in the springtime. Ned pushed the deer hide covering the entrance aside and let Susannah inside where a small fire burned in the center of the one-room cabin. A pot of the familiar stew hung over the little flame.

Ned snuffed out the flame of the torch with a leather cloth and entered the cabin. Susannah's arms wrapped around his neck and drew his lips toward hers. She had been longing for the lingering kiss for hours.

When their lips parted, Ned gazed at her, "I love you, Susannah Foster," he said.

She smiled up at him, "I loves you too," she said, then added, "I ain't never had a fam'ly name 'fore."

"Well, you got one now," Ned said. "At least in the eyes of this village."

"I don't care 'bout anyplace else."

"I want the whole world to know," Ned said, "and I got some ideas about how to do it."

"That sounds good long as Simon don' find out where we be," Susannah said.

"We're safe here," Ned said. "Now, we should consummate this marriage."

"I don' know what cons'mate mean, but I know what I wan' do," Susannah said while tugging the wedding dress over her head.

Chapter 31

August 7, 1787
Pennsylvania Statehouse

John Oliver watched as a steady patter of raindrops slid down the large window behind the dais where General Washington sat. Overcast skies together with the steady rain provided welcome relief from the relentless heat that had plagued the convention through the summer. There had been days when he had dreamed of open windows and a gentle breeze to move the stifling air around. In truth though, he knew there had been little in the way of gentle breezes on the other side of the nailed-shut windows.

Occasionally, he glanced across the room where Hugh Marlow sat ensconced with other delegates from South Carolina. Marlow was staring at him each time he looked. He was sure Marlow was seething since their first hearing before the magistrate on the previous Friday had resulted only in a delay of two weeks. Oliver had made a point of leaving the hearing without speaking to Marlow.

The convention had reconvened the day before to present the Committee of Detail's draft document to the delegates. They had adjourned until this morning so that the delegates would have time to read the draft.

Oliver had dutifully read the document the previous evening, then read several parts of it again. With frustration, he observed that after four months of work, not a single article or section enjoyed a consensus among the delegates, except perhaps the name of the nation. At least no one had suggested changing the name of the country from the United States of America as the Articles of Confederation had designated it.

He understood the need to create the draft document despite the lack of consensus. If they were to complete the task at all, delegates must now face the compromises they had dodged until now. Oliver wondered where each delegate would draw their line on compromise in the push for final approval. He was certain of one thing. Not a single delegate would be completely satisfied with the result.

The early morning had produced a long and somewhat animated discussion about the meeting time and frequency of the proposed legislative branch. Oliver's mind drifted during the interchange but would snap to attention when some statement stoked his interest.

Madison saw no reason they should fix a date in the constitution for the meetings, only that they be required to meet at least once a year. Others supported a fixed date while still others saw no need for requiring an annual meeting.

"I cannot think there will be a necessity for a meeting every year," Rufus King of Massachusetts said. "The great vice of legislatures is that they legislate too much."

Colonel Mason thought it essential that the legislatures meet often to preserve the constitution, "The extent of the country will supply business for them to act upon," he stated. "And if it does not, the legislature has inquisitorial powers as well as legislative powers, and they cannot suspend their inquisitions for long periods of time."

"Whilst I oppose the fixing of a date in general," Governor Randolph stated, "I see the necessity of it in the beginning. Afterwards, I propose we empower the legislature to change the date from time-to-time."

Randolph's proposal was seconded and then approved by the delegates.

Next, the delegates worked their way through a series of minor matters on which there was general agreement. Finally, they came to the matter of voting rights in the election of members of the

House of Representatives.

Gouverneur Morris moved to strike the language that aimed to match voting rights in the election of federal representatives to the rights granted by the respective states in the election of representatives to the state legislatures.

"We should limit the right of suffrage to 'freeholders'," Morris insisted.

James Wilson, another Pennsylvanian, leaped to his feet, "It would be most disagreeable for a person to vote for a state representative, but at the same time be denied a right to vote for a national representative."

Oliver Ellsworth concurred with Wilson, "The people will not readily support the national constitutions if it should disenfranchise them from rights they already have," he stated. "The states are the best judge of the circumstances and temper of their own people."

Colonel Mason was on his feet awaiting his turn to speak. "Eight or nine states have already expanded the right of suffrage beyond freeholders. What will those people think if they should be disenfranchised? The power to alter the rights of suffrage would be a dangerous power in the hands of a national legislature."

John Dickinson of Delaware supported the restriction. "Freeholders are the best guardians of liberty," he suggested. "The restriction of the right to them is the best defense against the dangerous influence of those multitudes without property and without principle. In time, our country will abound with such people."

"How shall we define a freehold?" Ellsworth demanded. "Ought not every man who pays a tax be able to vote for the representative who is to levy and dispose of his money?"

Gouverneur Morris believed they needed the restriction and it would be popular with most of the population. "If we give the vote to people with no property, they will sell them to the rich who will gain power from it. As to merchants and others, if they have wealth and value the right, then they can acquire it. If not, they don't deserve it."

"We all feel too strongly the remains of ancient prejudices and view things too much through a British medium. A freehold is the qualification in England, and hence we imagine it to be the only proper one," Colonel Mason said. "But every man having evidence of attachment to and common interest with the society ought to share in all its rights and privileges."

"The right of suffrage is certainly one of the fundamental articles of republican government and ought not to be left to regulation by the legislature," Mr. Madison stated. "A gradual abridgment of this right has been the mode in which aristocracies have been built on the ruins of democratic governments."

Madison's comments caught John Oliver's attention. Was the great Virginian advocating more democracy? Then Madison continued his speech.

"In future times a great majority of the people will not only be without land but any other sort of property," Madison continued. They will likely combine under the influence of their common situation; in which case the rights of property and the public liberty will not be secure in their hands."

Obviously, Madison had not changed his views. It struck Oliver as absurd that these three men — Madison, Morris, and Dickinson — had espoused a theory that only landed property owners would stave off the emergence of an aristocracy. What was an aristocracy other than the control of wealth and power in the hands of a few? It mattered not that they wouldn't pass out titles. The few would control wealth and power and would pass it from generation to generation.

As was often the case, it was Dr. Benjamin Franklin who offered the simple and logical reasoning for broad suffrage rights. "It is of great consequence that we should not depress the virtue and public spirit of our common people, of which they displayed a great deal during the war, and which contributed principally to its favorable outcome."

Later, when the states cast their decision on the matter, the delegates soundly defeated Morris' motion, with only Maryland supporting it. The matter had generated a lively debate, but in truth, most of the states had judged their policies for years and were pleased with their own approach to suffrage.

*****

Lake Champlain, New York

Susannah lay quietly on the soft pallet of straw covered with bear skin. She rolled over and put her head on Ned Foster's chest, reveling in the movement of his slow, rhythmic breathing. She waited patiently for the first sign of morning light seeping around the hide that covered the entrance to the little cabin.

In the distance, she heard sounds of the village coming to life for the day. Finally, the sun began to chase away the darkness. She listened again to Ned's breathing. Perhaps she shouldn't wake him, yet. But Susannah had come to understand her own need for sexual fulfillment. Until a few days ago, pleasure from sex was something she could only fantasize about. Now, she couldn't get enough of it.

With the lightest touch she could imagine, Susannah began to trace the edges of his manhood with her fingers. Her slender fingers traced little circles around each of his testicles, then followed the thin line of darker flesh to the tip of his shaft. His breathing became deeper and faster and his member responded to her touch.

"You sure have a nice way of waking a man up," Ned said, rolling onto his side to face her.

"I sure like wakin' you up," she said.

Susannah continued stroking his growing

erection while his hand gently fondled her buttocks. She pushed her thigh over his side and shuddered as his hand slid between her thighs, massaging her most sensitive spot. She pressed her lips against his and sensed his tongue invite her own to meet it.

The depth of the kiss and the wetness between her thighs made words unnecessary. She was ready and Ned knew it. He rolled her on her back and moved himself between her open legs. She guided his erection into her moist opening. Slowly, he pushed himself fully inside her, then pulled back until he was almost completely out. In again, then out. In again, out again. Gradually, the speed of his thrusts increased and the tingle of pleasure inside her grew.

He hovered over her, arms fully extended, His upper body moving little while his hips thrust ever faster. She grasped his buttocks in both hands to encourage the rhythm of his strokes. Her pleasure peaked just before his face took on the trancelike look she'd learned to expect before his entire body shivered with his pleasure.

He bent down and kissed her on the lips before finally withdrawing his spent member. As he pulled away, he gently kissed each of her nipples and her navel, before rolling onto his back beside her.

"You sure you gotta go away?" she asked.

"I'll only be gone a few days," he told her.

"You gonna miss me?"

"I'm going to think about you every minute,"

Ned assured her.

"You gonna think about what we just did," Susannah observed with a giggle.

"I sure am."

"Why you gotta send dat letter right now?"

"We need to have the state of Connecticut recognize our marriage," Ned explained.

Although they were married in the eyes of the Iroquois Confederation, Ned wanted the state of Connecticut to recognize it as well. He'd told her that state recognition would make her a citizen of the state, in which case a judge might take their side against any future fugitive slave hunters. He had composed a letter to John Oliver and planned to ride to Kingston so that Colonel Riley could see that it got to Oliver in Philadelphia. Natani would ride with him.

"We safe here," Susannah said. "We don' gotta go to Conni'cut."

"I want to have options, Susannah," Ned said.

Chapter 32

August 13, 1787
Kingston, New York

Ned Foster stuck a hand in his saddlebag to be sure the letter to John Oliver was safe and dry. A summer squall had swept through the hills near Kingston and drenched him and Natani as they rode the last miles to Colonel Riley's farm. They might have stopped in some dry place until the storm passed, but the trip had already gone longer than expected, and Ned was intent to get his letter on its way to Oliver as soon as possible.

After the rain passed, the sun broke through the few remaining clouds, warming the air and drying their soaked buckskins. They had traveled a different route from the ride north when he and Susannah had first gone to Odonida's village. Now, he began to recognize familiar landmarks.

"How much further?" Ned asked Natani.

"Over the next ridge we take the trail through the forest," Natani responded.

Ned Foster nodded and rode on silently toward the hilltop. The trail through the forest appeared on their right a short distance after the crest. Ned recognized it as the trail they had taken after Natani's small band had rescued them from Simon and the slave hunter. They would reach Natani's father's farm in half an hour.

When the farm came into view, Ned saw Colonel Riley leading a mule weighted with heavy green tobacco leaves toward his barn. The sight reminded him of John Oliver's farm in Connecticut, although Oliver's place would have had a dozen mules hauling the crop to large drying sheds.

"I didn't remember seeing tobacco plants when we were here," Ned said to Natani, who had stopped at the edge of the clearing to take in the sight of his father's farm.

Natani pointed to woods beyond the small lodge house, "Only a small patch over there by the woods," he said. "Father always grows a little tobacco for himself and friends."

"Tobacco is a lot of work just to have a pipe with friends," Ned observed. "A lot less trouble to buy it."

"He knows that," Natani said. "He's afraid store-bought tobacco might have been made by slaves. He won't support that."

"We grow a lot of tobacco in Connecticut without slaves," Ned Foster pointed out.

"You can tell him that," Natani offered, "but he's pretty stubborn."

"No," Ned laughed. "He can keep his protest. It's a good cause."

Natani gave his mount a nudge. "Let's go talk to the man," he said.

Colonel Riley had just entered the shadow of the barn entrance when Natani shouted to him. He stopped immediately and, after lashing the mule to a post in the barn, came out to meet them.

"Natani, I wasn't expecting you," Riley said, "but it's a good thing you've come." He looked from Natani to Ned Foster and nodded.

"Mr. Foster needs to send a letter to his friend," Natani said. "We didn't think he should go to the post office in Albany," he added.

"You were right not to go to Albany," Colonel Riley said. "There's been some trouble."

"We've been on the trail for several days," Natani said. "What's happened?"

"I was planning to leave in the morning to warn Odonida," Riley said. "A white settler's farm got raided four days ago. The country folk around Albany are sayin' it was Odonida's bunch."

"Our people didn't do it," Natani assured him. He and Ned were on the road when the raid took place, but he would have known if Odonida were planning anything of the sort.

"I know that," Riley said. "Even if Odonida wanted to raid a farm, Osieta wouldn't have allowed it."

"No. She wouldn't."

"Even so, there may be trouble," Natani's father warned him. "I went to town this morning. Farmers from all over the county been gathering in Albany since the raid. They're planning to march up to the lake and kill every Mohawk they find."

"We'll start back at first light," Natani said. "We'll get close to Fort Saratoga," he added. "I want to see what the soldiers are up to."

"I hope you can get there before them farmers," Riley said. "Now go inside and let your mother get some food in you. I'll hang those tobacco leaves and be right in."

A short time later the three men gathered around a table with Riley's wife, Emma. Ned savored the flavor of the thick stew and the ale that washed it down to erase the memory of the dried venison and turkey of the ride to Kingston. They would begin their journey back sooner than he expected, but he hoped there would be time for Emma's ham, eggs and biscuits before they departed.

"That letter must be mighty important," Colonel Riley observed to Ned.

"Yep," Ned acknowledge. Then he told the colonel and Emma about the marriage ceremony for himself and Susannah. He explained his hope of having the marriage officially recorded in Connecticut.

"The states are supposed to cooperate to capture escaped slaves," Ned explained. "But if Susannah is a citizen of Connecticut, they might refuse to help if Marlow demands it."

"Captain Oliver just might get it done," Riley said.

"Mr. Oliver is a quiet man, but he knows Connecticut politics as well as anybody," Ned said. "The thing is, we have to act fast, before this new constitution comes along. Right now, the state's sovereignty is superior to the Articles of Confederacy, but that probably won't be true once the new constitution is done."

*****

Ned Foster felt surprisingly stiff after sleeping on a feather stuffed mattress for the first time in weeks. He had rolled and tossed for hours before finally falling asleep. Then again, perhaps it was Susannah's absence that made him uncomfortable.

"Mamma's cooked breakfast," Natani said to him as he rubbed the sleepiness from his eyes.

The rain the previous day had brought cooler, drier air to the Hudson River valley. A million twinkling stars dotted the crystal-clear sky as the light of morning hadn't yet appeared in the eastern sky. As they walked toward the Riley cabin, the smell of cured ham and bacon cooking expelled the last vestiges of sleepiness from him.

The biscuits were just as he remembered, fluffy and soaked with fresh churned butter. Emma Riley had fried the smoky bacon crisp; the cured ham was moist and flavored with hints of salt and sugar. Emma was disappointed that he only wanted two of the fresh hen's eggs fried in bacon drippings, but Ned knew the long ride ahead would be difficult if he overstuffed himself.

"You'll want to stay off the main road to Albany," Gabriel Riley said as Ned and Natani strapped their little Mohawk saddles on the horses. Emma Riley had stuffed saddlebags full of cured ham, dried turkey, biscuits, apples, and pears, which they also threw over the backs of the animals.

"I wish these horses had had another day to rest," Natani said.

"The river's low this time of year," Colonel Riley said. "There's a good trail down by the bank."

"I know that trail," Natani said. "We'll circle around Albany, then pick up the river trail."

"Stay out of sight as much as you can," Riley said.

"Don't worry," Natani assured his father. "But I want to get close enough to Fort Saratoga to see what's happening there."

"Don't tarry too long. Those farmers may be on the road already," Riley said.

"I figure four days," Natani said. "Might be less

if the weather stays good and there's a good moon."

Colonel Riley wrapped his arms around his son, then shook hands with Ned Foster. "Good luck to you both," he said. "I'll get your letter to Captain Oliver, Ned."

As they rode away from the Riley farm, the sun was just above the eastern horizon. When they reached the main road to Albany, Natani stared hard toward West Point, then toward Albany. "I don't see anybody else on the road, but keep an eye out," he instructed.

Two hours passed without encountering any other travelers. At this pace, they could circle around Albany and reach the river trail on the north side before it became too dark to travel.

Natani suddenly pulled his horse to a stop and raised an arm to signal Ned to stop.

"What is it?" Ned asked.

"I thought I heard voices up ahead," Natani said.

There was less than fifty yards of road visible ahead of them before the road curved to the left and large trees blocked the view. Natani began walking his mount forward slowly before stopping again. He held one finger across his mouth to signal Ned to be silent. Seconds later Ned detected a young man's laughter from the road ahead.

Natani dismounted and waited while Ned did the same. He leaned close and said in a low voice, "I don't see any horse tracks, so they're either walking or they're coming this way."

Ned nodded.

"We can cut through these woods," Natani said. "If they're coming this way, they won't see us, and if they're walking toward Albany, we get around them."

Ned again nodded his agreement.

Natani picked a path with a slight incline. They led the horses for some distance before mounting and riding slowly through the massive trees. Ten minutes later, near the crest of a small hill, Natani and Ned dismounted again. They crept on foot to the top of the hill and looked down on the road.

Through the trees, they saw four men walking toward Albany. One man, the oldest, carried one of the long rifles that had been so successful during the war. The others carried muzzle-loading muskets of pre-war vintage. The wind was favorable so Ned could hear scraps of their talk.

"They say it's the best land in the state," one of the younger men said. *"We gonna get some of that land ain't we, daddy?"*

"We gonna get plenty of that land, boy," the older man said, *"Once we get them damn Indians off it."*

"We should a gone on to town day 'fore yest'day," one of the young men said. *"Them others is gonna get the best places."*

"We'll get good land, boy. Don't you worry."

The voices trailed off as the small party continued down the road.

"It's just what I thought," Natani said.

"What?"

"Some bunch of settlers faked a Mohawk raid to justify stealing our land."

"A farmer was killed," Ned pointed out.

"It was probably somebody they had it in for anyway," Natani said.

"You think it was those guys?"

"Probably not," Natani said, "but they knew what happened."

"What about the soldiers?" Ned asked. "We should tell them what we heard."

"Maybe," Natani said. "If we get there in time."

They mounted their horses and rode at a faster pace to get ahead of the old settler and his sons. A mile or so further on, they rejoined the road beyond a sharp bend out of the view of the settlers.

As they neared Albany, traffic on the road increased, and despite Natani's caution, they were noticed twice by other travelers. First, a farmer and his wife pulled to the side of the road as they passed. The couple had stared suspiciously at them but said nothing. As soon as they were out of sight beyond the couple's view, Natani removed his headpiece and necklace and stuffed them under his rolled-up blanket. Now, both men were wearing simple buckskins with no Mohawk markings. *Maybe it'll work*, Ned thought. After all, buckskins were not uncommon dress for ordinary woodsmen. Black men in buckskins was unusual, though. He was glad they'd only brought pistols and not bows, which would be hard to hide.

The next encounter was tenser than the first. A group of half a dozen men walked toward Albany. Like the other group they'd seen, these men were carrying weapons. This time, they spotted Ned and Natani before Natani could find a way around the men. As a group, the entire party turned to stare at the two men in buckskins. There was no choice now. Natani sat tall in the saddle and urged his mount slowly passed the group, clinging to the right side of the trail.

"You boys don't look like nobody I ever seen in Albany County," a man at the front of the troop said as Natani and Ned rode past them.

"Nope," Natani said. Despite being three-quarters Mohawk, his skin was lighter than most of the farmers who spent their days in the summer sun.

"Stop that animal a minute so's we can talk," the man instructed.

Natani stopped, as did Ned who was close behind him. "What you want to talk about?" he said with a cool stare.

"Where you boys from?" the leader demanded.

"Up north," Natani said.

"Ain't nothin' up north but Injuns."

"There's trappers up north," Natani told him.

"You fellas trappers?"

"Yeah."

"What about your friend there?" the leader nodded toward Ned Foster. "He don't look like a trapper."

"What's a trapper supposed to look like?" Ned asked.

"S'posed to be white," the man said. Then with another glare toward Ned. "That fella looks like he might o' run away from the plantation."

"He's a free man," Natani said.

The leader ignored Natani's statement. He looked at the other men in his troop, "I bet this fella's worth a fine reward from one of them Southern gent'men."

Several of the men in the group nodded their approval. Ned watched Natani scan the men with his eyes. He looked at Ned. "Go," he yelled.

Ned froze for a moment, unsure what Natani was telling him. But, as Natani pulled his horse to the left and charged directly at the leader, he realized they would have to make a run for it and hope the men's aim was poor.

Ned dug his heels into the horse's flanks and felt its rear end sink, then lurch forward at a gallop. He squeezed himself as low in the saddle as he could and yelled encouragement to his mount. He turned his head to the left and saw Natani close behind.

They were twenty yards clear before the noise of the first musket fire reached his ear. Three more fired in quick succession. One musket ball crashed into a tree on the right, but none of the others seemed close. He looked around again. Natani was still close behind.

At forty yards, Ned began to relax. He raised his head and let the horse set its own pace. Several more musket shots rang out but struck nothing around him.

They rounded a curve in the road. Ned slowed and let Natani pass in front of him. When they were well beyond the bend, Natani stopped. Ned stopped as well, and they looked back to where they had come from. The troop of farmers was not in sight.

"We're clear," Natani said, "but we need to get off this road."

"That was a wild ride," Ned said. "Good thing those guys can't shoot so good."

"All of them had muskets," Natani said. "Not a single long rifle among them."

"A lot of folks got killed by muskets in the war," Ned observed.

"Muskets are all right for something that's standing still at twenty yards," Natani said, "but they're useless for shooting a fast-moving target."

"That's good to know I guess," Ned said.

"Yep," Natani said. "Now, let's get off this

road."

Chapter 33

August 15, 1787
Near Albany, New York

Ned Foster lay awake for hours before Natani stirred as the first light of morning crept in from the east. His light saddle blanket had provided little warmth against a surprisingly cool upstate night, but that wasn't the thing that kept him awake. A large contingent of Albany County farmers had gathered in that city and were marching on the Mohawk village near Lake Champlain; the village where his new wife lay sleeping quietly at that moment.

He and Natani had surveilled the city from a grove of trees on a nearby hill, watching approaches from the south and west. Besides the two groups of men they had encountered earlier, they saw others enter the little city. These were stragglers from the far reaches of the vast county and probably feared they would be late to the action. There were a few experienced fighters, veterans of the war with England. But most would simply be eager to chase the remaining Indians off land they coveted for themselves.

Natani said there were thousands of farms spread over Albany County and guessed that one or two hundred men might already have left for the raid on Odonida's village. Also, there were about fifty militiamen occupying Fort Saratoga. Those men were remnants of the Continental Army still positioned to keep the peace on the frontier. Would they stand between the farmers and the Mohawk to preserve the peace? Or would they join the farmers to root out the Indians?

The political pressure to do the latter would be enormous. Representatives of the Iroquois Confederation had signed treaties with the state that gave the land to New York. But the European cultures — first the British and French, then the Americans — never understood the political makeup of the tribes, which did not recognize a central authority who spoke for all the bands. Though some chiefs had signed papers with the white man, Odonida and Osieta felt no compulsion to abide by those agreements.

Ned rose from his fitful night and stretched his painful muscles. Natani appeared to have slept well and was already leading the horses to the little creek they had camped next to.

He left the animals to drink their fill and dipped two wooden bowls into the fresh water for him and Ned. When he returned, they sat on the ground and ate some of the cured ham with a biscuit and an apple. They washed the food down with the cool creek water.

"We'll reach Fort Saratoga before noon today," Natani said, wiping his lips with his hand.

"What then?"

"If the soldiers are still at the fort, that means they won't join the fight," Natani said. "Or it might mean the settlers decided to pass by the fort and attack the village on their own."

"Would they do that?"

"Maybe," Natani said. "The soldiers are supposed to keep the peace. If the settlers make them choose sides, it would be awkward. Besides, there's enough of them they don't really need the army."

"The soldiers might force a peace settlement on them," Ned observed. "That ain't what they want."

"I know a place above the fort," Natani said. "We can see everything we need to see. There're always four canons at the fort. If any of those are gone, it means the soldiers have taken them north."

They followed the river trail for several miles before Natani changed course and followed an almost invisible trail through heavy woodlands and sloshy wetlands. They forded three small streams, stopping at the last to eat some dried meat and allow the horses to rest and drink.

By late morning, they were near the fort. Ned glimpsed the wooden stockade through thick foliage once as they circled to the northwest. Finally, Natani called a halt. They tied the horses to a branch at the bottom of a small hill, then kept low as they crept to the top where a small, rocky ledge provided a clear view of the fort not more than two hundred yards in the distance.

A few soldiers milled around the grounds inside the stockade. Two men, one on the north side and the other on the west side, paced back and forth along a walkway at the top of the wooden rampart enclosing the fort. Inside the ten-foot tall barrier, six large buildings were situated near the walls on the north, east, and west. The interior space included four smaller buildings and a large parade ground. Four canons were parked near the center of the parade ground. A half dozen horses stood in a small paddock behind a barn on one side of the central drill field. If the stockade held fifty soldiers, most of them would have to walk if they intended to move against the Mohawk village.

The placement of the canons puzzled Ned. From that position, they could only be fired at high angles in order to get over the fortress walls. But he noted platforms at each corner of the rampart that were wider than the walkway. Those would be where they would place the guns if Indians threatened the fort. But he wondered how long it would take to move them into place.

"The canons are still there," Natani said.

"That means they aren't going with the farmers?

"I think so," Natani said, "but let's watch a while longer. I want to see how many men are in the fort."

A short time later, two soldiers relieved the two sentries on the ramparts. The newcomers shouted back and forth to each other and to other men on the ground below, apparently a continuation of some game or argument from before their duty began. In any event, they paid little attention to the terrain surrounding the fortress.

Once, an officer appeared on the parapet and scanned the surrounding forests with a long spyglass. Ned and Natani ducked low as the telescope passed their position. The officer lowered his spyglass and nodded to the nearest sentry, satisfied there was no immediate threat to the stockade.

A short time after the sun had passed its zenith, a soldier emerged from one building and clanged a metal bar against a large bell near its entrance.

"I counted forty-two go into the mess hall," Ned told Natani.

"Good," Natani nodded. "There are probably a few more who were already inside or busy doing something."

"These guys don't look like they know anything about a bunch of farmers planning to raid a Mohawk village not far away," Ned said.

"That means the farmers went around the fort," Natani said.

"What now?"

"We ride as fast as we can," Natani said, "and hope we can get to Odonida before they do."

They rode away from Fort Saratoga knowing that time was against them. Most of the farmers were walking, but they had more than two days lead on Natani and Ned.

Chapter 34

August 16, 1787
Lake Champlain, New York

Susannah added corn, onions, and carrots to the big metal pot while Tabita continued to stir with a long, curved stick. The stew, which was over the main fire in the longhouse all the time, included rabbit, turkey, and venison meats together with the vegetables and was spiced with dried peppers and salt. A member of the clan — or the community — might feel hunger at any time and would expect the stew to be ready. It always was ready.

When Ned left for Kingston to send his letter to John Oliver, Susannah had moved back into their room in Tabita's clan house. When he returned, they would take their place as members of the clan. Ned would learn to hunt and fish with the men. She would master keeping the longhouse tidy, cooking whatever the hunters found, and, she hoped, raising their children.

She couldn't contain a giggle at the thought of Ned Foster learning to hunt with a bow and arrow. Fortunately, they wouldn't have to rely solely on Ned's bounty.

"What are you thinking?" Tabita asked, noticing her smile.

"Thinkin' 'bout how much ever'thing done changed." Susannah answered.

"You were a slave; now you're a Mohawk."

"I want to be Mohawk," Susannah said. "Mohawks is free."

"It's not always easy being a Mohawk," Tabita said. "This is our land, but they might not let us keep it. That's not really freedom."

"Well, it ain't slavery," Susannah said. "Dat's all I need right now."

Both women's heads turned toward the front of the longhouse at the crackle of a musket firing somewhere nearby. Seconds later, several more shots rang out. Shouts arose from outside the longhouse. Tabita grabbed her arm and drug Susannah toward the longhouse entrance.

Outside, the village was a swarm of confused men, women, dogs, and children, "Somebody is attacking the village," Tabita said.

"Other Indians?" Susannah asked.

"White people," Tabita speculated.

"Why dey attackin'?"

"I don't know."

Finally, Odonida appeared from the north end of the village and a semblance of order took over the chaos of the camp. He quickly assembled a group of a dozen men and boys and led them toward the south end of the encampment where the shots had come from.

"Most of the warriors are out hunting," Tabita said on seeing the small party of defenders.

"Ned and Natani ain't here either," Susannah said.

"This way," Tabita said, leading Susannah toward a group of women gathering in front of Osieta's longhouse.

As they joined the group, Osieta appeared from inside the longhouse and began speaking. Susannah still understood very little of the Iroquois language, but Tabita translated as soon as Osieta finished.

"Osieta says a group of white men is attacking the village from the south. There are only a few of them now, but two hunters came back to camp saying there is a much larger group coming behind them."

"What we gon' do?" Susannah asked.

"Odonida can stop them for a while," Tabita said. "But even if all the warriors were here, they probably couldn't stop a big bunch of white men with guns. The women and children will leave to the north. The men will follow when they can."

"We got to wait for Ned and Natani," Susannah insisted.

"Odonida won't be able to hold them back once the other bunch gets here," Tabita said. "Natani will know what happened and will come north to look for us."

The musket fire slowed noticeably, and Susannah looked in that direction, hoping maybe Odonida had turned back the attackers. Tabita must have guessed what she was thinking.

"It's just the start of it," she said. "There's more men coming and some of 'em might go around to the north and we'd be stuck here."

They rushed to the longhouse and gathered a few possessions for the trip, then joined a group of women and children gathered near the northern most longhouse in the village. There were about three dozen women, including several of the elders, and two dozen children. Boys who were old enough to have mastered the bow and arrow had joined Odonida in the fight, so most of the children were girls.

Osieta and the other elder women gathered and conferred for several minutes before Osieta communicated their decisions to the others. She pointed to Tabita with specific instructions.

Susannah looked at Tabita who nodded ascent to Osieta before relaying the instructions to her.

"Osieta and the other elders will take three of the canoes up the lake and cross into Canada," she explained. "The rest of us will leave on foot and make for the border."

Susannah knew there were several more canoes, but not enough for everyone. Then, Tabita explained. "We are leaving the rest of the canoes so some of the men can escape once we're safely away. The elders will negotiate safe passage with the bands in Canada."

As the three canoes drifted into the lake, the elders started smooth strokes with their short wooden paddles, quickly adding speed. They turned to the north, moving fast toward Quebec. Meanwhile, Tabita organized the women and children and began their march along the western shore of the big lake. She selected two young girls, perhaps fifteen or sixteen, to run ahead of the group to watch for the white invaders. Two other teenage girls took charge of Tabita's two little boys, so she was free to lead the caravan.

They moved quickly and silently, sticking to the main trail near the lake. The pops from the muskets soon resumed, more intense than before. Susannah looked back toward the village, but the thick forest blocked her view. Tabita heard the guns as well but didn't look. Her task was to lead them forward, not back.

A mile north of the village, Tabita halted the procession when the young scouts she'd sent ahead returned to the group. Susannah looked back to the village again. This time, a large column of smoke rose from the site. At least one longhouse was burning. No doubt the others would soon be burning as well.

The young girls spoke animatedly to Tabita, who raised a hand to slow them down. Finally, one girl breathing slowed enough to speak clearly, and when she finished, Tabita spoke to the whole group in a quiet but steady voice.

"What's happened?" Susannah asked after her speech.

"There are white men coming this way from the west," she said calmly.

"We trapped," Susannah sighed.

"No, we're not," Tabita said. "There's good cover in these woods. We'll lay quiet until they pass."

Tabita led them to a place in the woods where large maple and hickory trees created deep shadows around them. There, a rock outcropping created an indentation deep enough for the entire party to hide out of view from the trail. They didn't need instructions from Tabita to be quiet. There were over fifty people, including children, and many dogs, yet, there was no sound except the wind rustling the leaves in the trees overhead.

Only a few minutes passed before Tabita made hand signals for everyone to crouch even lower. The men were on the trail just below their position in the woods. Susannah slowed her breathing, listening to the crunch of twigs under the men's feet. She fought the urge to lift her head to see how many there were.

The sound stopped. Then one of the men spoke in a low voice.

"You boys be quiet now," he said. *"And watch out. If them Injuns run for it, they might come this way."*

Susannah held her breath. The men couldn't be more than twenty yards away. She pressed herself to the ground along with the others, all waiting for the sound of the men moving on. Then she froze with terror as a brown and white dog raised its head, ears perked, listening to a dog barking in the village a mile away. The dog gave a low snort of a bark and started to stand. A woman next to it wrapped a blanket over the animal and pulled it to the ground.

"What was that?" one of the white men said.
"I don't know," the leader said.
"Came from these woods," another man said.

Tabita pulled a long, bone knife from her waistband and lay on her elbows, knees bent, ready to spring. Other women in the group took the cue and also drew their knives.

"Look yonder," one man shouted.

"They getting' away in them boats," another man said.

"Let's get goin' or we'll miss all the fun," the leader said.

The men started moving toward the village again, this time they were walking fast, no longer concerned by the sounds of the woods. Tabita raised her head above the rock outcropping and stared toward where they had been. She stood up and brushed the twigs from her deerskin dress, then motioned for everyone to get moving again.

"We go now," Tabita said to Susannah.

Susannah just nodded. Through a gap in the trees she saw several canoes cruising north on the lake.

*****

The crack of a musket firing nearby caused Natani to pull his mount to a sudden stop. Ned almost collided with the animal before he could get his mare to stop. Both men leaped off their horses and pulled them into the shelter of trees next to the trail.

"Is somebody shooting at us?" Ned asked.

"I don't know," Natani said.

They kneeled beside the horses, listening as

more shots rang out. Ned crouched deeper, expecting musket balls to crash into the surrounding trees. But wherever the shooters were, Ned and Natani were not their target. Not yet, anyway.

Natani raised up a little and motioned for Ned to follow him. They led the horses to a spot about twenty yards into the woods and tied them to a small tree. Still crouched, they moved slowly through the woods, keeping the trail a few yards to their right. The going was rough in places as they pushed their way through dense underbrush. The boom of the muskets was closer now. The voices of white men came through the forest, too. Natani lowered himself to all-fours and crawled toward the sound with Ned close behind, their pistols loaded and ready.

Natani stopped next to a big maple tree and motioned Ned to a spot behind another maple. They peered around the trees and counted six white men hiding behind rocks and trees and staring into the woods left of the trail. One of the men was injured, propped against a tree with a Mohawk arrow still stuck in his right shoulder.

"Keep 'em penned down fellas," the leader instructed. "Two fire, two reload."

The man who gave the instructions to the others was leaning over the injured man. He twisted the arrow in the man's shoulder, causing a loud grown but not dislodging the projectile. The other men apparently understood the command as two of them fired their muskets toward a point in the woods while the other two reloaded. Then, they switched positions. A long rifle lay propped against a rock.

They watched the sequence twice. Natani timed the changeover, counting to twenty-five between when a musket fired and when it was ready to fire again.

Natani gripped his single shot pistol against the side of the tree and laid his shot and powder bag next to its base. Twenty yards was a tricky shot with a muzzle-loading pistol.

"You take the captain," Natani whispered.

Ned nodded. He had fired the pistol many times and knew his skill at this distance was limited. Also, he had never had to reload the weapon under pressure.

The two muskets boomed and as the two shooters dropped to their knees to reload, the other two rose and positioned for their next shot.

"Now," Natani said.

They raised their pistols simultaneously. Natani's shot caught the nearest of the standing riflemen in the left hip. As he grabbed for the hip, his musket discharged wildly into the air. Ned pulled the trigger of his pistol and watched a chunk of the tree behind the wounded man fly away. He'd missed, but none of the men had seen where the shots came from.

The leader crouched down, reaching blindly for his long gun while scanning the nearby forest looking for any movement or smoke. The uninjured shooter held his fire as he scanned the area. The two men who were reloading sprawled to the ground and tried to finish loading while flat on their bellies.

Natani finished his reload first and fired again, his ball glancing off a rock by the wounded gunman. This time, the smoke from his pistol hung in the air too long. As Ned leaned around the tree to fire his pistol again, two musket shots rang out. One ball crashed into the tree just above his head.

Ned ducked behind the tree and waited, expecting two more shots before they would all be reloading. When one more musket fired, Ned realized he hadn't heard the long rifle. There was a good chance that deadly rifle was aimed and waiting for a head to show from behind the trees.

He looked at Natani who had just finished reloading and was getting ready to take another shot. "Wait," Ned said.

Natani paused. Ned crouched low and leaped from behind the massive maple. When he hit the ground, he rolled to his right behind a smaller tree. He expected the loud report of the rifle to ring out, but it didn't. He came to his knees ready to shoot and saw why the man hadn't fired the rifle. A Mohawk arrow protruded from his throat, blood pumping out around it.

Ned steadied his hand and fired the pistol. This time his aim was true. The leader crashed to the ground, the long rifle clattering against the rocks. Natani held his fire as another of the arrows caught one of the other men in the chest. The three uninjured men looked at each other, threw down their weapons and ran down the trail as fast as they could.

Three Mohawk warriors emerged from the trees to their left and met Natani and Ned where the three attackers lay in the grass. Two were dead already. The third writhed on the ground from the wound to his hip until a Mohawk ax came down on his throat. Blood gushed from the gaping wound, then slowed as the heart stopped pumping. Ned wondered if he should feel disgust at the act, but he didn't. He had no idea what his new wife's fate at the hands of these men might be.

Natani, who had spoken at length with one of the warriors approached Ned. "They were out hunting," he explained. "They heard the muskets and smelled smoke from the village. They were on their way there when they ran into these guys."

"We've got to get to the village," Ned said.

"You wait here," Natani said. "I'll go get the horses."

Chapter 35

August 17, 1787
Philadelphia, Pennsylvania

Sara shifted her weight again but still she couldn't get comfortable in the plain wooden chair. Maybe it was the petticoats. She hadn't worn three petticoats under a dress in months. Now, she wondered why she'd done so today. But the notion of sitting in front of the Chief Magistrate of Philadelphia had made her quite nervous and the extra petticoats provided a sense of armament against the questions to come.

Yet, any sense of safety had vanished as soon as she entered the courtroom. Not ten feet away, Hugh Marlow was leering at her, a crooked smile turned up on one end and down on the other. Once, she tried to return his stare, but her resolve lasted only a few seconds before it melted into fear.

John Oliver had convinced her there was little chance the magistrate would side with Marlow's claim that she and Oliver had conspired to help Susannah run away. It was true that Oliver hadn't been part of the scheme, but she had, and he knew it. Still, without evidence from Susannah herself or Ned Foster, it would be nearly impossible to prove anyone else was in on it. There was also the fact that most Pennsylvanians detested slavery and the magistrate would probably be no exception.

The money Hugh Marlow demanded as compensation for enticing Susannah to run away from her horrid situation didn't bother Sara at that moment. Marlow's threat to investigate her life before she got to Philadelphia had the potential to ruin, or even end, her life. She glanced again at Marlow. He reminded her of the monster she murdered in Dublin those eight years earlier.

When she told Oliver what happened in Ireland and why she feared an investigation, he understood her fear. While the United States didn't have an extradition treaty with England at that time, Sara knew Lord Carlisle wouldn't feel bound by treaties anyway. A man like Hugh Marlow wouldn't worry about kidnapping her and taking her to Canada where she would face English justice.

She looked at Oliver. Despite everything she had told him, he still wanted to marry her. She wanted it too. She would sell Sullivan house and move to Connecticut with him. As long as she could stay out of Lord Carlisle's reach, she could have the family she dreamed of.

The magistrate, Gulliver Penn — a distant relative of the famous Penn family — directed Hugh Marlow to explain to him the basis of his claim. Marlow, who appeared without a lawyer, rose and spoke to the judge.

"Your honor, I came to Philadelphia in May of this year as a representative of South Carolina to the convention that is discussing modifications to the Articles of Confederation."

"Modifications?" Penn questioned. "The talk of this town is they intend to create a new nation."

"We assembled for the purpose of modification, sir," Marlow assured him. The fact that the judge knew of the direction the convention had taken despite their efforts to keep it secret was no surprise. Many of the delegates, for all their good intentions, couldn't resist the urge to expound their opinions to almost anyone who would listen.

"Go on then," the magistrate said. "We aren't here to discuss the convention."

"Yes sir," Marlow began. "When I arrived in this city, others had made arrangements for myself and the two slaves who accompanied me to live at Sullivan House, the establishment that Mrs. Sullivan operates. Mr. Oliver was also a guest at Sullivan House."

Marlow paused and stared at Oliver for a moment before continuing. "Mr. Oliver had a servant named Ned Foster, who stayed in a regular room, not the servant's quarters. In time, Ned Foster, with the aid of Mr. Oliver and Mrs. Sullivan, enticed one of my slaves, a girl named Susannah, to run away."

"Mr. Marlow," Magistrate Penn began, "it is my understanding that slaves don't particularly enjoy being slaves and they run away sometimes with no need for enticement."

"Susannah was happy with her situation," Marlow insisted, "until Ned Foster put ideas in her head."

"I wonder if Susannah would agree with that statement," the magistrate mused.

"It doesn't matter if she'd agree," Marlow shot back. "She is my property."

The judge turned to John Oliver. "Where is Mr. Foster now?" he asked.

"Mr. Foster has left the city, your honor," Oliver said.

"Is he with Susannah?" Penn asked.

"I believe he is," Oliver conceded.

"Is Ned Foster a slave also?"

"No sir," Oliver said. "Mr. Foster is a free black man."

The magistrate turned back to Marlow. "I concede there is a possibility that Mr. Ned Foster assisted your slave in her escape," he stated. "But I don't see any reason to assume that Mr. Oliver and

Mrs. Sullivan assisted in any way."

"Foster and Susannah had horses and money, your honor," Marlow offered. "The horses belonged to Mr. Oliver, and the money came from Mrs. Sullivan."

"Is that true, Mr. Oliver?" Magistrate Penn asked.

"No, your honor," Oliver said. "The horse and mule were Mr. Foster's property. Mr. Foster was in my employ for many years. I paid him a fair wage — in Spanish coin — plus room and board. He would have accumulated a fair amount of money over those years."

Relief swept through Sara because the magistrate hadn't asked her the question. She had given a small sack of coins to Ned Foster. She had also given money to Hennie to arrange their travel with the Quakers. If he had asked, she would have lied, but, so far, it hadn't come to that.

Judge Penn rested his left elbow on the desk in front of him and supported his chin in the palm of his hand while he stared at Hugh Marlow. "Mr. Marlow, do you have any other evidence that would show how Mr. Oliver or Mrs. Sullivan might have assisted Susannah in her escape."

"Yes, your honor," Marlow began. "My other slave is a man named Simon. Simon was supposed to keep an eye on Susannah, but he fell asleep at odd times. Simon believes Mrs. Sullivan put something in his tea to make him sleep. Also, both

Mr. Oliver and Mrs. Sullivan expressed their disapproval of slavery."

The magistrate smiled and sat straight up. "According to your earlier statement, Miss Susannah was happy with her situation," Judge Penn observed. "Now you tell me you had her watched constantly out of fear she would run away. Which was it, Mr. Marlow?"

"It was her first time away from Hallow Hill," Marlow explained. "She saw free niggers and white people who didn't hold with slavery. I thought she might get ideas."

"The facts suggest that she did get ideas," the judge said. "Most folks in this part of the country disapprove of slavery, Mr. Marlow; myself included. But disapproval does not constitute assistance to Miss Susannah. Moreover, you've not provided any evidence except your own speculation as to events, or Simon's speculation."

Marlow's face reddened more with every word from Judge Penn, but he said nothing.

"I see no reason to continue this action in any form," Penn continued. "Your claim has no basis under the laws of Pennsylvania, Mr. Marlow."

"My claim would be good in South Carolina," Marlow spat out, his face now glowing red.

"This isn't South Carolina," the judge pointed out. "However, you still may pursue the recapture of Susannah and Ned Foster. That is the only remedy available to you for your loss," Penn added.

Marlow regained control of his emotions before he spoke again. "Your honor, I have already tried to recapture the girl," he stated, "but Indians killed the slave hunter I employed."

"Where did this happen?"

"In New York, sir. Near Albany."

"The State of New York may have some interest in that," the judge observed. "As far as Pennsylvania is concerned, this matter is closed."

The judge stood up, confirming the end of the proceedings. Hugh Marlow huffed to the door to escape as soon as the constable who'd stood quietly at the back of the room, opened the way to the outside. He never turned to look at them, but Sara was sure he was already scheming his next move.

"That went well," Oliver commented as they stepped out into the morning sunshine.

"If possible, Marlow is angrier than before," Sara observed.

*****

Lake Champlain, New York

The sight that lay before him shocked Ned Foster. Piles of still smoldering rubble was all that remained of the majestic longhouses that had been the Mohawk village. They approached the smoldering ruins slowly, fearing the white farmers might still occupy the ruins. But after circling the desolated site, they determined that the attackers had disappeared, probably returned to their farms to await the land rush that would come.

"Why do you suppose they just left it?" Ned asked.

"They don't want to be around when the soldiers find out what happened," Natani explained.

"I thought they wanted the land?"

"They'll get the land anyway," Natani said. "The Mohawk have abandoned this place. After a few weeks, the state will stop asking questions and make the land available for settlers."

Near the southern edge of the village, they discovered a dozen dead Mohawk, including the chief, Odonida, and one of the young twins who had first greeted Ned and Susannah. They searched the rest of the village but found no evidence of the women and children. All the village canoes were gone as well.

"The rest have gone north," Natani said.

"Will they be all right?" Ned asked.

"The farmers got what they came for," Natani observed. "I don't think they would've chased after the women and children."

Natani must have heard Ned's long sigh of relief. "That doesn't mean they are out of danger," he pointed out. "They will have to find their place among the tribes in Canada."

Ned looked back at the destroyed village. "We

need to be on our way to find them," he said.

"We leave in the morning," Natani said.

Chapter 36

August 22, 1787
Pennsylvania Statehouse

For three months, the convention had steadfastly avoided head-on conflict over the matter of slavery. The practice was nominally legal in every state except Massachusetts, though Pennsylvania and Connecticut had adopted laws that eliminated the practice over a period of years. But, in fact, slavery was rare in most of the Northern states. In seven or eight of the states, public support for the elimination of slavery was overwhelming. Yet the delegates would not take on the issue. Instead, they suggested limiting or taxing the importation of slaves. To placate the Southern states, the Committee on Detail report had specifically excluded slaves from an import tax and made no suggestion as to ending their importation.

To Oliver, this was objectionable on both moral and economic grounds as the importation of raw materials and equipment for Northern manufacturers would be taxed but the machinery of the plantations would not. He was disappointed that members of his own Connecticut delegation were willing to go along with the scheme.

Roger Sherman of Connecticut was speaking. "I object to the slave trade," he said. "Yet the states now possess the right to import slaves and I see no public good to be attained by taking it from them."

Somewhere in the room a voice shouted agreement. Sherman continued, "The abolition of slavery seems to be happening in the states anyway, and, in time, will surely be completed. It is expedient now that we have as few objections to this new government as possible and thus complete our business."

Colonel Mason of Virginia took the floor. "Maryland and Virginia have already prohibited the importation of slaves," he began. "North Carolina has done the same in substance. All that will be in vain if South Carolina and Georgia are at liberty to import. The Western people are now calling out for slaves for their new lands and they will get them through South Carolina and Georgia."

Mason continued, "Slavery discourages arts and manufacturers. The poor don't want to do labor they believe to be slave work, and they discourage the immigration of white people who really enrich and strengthen a country. The practice produces the most pernicious effect on manners as every master of slaves is a petty tyrant."

Once again, Colonel Mason was a puzzle to Oliver. Often, his words suggested strong opposition to slavery, but, at the same time, he was one of the largest slave holders in all the states. He wondered if Mason considered his own manners pernicious and himself a tyrant.

Oliver Ellsworth spoke next. "I have never owned a slave and thus cannot judge its effect on character," he said. "However, if we are to consider it in a moral light, we ought to go further and free those already in the country. But we should not meddle with the rights of those states that must import slaves to meet their need. As our population increases, poor laborers will be so plentiful as to render slaves useless. As to the danger of insurrection from foreign influence, that will be a motive for kind treatment of the slaves."

"If slavery be wrong, it is justified by the example of all the world," Governor Pinckney of South Carolina said. "France, England, Holland, and all the other modern states give it sanction directly or by trade."

General Pinckney, also of South Carolina, added the suggestion that importation of slaves was an economic benefit to the nation as a whole since it increased production, shipping, consumption, and revenue for the treasury. He conceded the fairness of taxing the importation of slaves just as other imports but suggested that South Carolina would not join the union if they proposed imposing such a tax.

James Wilson of Pennsylvania believed that exempting importation of slaves from tax while taxing all other imports effectively gave sanction to the practice. Elbridge Gerry of Massachusetts echoed that sentiment.

John Dickenson of Delaware offered the strongest rebuke yet. "It is inadmissible on every principle of honor and safety that the importation of slaves should be authorized to the states by the constitution," he said. "The true question is whether the national happiness will be promoted or impeded by the importation, and this question ought to be left to the national government, not to the states particularly interested." He went on to describe how England and France permitted slaves in their colonies but banned them in their homeland. "Greece and Rome were made unhappy by their slaves," he added.

"It is wrong to force anything down that isn't absolutely necessary," Hugh Williamson of North Carolina said.

"If two or three states will not agree to the constitution if it limits or taxes importation of slaves, there is at least an equal number that will not agree to the exemption," Rufus King of Massachusetts said. "As they tax every other import, it is an inequality that cannot fail to strike at the commercial interests of the Northern and middle states."

"Only the general government should have the power to set taxes or to exempt taxes," John Langdon of New Hampshire insisted.

"Candidly, I do not believe South Carolina will stop importation of slaves any time soon but will stop it occasionally as it has done in the past," General Pinckney stated. "However, I move that we have a committee study the notion that importation of slaves might be made liable to an equal tax with other imports. I believe that to be fair, and it will remove one difficulty that has been started."

"It is in vain to believe that North Carolina, South Carolina, and Georgia will agree to any plan unless their right to import slaves is untouched," John Rutledge of South Carolina said. "However, I second General Pinckney's motion."

"Perhaps the committee can find a sensible answer," Governor Randolph interjected. "I could not support the clause as written," he added. "It would revolt the Quakers, the Methodists, and many others in the states having no slaves. On the other hand, two states might be lost to the union. Let us then give the committee a chance to find a middle ground."

They appointed a committee of eleven delegates to study the matter and propose a solution. The composition of the committee — only two men from South Carolina or Georgia — encouraged John Oliver to believe they would propose something better than the original clause.

For the remainder of the day, the session dealt with more mundane issues such as ex-post-facto laws and bills of attainder. Oliver was relieved when the gavel finally sounded adjournment for the day. Escaping the company of these gentlemen in favor of the company of the lovely Sara Sullivan was the only thing on his mind now.

*****

Sara placed a loaf of bread in her basket and tucked a white muslin cloth around the edges. The baker smiled when he saw the Spanish coin she offered in payment. "Thank you, Mrs. Sullivan," he said as she walked out the door onto Market Street.

She walked along the shady side of Market Street where shadows of the buildings on the west side of the street stretched all the way across the wide street in the late afternoon. At Fourth Street, Market turned into a divided boulevard with a wide median of trees, shrubs, flowers, and patches of grass. The park was a point of pride in Philadelphia, but at the end of a long, dry summer, the grass was brown, and the flowers were well past their blooming. In a few weeks, temperatures would cool, and the leaves of the oaks and maples would show their colors before they vanished for winter.

She paused a moment, reflecting on the first time she'd seen the park. The coloring of the leaves had barely begun on that late September morning, offering only a hint of the reds and yellows that would appear over the next several weeks.

Sara had seen nothing quite like Philadelphia. Everything seemed new; beautiful in some places, and incredibly rustic in other places. There was wealth, but without the majesty of European wealth. There was poverty, but without the desperation of European poverty. Every person — at least every white person — envisioned finding a prosperous place in this new society.

Just as she started to walk on toward Third Street, she noticed a movement in the park. A man who'd been leaning against an oak tree moved out of the deep shadow and into a narrow strip of sunlight. A wide brim hat cast a shadow over his face, but still there was something familiar about him.

Sara's heart suddenly pounded faster. She froze where she stood, staring at the man thirty yards away from her. Philadelphia was a major seaport, so it was not unusual to see strange men about the town. A woman alone at night could be in danger from such men, but in broad daylight, there was little to fear. Still, a chill shivered down her spine. She couldn't see his eyes, but she knew he was watching her. And there was that something familiar. Maybe he wasn't a sailor.

After losing his claim before the magistrate, she knew Hugh Marlow would be even angrier than before. He blamed her and John because Susannah had run away with Ned Foster. She tried to calm herself. The man in the park could simply be resting there during a long day. On the other hand, he might be another of Marlow's hired henchmen.

Sara walked again toward Third Street, slower this time. She glanced back several times. The man was moving at the same pace as her, still only a few yards away in the park. Instead of turning left to Sullivan House as she usually did after crossing Third Street, Sara walked on to a tea shop a few doors farther on. She knew there was plenty of tea in the cupboard at Sullivan House, but she bought a wooden box of black tea anyway.

She paid the shopkeeper and left. The man had once again leaned against a tree in the park. Obviously, he had made no attempt to disguise the fact that he was following her. She supposed that was the point. The man intended to frighten her and it was working.

After walking fast to the corner of Market and Third Street, she turned right toward Sullivan House halfway down the block. She didn't look back until she reached the gate in front of her house where she quickly glanced back. The man stood still, staring at her from a short distance behind. Part of his face was visible now, darkly tanned and adorned with a thin, curly beard.

Sara rushed through the gate and into the front entrance of the big house. She closed the door forcefully and slid the bolt into place. Then she turned and saw John Oliver watching her from his favorite chair in the parlor.

"What's wrong?" Oliver asked her.

"There's a man following me," she said.

Oliver walked to the window and saw a man leaning against a gas lamp post on the opposite side of the street. Without a word he walked to the door, unbolted it and stepped outside. Sara peeked through the window to watch, but as soon as Oliver appeared on the porch, the man casually walked back toward Market Street.

"He's gone," Oliver said when he came back inside.

"He meant to frighten me," Sara said. "I think Hugh Marlow sent him."

"Hugh Marlow doesn't take well to losing," Oliver observed.

Chapter 37

August 23, 1787
Southern Quebec

Susannah's feet ached from days of trudging through woodlands and wetlands between the village on Lake Champlain and the great river that lay before her now. They had camped on a hillock overlooking the river. In the early morning light, she observed a little town in the low-lying land on the other side, smoke rising from its many chimneys.

When Tabita had told her they'd crossed the border into Canada, Susannah looked around in surprise. Nothing looked different. Nothing obviously delineated Canada from New York but Tabita assured her it was different. At least for now, the British authorities were tolerant of the Iroquois tribes, which had occupied the area for centuries. The French, who had nominally possessed Quebec since the early 17th century, made alliances with the indigenous people. The British, who took control of Quebec in 1763, didn't want to make new enemies of the tribes who vastly outnumbered white settlers.

A few hours after they crossed the border, a troop of British soldiers stopped them. They questioned Tabita about where they came from and where they intended to go. When Tabita explained what happened at Lake Champlain, the soldiers offered to escort them to the river, which they called the St. Lawrence River, where they believed Osieta was conferring with other elders.

So, Tabita's troop of women and children made their way to the river with an escort of a dozen British redcoats. At first, Susannah worried that the soldiers might take notice of a young woman who looked different from the others, but, if they noticed, none of them said anything. When they reached the river, they found Osieta's camp in hours. The redcoats waved and went on their way.

It was late on the previous day when Tabita's caravan met up with Osieta and the warriors who had escaped the Lake Champlain village. They received the sad news of Odonida's death and that of Osieta's grandson. Osieta had no news of the hunting parties who had been away from the village during the attack, nor did they know what might have become of Natani and Ned Foster.

Osieta got permission from a council of

matriarchal leaders of the region to establish a village on the south side of the river about ten miles to the east of Montreal. She and the rest of the female elders would select a new warrior chief from the remaining men.

"What's happened to Ned and Natani?" Susannah asked Tabita. The other woman must be as worried as she but gave little indication of it.

"They will find us if they didn't get caught by those men," Tabita said.

The casualness with which she said this startled Susannah. "You think dey might've got caught?" She had refused to consider that possibility up until now.

"No," Tabita answered quickly. "Natani knows the woods a lot better than they do."

"Dey was a lot of them men," Susannah pointed out.

"Yeah," Tabita acknowledged.

*****

Philadelphia, Pennsylvania

Sara Sullivan took a sip of the hot tea and sat her cup down on the little table next to her settee. Again, she studied the envelope on the table. She recognized the pale gray paper of the stationary set she had packed in Ned Foster's saddlebag. Hennie handed the letter to her an hour earlier, having retrieved it from the post office on Market Street. It was addressed to John Oliver at Sullivan House and she was sure it came from Ned.

Her first instinct was to rip open the envelope and learn what had become of Ned and Susannah, but she didn't do that. Despite their intimate relationship, Oliver was a guest of Sullivan House and she would never invade the privacy of a guest in such a manner. He would be home soon, and they could open the envelope together.

She took another sip of the tea and folded her bare feet underneath her. They had talked of marriage and she longed to have that dream come true. But there were obstacles to their union that would make marriage difficult and maybe dangerous. She could never disclose her true identity so any marriage documents would by necessity include some falsehoods. Also, Oliver's marriage to Rebecca Black was a problem. A judge in England had declared that marriage voided but the declaration might be meaningless in Pennsylvania or Connecticut.

Pennsylvania or Connecticut? That was another question. She had built a life as a successful businesswoman in Philadelphia and Oliver was a prosperous farmer and lawyer in Hartford. She supposed it would be easier for her to sell Sullivan House and move on than it would be for Oliver to leave his lifelong roots in Connecticut. In fact, Mr. Martin had suggested that she sell the house to him, so he could move his wife and family to where his new trading business was flourishing.

She heard the front gate open and close and hurried to the window to be sure it was John Oliver and not the man who had stalked her. She saw Oliver and rushed to the door to unbolt it.

He looked tired when he folded her into his arms and kissed her. When they parted Sara said, "A letter came for you. I'm sure it's from Ned."

John Oliver popped the wax seal from the letter and read silently. Halfway through the first page, he smiled. "They've married," he said.

"How could they do that?" Sara asked.

"They were married by a Mohawk chief," Oliver told her.

"Mohawk?"

"The Mohawk are one of the five tribes of the Iroquois Confederation," he explained.

"Is that legal?"

"Good question," Oliver said, as he continued reading.

Finally, he folded the paper and tapped it against his hand. "Ned suggested a very good solution," he said.

"What solution?" Sara asked.

"He suggests getting a judge in Connecticut to declare the marriage legal," Oliver began. "That would make Susannah a citizen of Connecticut. Slave hunters wouldn't be able to take her out of the state."

"That would be wonderful," Sara said.

"Well, that's the theory anyway," Oliver said. "Slave hunters aren't really a law-abiding bunch."

"Will the judge do it?"

"I know one who will," Oliver said. "He's my cousin."

*****

Southern Quebec

Natani delayed leaving the village site while he sent warriors out to look for others who had been away hunting. While the others were gone, he and Ned built a large funeral pyre and moved the bodies of all the dead Mohawks to it. When the others returned, they would send their fellow warriors to the Great Spirit.

He doubted the farmers would return while they stayed at the village. They would go back to their farms and wait for news of the raid, pretending ignorance of the attack. But Natani wanted to alert the soldiers at Fort Saratoga about what happened, so he sent a young warrior to the fort on horseback to inform the commanding officer.

Three days passed while they waited for the warriors to return. The odor of the dead grew stronger as each day passed, but Natani was determined to honor them in the best way he could.

Late on the third day, Natani counted fifteen

hunters who had returned with the scouts he'd dispatched. He gathered them all before the funeral pyre. He spoke passionately. Although Ned didn't understand the words, he could see how much Natani and the others respected the old chief.

While the pyre burned, dispatching the Mohawk souls to the great beyond, the young warrior who had gone to Fort Saratoga rode back into the remains of the village. He went immediately to Natani and spoke to him for several minutes.

"What did he say about the soldiers?" Ned asked after the young man left to pay his respects to the dead.

"The soldiers have decided to believe Odonida led the raid on the farm that started this," Natani said.

"That's not surprising I guess," Ned offered.

"No, it isn't," Natani sighed. "The commander also warned us to get out of here quickly. They will be escorting a party of surveyors around in a few days."

"We should go find our wives," Ned said.

Natani glanced at the funeral pyre where the flame was slowly dying away. "We shall leave this afternoon," he said.

They left before the fire was out and made it to the north end of the lake before camping for the night. The next day, they crossed the border into Canada and began looking for clues as the where the others might have gone. Natani and Ned had the only horses among them, so they elected to walk along beside the animals.

Near midday, Natani halted the march and pointed to a column of British redcoats watching them from a ridge above the trail. Ned reckoned there were fewer of the redcoats than Natani's twenty-one warriors, but the redcoats had rifles and muskets and horses.

"What should we do?" Ned asked.

"I don't know," Natani said. "I think you and I should go up and talk to them."

Natani took a piece of white cloth from his saddlebag and waved it over his head. Then he began walking slowly toward the base of the hill, Ned a few steps behind. Two of the redcoats dismounted and walked down the hill to meet them.

"Greetings, captain," Natani said to the man in the most ornamental uniform.

"I'm Lieutenant Anderson," the officer responded, "not a captain."

"My apologies, sir," Natani offered.

"Your English is extraordinary," Anderson said. "Where did you learn it?"

"My father is half English," Natani told him.

"I see," Anderson said. "Do you mind telling me where you and your men are going?" His eyes shifted from Natani to Ned Foster and back to Natani.

Natani told him about the attack on his village

near Lake Champlain. "We are looking for the others who escaped," he added.

"I can help you with that," the lieutenant said. "We escorted a group of women and children up the river a few days ago. They camped just across the river from Montreal."

"Thank you, Lieutenant Anderson," Natani said. "We'll be on our way, then."

"All right," Anderson said. "But I would like to remind you it was New Yorkers that raided your village, not Canadians."

"I understand," Natani offered.

"One more thing," Anderson said with his eyes on Ned Foster. "Is this man a runaway?"

"He is a part of our tribe," Natani said.

"Yes, but is he a runaway?"

"I'm not a runaway, Lieutenant Anderson," Ned spoke for himself. "I am a free citizen of Connecticut. I have a paper in my bag."

"It doesn't matter," Anderson said. "I just want to know if I need to be watching out for slave hunters. They aren't supposed to come into Quebec, but sometimes they do."

"Are there any slaves in Quebec?" Ned Foster asked.

"I suppose it's still legal," Lieutenant Anderson said, "but I've never seen a slave in Canada."

"Thank you for that information, Lieutenant," Ned said.

"Safe travels, gentlemen," Anderson said. "And no trouble, please." The lieutenant and his companion turned to go back up the hill to his troop.

They reached the river early the next afternoon and followed its shore northward until the little town of Montreal came into view on the other side. They smelled the campsite before it came into their view as the scent of roasting venison drifted down the river valley. Natani's pace quickened as if the aroma drew he and his men to it.

*****

Susannah sat with her back against a large rock and studied the settlement on the other side of the river. Until a few months ago, she thought all white culture was like Charleston with its stately mansions along the battery, or like Hallow Hill with its massive white columned porches. Those things that hid the ugliness that lay behind them. Elegance and beauty for the masters. Ugliness and misery for everyone else.

Susannah wondered what those white people on the other side of the river were really like. Of one thing she was sure. This place looked nothing like South Carolina. She'd asked Tabita if those people had slaves.

"I don't know," Tabita had said. "I don't think so."

In her mind, Susannah had never imagined a

place where slavery didn't exist. Then, in Philadelphia, she'd seen free black people. They were desperately poor and lived among others who still were slaves. She wondered if such desperation was the price of freedom. Then she met Ned Foster, a man who had been educated by a British nobleman named Lord Black. A man named John Oliver had given Ned freedom. He carried himself with a bearing and confidence that made him respected, an equal to any. Now, all she could do was hope he would soon return to her.

A sudden burst of cheering and loud greetings interrupted her thoughts. Susannah jumped to her feet and sprinted toward the camp. She soon realized a whole group of men had come into the camp and the others were joyous to see them.

Susannah stopped at the edge of the crowd. There was only one man she was looking for. There he was. Her feet were running again. She threw herself into his arms.

Chapter 38

August 25, 1787
Pennsylvania Statehouse

The day before, a Friday, had dragged on-and-on through endless debate on matters of interest to no one except bankers and financiers. Despite occasional cups of strong tea, John Oliver found it difficult to keep his eyes open.

The day had begun on a promising note when the secretary read the report of the committee of eleven to the gathering.

Strike out so much of the 4th section of the 7th article as was referred to the Committee and insert, "The migration or importation of such persons as the several States now existing shall think proper to admit, shall not be prohibited by the Legislature prior to the year 1800 — but a Tax or Duty may be imposed on such migration or importation at a rate not exceeding the average of the Duties laid on Imports."

In essence, the committee suggested allowing the Southern states a few years to adjust to a new reality in which they could not import new slaves, assuming the legislature would enact such a prohibition once authorized to do so. But Oliver thought it a virtual certainty the legislature would do so given its mix of Northern states and Southern states such as Virginia, Maryland, and perhaps North Carolina that would not oppose the move. In the meantime, the import duty might serve as some deterrent against importation, or, at least, as an offset to the incentive created by the three-fifths compromise.

But the president deferred discussion of the report until Saturday so they could address other matters. Even today, disagreement over debt payments and maritime regulations had taken much of the morning, before they finally took up the committee report.

Gouverneur Morris spoke first. "The clause should be amended to read 'importation of slaves into North Carolina, South Carolina, and Georgia shall not be prohibited before 1800'. This would be most fair as it informs all that this part of the constitution was an accommodation to those states."

"I have no objection to using the term 'slaves',"

Colonel Mason stated, "but I do oppose naming the states, lest it give offense to those people."

"We should continue to use the description rather than the term 'slaves'," Roger Sherman of Connecticut said. "The old congress would not use the term since it was not pleasing to some and the same situation continues."

John Dickenson insisted the clause should be confined to those states which had not, of their own accord, prohibited the importation of slaves. In addition, he proposed that the prohibition against legislation be extended until 1808. After further discussion, they agreed to change the year to 1808, but not to name specific states. Still, the delegates declined to use the word "slave".

More controversy arose from the second part of the clause as well. Some delegates believed that setting a duty on importation of slaves was tantamount to declaring them as property and not as humans. Others feared the lack of a duty would encourage more importation. After much debate, they decided to set the duty at ten dollars per person imported.

Will anyone be happy with this? John Oliver thought. In twenty years, the legislature, in all probability, would enact a prohibition on further importation of human slaves. But it wouldn't mean an end to slavery. He doubted it would even mean an end to importation since there were already slave markets in the Western territories, where enforcement would be difficult. Still, he supposed it was a start.

The tax to be imposed was a pittance. It would do nothing to discourage the trade since the vast majority of people taken from Africa were destined for South America and the Caribbean where working conditions required a constant flow of new bodies. In theory, the United States would not contribute further to the problem after 1808, but he doubted it would prevent the colossal struggle he feared in his nation's future.

The convention had made its decision and Oliver doubted there would be any more discussions on the matter of slavery. In the quest to form a union, they had steadfastly avoided confronting the one issue that made a lasting union impossible. The cancer would continue to fester. South Carolina would not surrender its lust for slaves and Massachusetts would not quash its growing abhorrence of the practice.

He knew the convention would continue for some time. There still were many issues to be resolved and put into final form, including matters of great importance such as presidential impeachment and succession, or regulation of interstate commerce. There had been a fleeting discussion of including a 'bill of rights' in the document, but most of the delegates had insisted none was needed.

But John Oliver had come to the convention seeking a definitive plan for the elimination of slavery and there would be no such plan in the final document. He could not help but feel that his efforts had been wasted. Perhaps it was time to return to Connecticut.

*****

Sara was still hesitant about going out after the strange man had followed her home. But she had a business to run and Mr. Martin had just arrived to take up his room for the next several days. She needed to stock up on cheeses, ham, butter, and jams. She would need to get fresh bread every day, as well, and Mr. Martin liked his ale and an occasional mug of rum.

The afternoon was sunny and warm. As usual, Sara chose comfort over the customary fashion for ladies, which would have included sleeves to the wrists, gloves, and three or four petticoats. Instead, she wore a blue dress of light cotton with elbow-length sleeves, without gloves, and only one petticoat. Also, she didn't cover her hair with the broad-brimmed hats many ladies wore. Not only was she more comfortable, but she liked the tint the sun gave her arms and face.

She paused at the corner of Market Street and studied the people in both directions and across the street in the park. Satisfied that her stalker was not around, she turned right and started toward the cheese shop a short way along Market.

After only a few steps, her heartbeat suddenly raced as she heard heavy footsteps behind her. She resisted the urge to turn around and look. It must be someone else. She hadn't seen the man. Still, her pace quickened.

"Good aft'noon to ye, Sara Byrne," a voice came from behind her. She hadn't heard that voice in eight years, but there was no mistaking it.

She stopped, then turned slowly around, "Danny?"

"S'prised to be seein' yer dear old brother are ye girl?" the man said.

"What are you doing here?"

"Aye, a bit of a tale, that," Danny said. "I s'pose ye never expected to see the likes of me again."

"I figured you for dead by now," Sara said.

"Aye," Danny nodded, "and ye wasn't wrong by much."

"Well, I don't want anything to do with you so leave me be."

"Well now, ain't that a hurtful way to welcome family," Danny said.

"You're not welcome," Sara spat out.

"Aye," he nodded, "but we got a bit o' b'ness to converse, so I ain't leavin'."

"It was you followin' me t'other day, wasn't it?" Sara said, her old accent emerging in her anger.

"Like I say, we got b'ness to converse on, lass," Danny said. He nodded toward a bench in the park. "There looks like a good place to converse."

Sara looked up and down the street. She hoped for the comfort of a crowded boulevard but was disappointed. She could simply walk into the nearest shop and Danny wouldn't follow her. But he wouldn't go away, either. He knew what had happened in Dublin and there would be a price for his silence.

"All right," Sara said. She was already walking toward the park.

"Are ye a bit curious 'bout yer dear old family?" Danny asked once they were seated on the bench.

"Not really," Sara said. "But you're probably going to tell me anyway, so go ahead."

"Aye," Danny said. "Well, yer dear papa passed away some years ago. No s'prise that, I'm sure."

"No."

"Yer brother Steven's passed too," Danny said, "at the end o' the hangman's noose."

"No surprise," Sara said.

"Aye, no s'prise a'tall," Danny said. "Stevie was mean when the Bushmills took hold o'em. He got a bit too rough wi' a lass."

"She died?"

"Aye," Danny confirmed, staring down at her. "I s'pose ye could say murder runs in the family."

"How did you find me?" If Danny found her, it was possible for Lord Carlisle to find her as well.

"Aye," Danny said. "I s'pose t'was a fortunate encounter with a Porta'gee seaman. Ye see, when

Stevie's troubles happened, there was some question as to me own involvement in the matter. I laid low for a while 'round Dublin, but after they hung Stevie, I thought I best be movin' on."

"Is there a price on you?" Sara asked. Maybe he wasn't in such a good position to use the leverage he had on her.

"I s'pose there is," he mused. "Anyway, I signed on to a freighter headed 'round the Cape to India. Well, I tell ye, I din't care much for that passage. When I got back to Africa, I joined a slaver goin' to Cuba. That's where I run into the Porta'gee what told me 'bout transportin' an Irish gal to Philadelphia. Started me thinkin' how nice it'd be to find me dear sister."

"So here you are."

"Aye."

"I guess you want money," Sara said.

"Well, we bein' the only family remainin', and ye lookin' mighty prosp'rous, I think it a fair thing."

"What if I don't give you money?"

"Aye, well, theys others wantin' to find ye too. Lord Carlisle's offerin' a pile o' good British money for ye."

"Pennsylvania doesn't have an extradition treaty with England," Sara said, remembering what John Oliver had told her.

"Well, I don' know what all that means," Danny said. "But, Carlisle ain't the only one interested in

Sara Sullivan."

"Who else?"

"There's a gent right here askin' lots of questions 'bout the pretty Irish lady," he told her. "Name's Marlow."

"How much do you want?"

"I like this place," Danny said. "I think this'd be a good place to settle if I had a thousand in Spanish gold."

"All right," she said. "Meet me here Monday at noon."

"Day after tomorrow then," Danny said. He tipped his hat as he stood and walked away.

She remained on the bench for several minutes. She would pay Danny the money, but she doubted that would be the end of it. He would be back for more and he planned to stay close to her from now on. She was glad she had already told John Oliver the whole story. Danny would think she was alone with her plight, but she wasn't.

Chapter 39

August 27, 1787
Philadelphia, Pennsylvania

Sara rehearsed the story she would tell her agent while she walked to his office on Chestnut Street. She had never withdrawn such a large sum before. In fact, she wasn't even sure the agent could have one thousand dollars in Spanish gold available on short notice. It had taken two days to secure the funds when she purchased Sullivan House, but that had been over three thousand.

She paused in front of Samuel Morris' door and smoothed the front of her dress with her hands. In her prior dealings with Morris, he had proven to be a stickler for propriety. He was fastidious in his attire, which usually made her feel underdressed no matter what she wore. Well, her best gray dress, with three petticoats and hat would have to be good enough. She wanted to get this business with Danny concluded as quickly as she could.

Inside, she waited for a short time while Morris finished some business with another client, then she took a seat across the desk from him. Morris was a jack-of-all-trades where financial or administrative matters were concerned. For some, he was an attorney. For others, a banker. She knew he often lent money at steep interest rates, but Sara had always found him to be steadfastly honest in her dealings.

"A thousand in Spanish gold is a large sum, Mrs. Sullivan," Morris said when she told the amount she needed.

She spun through the story she'd concocted. A relative in Dublin desperately needed her help. She needed the money quickly in order to get the package on a vessel bound for Ireland due to leave that night. She hadn't checked to see if there really was such a vessel destined for Dublin, but she doubted Morris would check either. In any event, ships left the port every day and surely one of them included Dublin on its itinerary.

She worried that her story sounded too practiced, but Morris didn't seem to notice. He left the room for several minutes, then returned with two small bags. "Do you have pockets, Mrs. Sullivan?" he asked. "Or perhaps a reticule?"

"Pockets," Sara said, raising the corner of one of the two satin bags strapped around her waist.

"Good," Morris said. "Put one bag in each pocket. They are quite heavy as you have no doubt observed; each one is over two pounds."

She stood up and dropped one of the heavy bags into the pockets that hung against each hip. The weight caused the pockets to sink into the folds of her dress so they were less obvious.

"Good, the pockets are hardly visible," Morris said. "It's important that you walk normally," he added. "There are men who watch for people with heavy pockets or bags."

As she walked to the park on Market Street, she wished Morris hadn't said anything about walking normally. Now it was all she could think about, constantly trying to measure her steps and glancing around for furtive looking individuals.

Seeing Danny waiting for her on the park bench was a relief. As she approached him, anger began to replace the apprehension she had sensed during the walk.

"Good mornin' to ye, dear sister," Danny smiled as she took a seat next to him on the bench. "Yer pockets look a bit heavy, lass," he added. "Luck be with ye there was none like me about watchin' for such things."

She thought of Morris' warning. Her brother, Danny, was just the sort of man he was talking about. Of course, Morris didn't realize that even upon reaching her destination safely, she would still be robbed.

She took the two bags of gold from her pockets and placed them on the bench between them. "Take your money and leave me alone," she said.

He picked the bags up one at a time and felt their weight in the palm of his hand. "Aye, lass," he said. "Father O'Malley would be pleased with ye; what with helpin' family and all."

"Father O'Malley would be stealing a share for himself if he was here," she spat out.

"Ye could be right 'bout that," Danny agreed.

"Take the money and leave Philadelphia," she said.

"Aye, but you see, lass, I've come to like this town," Danny said. "I think it'd be a fine place to make me home."

"Go away," Sara spit out, her voice shook with anger.

"It be a costly place, though," Danny continued, ignoring her entreaty. "I'll be needin' a bit of this every month or so," he added, again balancing one of the bags in his hand.

"I thought so," Sara said. "How much?"

"I figure a hundred a month 'ill do nicely."

"You'll be a rich man in this town," she said. She had no intention of giving Danny money for the rest of her life, but it was better if she didn't tell him that just yet.

"We'll talk 'bout such matters soon," Danny said as he rose to leave. "I know where to find ye," he added. "Know where to find the Marlow fella, too."

Sara shook with anger and fear as her brother walked away in the direction of the docks. Stevie had been the mean one; the one who would take a swing without hesitation or rip her shirt away if he was in a mood to see her breast. But Danny was the conniving one, the one who plotted out plans and then followed through.

*****

Sara was surprised to find John Oliver at Sullivan House when she returned. It was barely two o'clock and the convention rarely adjourned before six.

"You're home early," she said.

"I've resigned from the Connecticut delegation," Oliver said. His tone was flat and emotionless.

"Oh?"

"There is nothing more for me to contribute," he said. "The convention has chosen a path and I cannot endorse that path."

"You were naïve to think this convention would solve slavery," Sara said.

"I didn't expect a solution," Oliver said. "I expected more of an effort though."

"What happens next?" Sara asked.

"They will finish the document and send it to the states for ratification."

"Will the states ratify it?"

"Most will," Oliver said. "Some delegates believe their states won't ratify unless there is a 'bill of rights' written into it, but Madison and Hamilton — and some others — are opposed to including it."

"Was it all for nothing?"

"No," Oliver said quickly. "We will be a stronger union than the Articles of Confederation made. Slavery will remain but it was already a fact. We can defend ourselves if the British decide to come back."

"What's next for John Oliver," she asked.

"I have land and clients in Connecticut that need my attention," he said.

"Of course."

"We've spoken of marriage," Oliver said. "I think the time has come for it."

"Yes."

"Can you leave Philadelphia and Sullivan House?" he asked.

"Not only can I leave, I must leave," Sara said.

She sat next to him on the parlor settee and told him the story of Danny's sudden appearance, his demands and threats, and her desire to get away.

"What about Sullivan House?" Oliver asked.

"Samuel Morris will take care of selling it," she

told him. "Mr. Martin has expressed an interest in purchasing the house in the past. Perhaps he still wants it."

"I spoke to Martin at some length last evening," Oliver said. "He would like to move his family to Philadelphia."

"That's it then," Sara said. "When can we go to Connecticut?"

Chapter 40

September 27, 1787
Hartford, Connecticut

Hartford mornings were cooler than Philadelphia. Autumn had arrived in New England earlier than it did in the Delaware Valley. *That's fine with Mrs. John Oliver*, Sara thought.

She rolled to her right, pulled the cover over her bare shoulders and laid her head on his chest, her breast pressed into his abdomen. A soft moan from Oliver told her he wasn't quite awake yet. That was fine. He would wake soon. No hurry.

The clank of the teapot on the stove downstairs told her Hennie was up. In the first days after they arrived in Hartford, the tension between Hennie and Miss Mary was thick, Miss Mary having been cook and housekeeper since John's father built the house more than thirty years earlier. They made peace when Miss Mary realized Hennie liked to rise early while she preferred to sleep in.

It was difficult to believe only thirty days had passed since they decided to leave Philadelphia. Samuel Morris had gladly taken charge of Sullivan House, delighted at the prospect of another commission. Mr. Martin was indeed interested in buying the property but wouldn't secure the funds until he sold the new shipment of goods coming from Trinidad. Also, Morris would handle selling their horses, tack, and the little one-horse carriage she had rarely used.

They had managed to leave Philadelphia without alerting Danny or Hugh Marlow, although both would find out soon enough. A few gold coins had convinced the captain of a coastal schooner to let them settle on board well before dawn. Luckily, none of the other passengers took any notice of them on the cruise to New York and then Boston, where Oliver arranged for two coaches to carry them and their luggage to Hartford.

John Oliver's sudden return to Hartford had caught Miss Mary and the rest of his employees by surprise. On top of that, he'd returned without his long-time valet, Ned Foster. Instead, a young woman with stunning red hair and green eyes, along with her somewhat eccentric servant, arrived in Hartford alongside their long-time employer.

Miss Mary said nothing when Oliver announced his intention to marry the woman, but her raised eyebrows told Sara she would need to win the lady's approval. By noon the following day, it seemed the whole town — Hartford was much smaller than Philadelphia — knew John Oliver had returned with a mystery woman he intended to marry. The entire day had been a parade of prominent townspeople eager to welcome Oliver home and to satisfy their curiosity about the woman.

The next day, they went to see the judge. Although Oliver had told her the judge was a cousin, they were, in fact, not closely related. Thomas Barnes was a few years older than Oliver. He moved slowly on a wooden prosthetic leg, the result of a severe wound at the Battle of Brooklyn.

The first order of business was Ned Foster's marriage. After reading Ned's letter, Judge Barnes said he couldn't see any precedent in Connecticut law for recognizing an Indian marriage. On the other hand, there was no precedent for not recognizing it either.

"We'll conduct a proxy marriage," Judge Barnes said.

"How do we do that?" Oliver asked.

"You will be Ned's proxy and Mrs. Sullivan will be proxy for this girl, Susannah," Barnes said.

He called a court clerk into the office to record the simple marriage ceremony, which took only a minute or two. In a few days, the marriage of Ned Foster and Susannah Foster would be recorded into the official records of Connecticut.

Next, Oliver presented the decade old letter notifying him that a judge in England had dissolved his marriage to Rebecca Black. It was a simple matter for Judge Barnes to recognize that dissolution in Connecticut's records as well.

"There's one more thing, Tom," Oliver said to the judge.

"What do you need, John?"

"Another marriage," John Oliver said. He took Sara's hand in his own and lifted them to show Judge Barnes.

The judge called the clerk into the office once again to act as witness and to record the marriage. The couple stood before Judge Thomas Barnes and repeated the vows as he instructed. Sara was surprised when John took a gold band from his pocket and slipped it on her finger. Later, she learned the ring had belonged to his mother. That was ten days earlier.

John shifted toward her as he began to awaken. She rolled onto her back.

"Are you awake, Johnny?"

"I am," he answered.

She took his hand and laid it flat on her belly. "Do you feel anything?" she asked.

"Stimulated," he answered.

"Ha," she laughed. "We'll take care of that. But there is something else in there."

"Oh?"

"I'm pregnant."

*****

Montreal, Quebec

The little bookshop caused Ned Foster's heart to beat faster. He found newspapers from Paris and London that were no more than two months old. Editions from New York and Boston were as recent as two weeks.

The nearby shelves were crowded with leather-bound books in French and English. Ned recognized many titles he had read from Lord Black's or John Oliver's libraries. And he saw quite a few he hadn't read.

"Can I help you?" a voice came from the rear of the shop.

"Is this your shop?"

"Yes." He was older than Ned expected, with thin white hair above a round face with red splotches on his puffy cheeks. A pair of spectacles seemed to hover above his sharp nose.

"The man at the bakery said you were looking for an educated man to help in your shop," Ned answered.

"Are you an educated man?" the shop owner asked.

"Better than most, I suppose," Ned answered.

"I've not seen you about in Montreal," the man said. "Are you new in town?"

"My wife and I came with a band of Mohawk," Ned explained. "We're camped a few miles east."

"The Mohawk don't usually look for work in town," the owner commented.

"I suspect you can look at me and realize I'm not really a Mohawk," Ned said with a smile.

"I didn't think so," he said. "What's your story?"

"What's your sentiments on the matter of slavery?" Ned asked.

"It's abominable," he answered. "Are you a runaway?"

"No," Ned said, "but my wife is."

"I see."

Ned told him the story of his travel to Philadelphia with John Oliver and of seeing Susannah for the first time. He held nothing back in describing their escape and how they came to be with the Mohawk.

"I heard about an Indian village being burned down in New York."

"The Mohawk have been good to us, but I miss this," Ned Foster said with a wave of his hand to the shelves surrounding them.

"An educated man would miss it," the shop

owner agreed.

"It's more than that," Ned continued. "Susannah is with child. I want the child to enjoy these books the way I have."

"The job doesn't pay much," the man said. "But there is a nice apartment above and a midwife just down the street."

THE END

Author's Note

Many scenes in this novel take place during sessions of the Constitutional Convention of 1787. Representations of events and statements in those scenes are primarily based on detailed notes recorded by James Madison and published in 1840, four years after his death. Madison's notes along with those of several other participants and the official journal of the convention were compiled by Max Farrand in *The Records of the Federal Convention of 1787 (3 Volumes)*, published in 1911. John Oliver, Hugh Marlow, Luther Moore, and Stephen McGrew are fictional characters and any statements, thoughts, or actions attributed to them are purely the creation of the author. Other delegates mentioned in this work were real and quotes attributed to them are based on Madison's notes.

The Constitutional Convention of the United States took place between May 25, 1787, and September 17, 1787, in Philadelphia, Pennsylvania. In total, fifty-six delegates from twelve states (Rhode Island did not send delegates) took part in the proceedings, some arriving long after the Convention began and others leaving before it concluded.

Ostensibly, the gathering was intended to revise the Articles of Confederation under which the thirteen colonies had united after the conclusion of the War of Independence from Britain. The Articles had proven to be inadequate in that they did not provide stable mechanisms for national defense, trade regulation, international relations, growth management, or fiscal administration. A recent episode, known as Shays Rebellion, had focused a bright light on the young nation's inability to mount a defense of its territory.

Shortly after the Convention opened, though, Governor Edmund Randolph of Virginia presented the Virginia Plan. At that point, the delegates realized that James Madison, the driving force behind the effort, intended to scrap the Articles altogether in favor of a completely new Constitution. In the weeks that followed, the delegates fiercely debated the plan until finally agreeing on a series of compromises which became the Constitution of the United States.

We Americans have come to think of these men as the "Founding Fathers", but most of them would be astonished to learn that the union they formed has survived for almost two and a half centuries. Much of what we consider our essential rights and freedoms today are the result of amendments to that basic document. The Bill of Rights, voting right for people without property, ending slavery, and women's suffrage all resulted from the amendment process. The men and women who drove those amendments are also founding fathers and founding mothers.

Acknowledgments

Special thanks to my wonderful wife, Celia, for her encouragement, patience, and valuable feedback.

About the Author

Fred McKibben is the author of the Gardeners trilogy, *Hot Times in the Garden of Eden, The Salt Castle,* and *The Carnival Road*. The series has been described as suspense with strong elements of science fiction, politics, history, anthropology, and romance. The allegorical story is particularly relevant in the current political environment where the rise of strongman rulers portends the loss of individual freedom, knowledge growth, and creativity. The full series is also available as a compilation titled *Seven Deadly Sinners*.

In addition to the Gardeners trilogy, Fred has written *The Shadow of Death* (2016) and *Sweet Dreams* (2017). Both are murder mysteries featuring Eddie Rose, a semi-retired insurance investigator.

Fred lives in Southern Spain with his wife, three dogs, and a horse. After many years as a finance executive and entrepreneur, he decided to try his hand at writing fiction. *A More Perfect Union* is the first of a planned series of historical novels set in the early United States.

Other Books by Fred McKibben

Hot Times in the Garden of Eden (The Gardeners #1)

The Salt Castle (The Gardeners #2)

The Carnival Road (The Gardeners #3)

Seven Deadly Sinners (The Gardeners Story)

The Shadow of Death (an Eddie Rose mystery)

Sweet Dreams (an Eddie Rose mystery)

www.ingramcontent.com/pod-product-compliance
Lightning Source LLC
Chambersburg PA
CBHW071231290426
44108CB00013B/1372